THE HISTORY OF
AMERICAN
CERAMICS

by Elaine Levin

THE HISTORY OF

1607 to the present

AMERICAN CERAMICS

from pipkins and bean pots to contemporary forms

Harry N. Abrams, Inc., Publishers, New York

To Bill
for his love, confidence, and persistence
and
In memory of Becky Levin and Hope Silver

page 1: WILLIAM GRUEBY. BEAVER TILE. *Astor Place subway station, New York City. c. 1904. Earthenware*

The beaver is a heraldic emblem of the Astor family of New York City; hence its choice in the tiles at the subway station named after the Astors. The city's first subway opened in 1904, its stations decorated with custom-designed tile produced by William Grueby and Rookwood.

page 2–3: ROOKWOOD POTTERY. FIVE VASES. *Earthenware. (left to right:) Lady vase. 1901. Height 8¾", diameter 3¼"; Geese vase. 1901. Height 10⅜", diameter 5½"; Kitten vase. 1902. Height 7⅝", diameter 4"; Indian vase. 1898. Height 7½", diameter 8"; Maria Nichols (decorator). Vase with grasses. 1882. Height 7¾", diameter 7⅝". Private collection*

PROJECT MANAGER: Leta Bostelman
EDITOR: Ruth A. Peltason
DESIGNER: Darilyn Lowe
PICTURE EDITOR: John K. Crowley

Library of Congress Cataloging-in-Publication Data
Levin, Elaine.
   The history of American ceramics, 1607 to the
present.
   Bibliography: p.
   Includes index.
   1. Pottery, American. I. Title.
NK4005.L48 1988   738′.0973   88-3332
ISBN 0-8109-1172-8

Printed and bound in Japan

CONTENTS

ACKNOWLEDGMENTS

A volume of this nature and length requires a variety of resources. I'm fortunate to have had not only great support from many people, but also their encouragement over a longer time period than anyone expected this book would have required.

My initial research and queries about publishing were greatly facilitated by advice from Mel Bernstein, Miguel Angel Corzo, Sandra Dijkstra, Ann Gavel, Janet and Michael Mayer (who were also my hosts in New York), Betsy Richman, Charlotte Speight, and Susan Wechsler. Valuable assistance came from Susan Myers and Regina Blaszczyk at the Division of Ceramics and Glass of the National Museum of American History, Smithsonian Institution, Washington, D.C. Among the many people and institutions I consulted I'm especially indebted to Hazel Bray, formerly Curator of Crafts at the Oakland Museum, California; Susan Strong, Assistant Dean, New York State College of Ceramics, Alfred University; the Archives of American Art, Smithsonian Institution; Victoria Peltz, Supervisor, Cowan Pottery Museum, Rocky River Public Library, Ohio; and Linda Poe, Special Collections, Howard Tilton Memorial Library, Tulane University. Each one answered my numerous questions and made available important archival material. William Hunt, Editor, and Spencer Davis, Publisher, of *Ceramics Monthly*, were most gracious advisors and a source of constant encouragement and support. I have been given access to the storage areas of numerous museums for my research and have received considerable assistance from museum photographic services; from that long list I must single out the Everson Museum of Art in Syracuse, New York, and Barbara Perry, Curator of Ceramics.

A number of galleries have been forthcoming with special material; in particular, the Rena Bransten Gallery, the Braunstein/Quay Gallery, and the Fuller Gross Gallery (formerly Hansen Fuller Goldeen Gallery), all in San Francisco; the Leo Castelli Gallery, the Frumkin/Adams Gallery (formerly the Allan Frumkin Gallery), and Meagan McKearney of the Jordan-Volpe Gallery, in New York; the Jan Turner Gallery of Los Angeles and the Garth Clark Gallery of Los

opposite:
PAUL SOLDNER
UNTITLED PLAQUE
1978. Raku fired, stencils, stains, 16½ x 23 x ¼". Private collection

Angeles and New York; the Helen Drutt Gallery of Philadelphia; Ree Schonlau of the New Gallery in Omaha, Nebraska; and the Esther Saks Gallery and the Alice Westphal Gallery in Chicago.

A group of colleagues, friends, and relatives served this project in both official and unofficial capacities. Regina and Joseph Scheer, Mace and Clare Levin, and Hy and George Levin loyally sent me catalogues and pertinent information on ceramics from their trips around the country and abroad. For a number of years, Bernice Sisson filled my files with significant clippings from newspapers in the East Coast. Frances Baer and Blair Levin conscientiously clipped newspaper articles from northern California and North Carolina. Liliane Corzo graciously translated articles in German. Rebecca Levin, Debra Lucas, Yvonne Madrigal, and Ellen Sisson Rosen assisted with research and many typing chores. Special photographic help came from Morley Baer, Nancy Kaye, Erik Lauritzen, and Jeffrey Levin. Clare Levin and Norma Moses assisted with my own photographic efforts. Many collectors of ceramics, among them Betty and Robert Hut, Stephane Janssen, Joan Mannheimer, Forrest L. Merrill, Betty and Stanley Sheinbaum, and Gwen Laurie and Howard Smits were most gracious with access to their homes, allowing photography, and generous with necessary detailed information.

Assembling a mountain of factual details in readable, coherent order would not have been possible without some special help. Judith Schotz gave a critical reading to the first section of the book and diligently checked the footnotes and bibliography. Michael McTwigan edited an early version of the manuscript and offered valuable suggestions; my son, Jeffrey Levin, gave the book a most careful and thoughtful editing; his advice and writing skills were essential to maintaining my historical perspective. I'm also most grateful for his constant reassurance. I learned a great deal about visual material from John Crowley, my photo editor at Abrams, who was always available and optimistic about the book's progress. Ruth Peltason, my editor at Abrams, determinedly kept me focused on the main narrative. She spent endless hours on the details involved with this material. Her questions, graceful editing, and critical appraisal have been invaluable and I'm most appreciative.

Essential to this project was the cooperation of the over 100 contemporary artists whose work I discuss. They have answered my letters with helpful details, welcomed me to their studios, made time for interviews and lengthy phone conversations. I could not have asked for more confidence and enthusiasm.

My immediate family deserves special praise for their patience, unwavering support, and for keeping both their and my sense of humor. Cheering me ever onward were Jeffrey Levin, Nancy Kaye, Dr. Patricia Friedman, Blair Levin, Carol and Michael Brady, and Rebecca Levin. Most of all, a project consuming so much effort would not have been possible without my husband, Bill. Besides his proofreading, his considerable editorial skills, and indispensable advice, he believed wholeheartedly in the value of this book. He drew the line, however, at doing my typing.

Elaine Levin

PREFACE

I began working with clay in the mid-1960s determined to realize a long-held ambition—to throw on the potter's wheel. The exhilarating experience of accomplishing that eventually led me to question the unusual forms ceramists were then producing. Previously, I thought of clay as a simple craft serving functional needs. During the sixties, I watched it evolve into what appeared to be a complex mosaic of wheel-thrown shapes distorted, paddled, scarred, and assembled into curious sculptures. What was happening? How did the political and social turmoil of the 1960s affect artistic expression (and even my own work)? I decided to research the past in order to understand the present.

What I did not realize was that exploring 380 years of American clay and the potters who shaped it would soon become more engrossing than making pots. At first, the answers to some of my questions involved the nature of clay, a primordial material, easily accessible and underfoot in most parts of the country. Clay is adaptable; handbuilt, thrown, or formed by industrial tools, it can serve functional needs; some of the same methods shape it into sculpture.

But then I found other answers in the unique history of America, especially in the lives of the early settlers. Even though the sixteenth- and seventeenth-century potter initially produced ware similar to that of his native land, he had to alter his methods and designs to suit the functional and cultural needs of this new society. From the beginning, potters had to improvise; clay, glaze materials, even bricks for the kiln did not perform exactly as they had in Europe. The wheel, kiln, and hand tools of the farmer-potter had to be made from the supplies at hand. The generations of potters who followed—whether immigrant or native-born—continued to alter ceramics and improvise. Stylistic developments imported from Europe, such as the Empire Style, Art Nouveau, and Art Deco, yielded to an American interpretation when they crossed the Atlantic Ocean. Indeed, at the present, influences as diverse as those from the Orient and Africa have been so completely integrated that work reflecting these ideas often appears quite distant from its source. The

Americanization or assimilation of influences is a recurring theme in this history and is related to the fact that ours is a multi-cultural society. The term Yankee ingenuity might well apply to the ability that ceramists have historically employed: borrowing and modification from different sources to achieve particular purposes. It all leads up even to contemporary ceramists, who have crafted and defined their own American iconography.

The ability to meet new situations has historically tested the self-confidence of American potters. In the 1700s, colonial rule downgraded the colony's products and placed them in competition with the European industrialization of production (which this country could not match until the mid-nineteenth century). Both forces combined to forge an inferiority complex toward American products, including ceramics. That condition began to change with the opening of the Philadelphia Centennial of 1876. When displayed with European and Oriental ware, American ware compared rather favorably, especially for a young country without a long ceramic tradition. Indeed, it was not until the late nineteenth century that ceramics made during the previous two hundred years earned the respect due an important part of the American heritage. Only after art historian Edwin Atlee Barber researched and wrote about Pennsylvania sgraffito-decorated redware in 1903, did private collectors and museums realize the ware's significance. That pattern of research, writing, and recognition set in motion by Barber has continued to shape contemporary attitudes.

In recent times, almost every type of American ware, from handthrown eighteenth-century redware and stoneware jugs to molded factory dinnerware of the 1930s, has found an appreciative audience. Organizations such as The American Art Pottery Association and the Art Deco Society have encouraged collectors and kept the public informed. The National Council on Education for the Ceramic Arts (known informally as NCECA) and the American Craft Council have brought educators, ceramists, collectors, and students together for the study and advancement of ceramics. In part as a result, the work of potters such as George Ohr, a turn-of-the-century Mississippi eccentric, along with the folk potters of the South, have been rediscovered. Rockingham, spongeware, and common kitchen yellowware are now acknowledged as sturdy and often exuberant examples of nineteenth-century Americana.

My personal search for information led to placing these developments in a historical perspective. In that context, I realized that cultural factors frequently have determined stylistic directions, a point which helped clarify my earlier confusion. In looking back through time, many of the conditions leading to the contemporary ceramic climate were present over a century ago. Today we find ceramists functioning in many different ways—in a rural or urban studio or on an Indian reservation, teaching at universities and art schools, designing for the ceramics industry, and exhibiting work at fairs, in galleries and museums. All these elements have contributed to the unique tradition that is American ceramics, a diverse art form that has evolved along with an equally diverse society, and has earned its place within the mainstream of American art.

opposite:
1. GOTTFRIED AUST
PLATE
Late 18th century. Moravian earthenware, green, brown, and red slip over white slip wash, diameter 13⁹/₁₆". Courtesy Old Salem Restoration, Winston-Salem, N.C.

Part I

From Folk Pottery
to Industry 1600–1876

Chapter 1

A Handcraft Foundation for Clay

From its earliest beginnings in the seventeenth century, ceramic development in America was as diverse as were the newly arrived settlers from all parts of Europe. Whether English, French, or German, these settlers brought with them the techniques and tools of their craft typical of their native homelands. Dispersed among the growing colonies, the potter learned to adapt his methods and materials to the conditions imposed on him by this new frontier; form and design were no less required to suit the needs of the settlers in their new country. With the eventual rise of a merchant class and the sophistication of the colonies, there grew a market for more stylish, high-quality ware. The American potter had but one example to follow, and so he looked to European-designed imports, which he did his best to imitate. While the results were frequently less sophisticated, they displayed an ingenuity in the use of American materials. Imitation as a reaction to foreign influences and modification according to the needs of the American environment continued well into the middle of the twentieth century.

Adding to the process of imitation/modification was an element unique to this new culture. The European colonists were occupying territory already settled by native Americans, the Indians. Just as varied in their traditions as the settlers, the Indian tribes along the eastern coast—from the Pequot or Mohegan tribes of the Connecticut River Valley to the Catawba tribes of South Carolina—produced functional pottery. Although relations between the native Americans and the Europeans obviously varied from colony to colony, during the early years of small settlements, the Indians did not feel threatened. In the South, Indians would show potters where to find local clay deposits. Others taught the newcomers some of their farming practices. New Englanders, who learned to plant, harvest, and prepare corn and beans, added succotash and baked beans to their diet which they cooked in vessels modified for long hours of baking—the pipkin and bean pot.

opposite:
2. WILLIAM PECKER
HERB POT
1780–1820. Red earthenware, brushed with dark brown manganese, covered with a lead glaze, height 6½". Division of Ceramics and Glass, National Museum of American History, Smithsonian Institution, Washington, D.C. Gift of Lura Woodside Watkins

Decorative color splotches at this time were made by anvil dust, copper filings, or manganese which the potter collected from the local blacksmith. When sprinkled over the lead glaze, these minerals melted in the firing and flowed down the side of the pot.

above:
3. WINE CUP
First half of 17th century. Red earthenware, height 3". Division of Ceramics and Glass, National Museum of American History, Smithsonian Institution, Washington, D.C.

In time, life among the colonists and Indians grew antagonistic as bitter disputes over territory erupted into sporadic warfare which continued until the West was settled. Only at that point, by the end of the nineteenth century, did native American culture become of interest generally, and to potters in particular. Indeed, the Indian tribes of the Southwest and their extensive pottery tradition emerged first as archeological curiosities; it was later on that they had such impact on American designs and firing practices.

Early Redware in the Seventeenth Century

Long before the influence of the Indians, the seventeenth-century immigrant potters established themselves as essential members of their settlements. The importance of clay to a colony is exemplified by a report filed in London in 1588 noting that the Viriginia area considered for colonization had clay resources suitable for making bricks.[1] Nineteen years later in 1607, the first English settlers arrived in Jamestown.

Redware of Virginia and the South

Earthenware clay deposits and wood needed to fire the kilns were underfoot and in the surrounding Virginia forests. Because of the fragility of crude, low-fired clay, extant examples of seventeenth-century ware are limited, but research conducted at abandoned kiln sites in Jamestown indicates pottery production began around 1625.[2] Shards from excavation sites reveal that red earthenware was fashioned into storage jars, jugs, pitchers, bowls, and mugs, all of it lead-glazed on the inside to make the porous clay watertight. A mixture of litharge, sand, and lead was ground together in a hand-operated mill. When this glaze was brushed on the inside of a vessel and fired in the kiln, the shiny, transparent surface brought out the warm brown color of the clay. Kiln construction differed according to the potter's background, but all were simple structures having an opening at one end (closed during the firing) and a chimney at the other. The ware was stacked inside, wood was piled around it and ignited. Understandably, the temperature was difficult to control; a firing could take from thirty to forty hours and as much as a week was required for the pottery to cool before it could be removed from the kiln. What with much guesswork and unpredictability of the firing, much of the ware was destroyed.

Decoration on early redware was unpretentious, limited to designs created by a finger impression in the clay or by straight or wavy lines made with a sharpened stick, a technique termed incising, done while the pot revolved on the wheel. At this time, English potters used a wheel powered by a lever attached to a crank in the wheel shaft which the potter moved back and forth with his foot as he leaned against a wall.[3] Generally, Continental potters used a wheel which consisted of two horizontal disks joined by a shaft, allowing the lower disk to be revolved by the potter's foot while his hands shaped the clay on the upper disk. The colonial potter continued this

4. YELLOWWARE PIPKIN
New Jersey or Pennsylvania. c. 1880–90. Yellow earthenware with a clear alkaline glaze, height 5½". Collection Samuel Herrup, N.Y.

The pipkin, which had a hollow handle, was a popular form that continued in use from the seventeenth century to the nineteenth century. Because of earthenware's fragility, early redware pipkins are rare. This nineteenth-century yellowware example is similar to its predecessors.

tradition along with methods of throwing and refining the vessel. A common tool was a thin piece of wood held against the vessel's surface to level the indentations made by the potter's fingers as he pulled the clay into shape. Production that exceeded the needs of the potter's family was exchanged with neighbors for other goods or else peddled to nearby villages. Usually middle class and a respected member of the community, as time progressed the early Virginia potter held positions of responsibility in his church or local government.

In many areas of the Deep South, pottery production varied in quality and remained a part of the work on small farms. Adequate but undistinguished ware was made since it was not a craft favored by plantation owners. The cash crops of cotton and tobacco depended on the slave trade—blacks brought from Africa—which was increasingly important to the economy by the late seventeenth century. Gradually, slaves who learned to produce earthenware for functional needs replaced the indentured servants who had paid their way to America by contracting to work for a family. When potters found slaves adaptable to making ware, many white apprentice potters—unpaid young boys who wanted to learn a trade—also had to look elsewhere. Lacking initiative or incentive to come up with new decorative ideas, the potter-slave in southern society was further thwarted by the rising affluence; plantation-made pottery was relegated to kitchen use, which kept it sheltered from mainstream influences.[4] As plantation owners prospered, the demand for quality ware from England and the Continent rose and it became the preferred tableware for wealthy southern families.

EARTHENWARE IN THE NORTHEAST

A different tradition evolved in the Northeast. Like their southern counterparts, the English potters accompanying the small band of farmers and tradesmen who arrived in Plymouth in the 1620s found abundant supplies of the two essentials for pottery production—deposits of earthenware clay and kindling wood. Working on a treadle or kick wheel in a corner of his barn, the New England potter threw functional ware for his household and the neighboring community. Jugs for storing milk, butter, and cheese were common containers. Ovoid, wide-mouth jars functioned as pitchers with the addition of a loop handle and a spout, a shape derived from English and European medieval ware dating back to the Roman period in England. Earthenware plates developed later because wood trenchers—square blocks of wood dug out by hand—held the family dinner, often the only container for a family of four. Pewter porringers had been brought from England along with mugs made from animal horn.

In New England, too, potters used a lead glaze on their ware. Parallel or wavy lines beneath the rim added a decorative touch. On occasions when the vessel's exterior was also glazed, the potter often applied deep brown or dark green splotches of color.

Legal documents of the Massachusetts Bay Colony mention some of the potters of this period; among the earliest were John Pride

5. CROCK WITH HANDLES
New England, Essex County. c. 18th century. Incised decoration red earthenware, height 8¼", diameter 11". Division of Ceramics and Glass, National Museum of American History, Smithsonian Institution, Washington, D.C.

and William Vinson of Salem, and Philip Drinker of Charleston, producing pottery by 1635. Referred to as "pot bakers," these men made roof tiles and bricks as well as jugs and crocks. As other potters gravitated to Essex County, Massachusetts, the area became the first pottery center in the New World.

New England cupboards continued to display unsophisticated redware pottery for common use, but by the mid-seventeenth century a merchant class had developed, and like the prosperous southern plantation owners, they too created a demand for better made, imported ware. The growth of the merchant class also shifted the balance of power away from the clergy, which previously had exercised Puritan restraint over the acquisition of luxuries.[5] Between 1660 and 1675 there was a marked increase in the importation of finer wares, especially tin-glazed earthenware. A better grade of earthenware, this pottery dates back to ancient times. It was brought to Europe in the eleventh century by the Moors via Spain. By the fourteenth century, it was used in Italy, where it was known as majolica. It eventually became an important industry in Delft, Holland, which became the center for production beginning in 1602 to imitate and compete with the importation of Chinese porcelain. It consisted of a dense white glaze which covered the clay body and provided a surface for painting. As its popularity grew, European potteries employed the style, where it was known variously as English Delftware, faience, or majolica. American potters did not learn the technology to produce similar wares until the next century; until then they could not successfully compete with imported sophisticated pottery.

Slip- and Sgraffito-Decorated Redware, Late Seventeenth to Early Nineteenth Century

Before the end of the seventeenth century, New England potters added slip-cup designs to their decorative vocabulary. The slip-cup, a popular tool in England, was a small, earthenware vessel with a hole in the bottom or the side. Holding a finger over the top hole, the potter filled the container with slip, a liquid mixture of white or pipe clays and water. As he released his finger the slip could be trailed in a simple pattern over the surface of the ware. Slip was also brushed on to completely cover the surface. The earlier, decorative process of sgraffito was combined with slip by scratching lines into the light-colored slip, thereby exposing the dark clay below. The contrasting design was then covered with a clear lead glaze and fired. New England slip decorations on redware never progressed to the complex designs and colors of their German neighbors in Pennsylvania because these colonists had left England in the early 1600s, before such ware became highly developed.

PENNSYLVANIA GERMAN REDWARE

Adding to the the slip- and sgraffito-decorated redware tradition were a group of immigrants who brought a rich German heritage of

earthenware designs to Pennsylvania. After 1681, when Quaker William Penn received a charter from Charles II to colonize Pennsylvania, immigrants from the upper Rhine and Palatinate area of Europe began arriving in Philadelphia, settling in a section appropriately named Germantown. As the new settlers began to out-populate the Quakers, they were forced to leave Philadelphia for the surrounding counties further west. Skilled farmers, they worked the rich land into farms distinguished by the superior size of their barns, extensive, well-cared-for orchards, and luxurious meadows. At its apex in the mid-nineteenth century, their pottery reflected this opulence.

The antecedents of Pennsylvania German earthenware are found in the highly developed late-seventeenth-century slip-decorated European folk pottery, which was then at the height of its popularity. This ware was characterized by easily identified symbolic motifs appealing to simple tastes. In the colonies of the late 1600s, where the need for common pottery remained but was not as pressing as it had been for the early settlers, a more decorative style had an oportunity to develop. The Germans' adjustment to American life included adding New England-style baked beans to their diet and the bean pot to their vocabulary of shapes. The English brought the meat pie to America and with it the pie plate; the Germans adapted the pie to their bountiful orchards and added the fruit pie to the American

above left:
6. WOODEN SHAPING RIBS
c. 19th century. Used by Old Salem potters. Courtesy Old Salem Restoration, Winston-Salem, N.C.

above right:
7. THOMPSON POTTERY SLIP CUP
Morgantown, West Virginia. 19th century. Division of Ceramics and Glass, National Museum of American History, Smithsonian Institution, Washington, D.C.

A slip cup was used for decorating pottery. The potter would draw the slip cup across the surface of the vessel, making a variety of slightly raised designs. When fitted with a quill, the potter could use the slip cup to draw complex lettering and intricate designs.

8. GEORGE HUBENER,
MONTGOMERY CO.
DISH
*1786. Earthenware, with slip
coating, clear lead glaze, diameter 12½". Philadelphia Museum
of Art. Gift of John T. Morris*

diet.[6] The requirements of apple butter pots, flower pots, vinegar or molasses jugs, and dishes for vegetables and meat dictated the range of forms the German potters produced.

Ornamental pie plates were formed by shaping the clay over a convex, curved form. Using a slip-cup fitted with a quill, the Pennsylvania German potters painted their plates with a tulip design, a favored central European motif, and later drew inspiration from American flowers and foliage. Eagles, ducks, and swans were also popular but, like human figures, were not especially well drawn. The oldest example of Pennsylvania slipware dates from 1733, and is a barber's basin decorated in a conventionalized tulip design with an inscription in German, which translated is: "Clean and shave me nice and fine/That I may please my beloved one."[7] Traditional German proverbs were common inscriptions on plates made for special occasions. In Montgomery County, George Hubener's elaborately decorated and inscribed earthenware featured two circles of lettering, usually with the names of the persons for whom the plate was intended. Two doves united by one body, a symbol of love and union, appear frequently in Hubener's work, which was produced between 1785 and 1798. David Spinner, a member of a prominent Bucks County family whose ware dates from 1801, was one of the area's foremost potters. Like his contemporaries, he had no formal training in drawing, yet his plates were animated and lively. Horses with thin necks, small heads, and heavy flanks, prance or dash across his plates, carrying uniformed soldiers or gentlemen engaged in hunting.

MORAVIAN REDWARE IN NORTH CAROLINA IN THE EIGHTEENTH CENTURY

According to oral tradition, Peter Craven was the first potter on record from North Carolina. Originally from Staffordshire, England, Craven began farming in Randolph County around 1764. However, property inventory records from that time confirm only that Peter's grandson John Craven made pottery and began the Craven craft dynasty in the early 1800s. Succeeding generations of Craven potters eventually moved to other southern counties and states.[8] More complete records identify the earliest group of North Carolina potters as Moravians, immigrants from central Europe and Germany, who had previously settled in Bethlehem, Pennsylvania. In moving to the Piedmont section of North Carolina in 1753 where they planned to establish their own viable religious community of organized, noncompetitive craftsmen and farmers, the Moravians also brought with them the fine Pennsylvania German redware tradition, which they had established there. Among the settlers of Bethabara, the first of the planned, self-supporting communities, was Gottfried Aust, a Moravian potter who had served his apprenticeship first in Germany and then in Bethlehem, Pennsylvania. Aust built his pottery according to the directives of the ruling Collegium, which regulated output and prices to prevent unfavorable competition among craftsmen. Like Pennsylvania German ware, Aust's designs are derived from the folk culture of central Europe, but the exuberant plant forms that

9. Attributed to DAVID SPINNER
DISH
c. 1800–11. Earthenware with slip covering and clear lead glaze, diameter 11⅝". Philadelphia Museum of Art. Gift of John T. Morris

dominate his slip-decorated plates have a special vigor. His palette of slip colors delineates sectioned seed pods and fish scales, motifs also common to the pottery of Czechoslovakia, Rumania, and Staffordshire, England, of an earlier period.[9]

Although Moravian craftsmen were a tightly knit community, they traded a good deal of their ware to outsiders, and so were open to new ideas and techniques which would attract more customers. In 1773, William Hanley Ellis, an itinerant English potter familiar with Queen's ware, came to Salem, the third Moravian settlement. The town had been built especially for craftsmen, and Aust, who had moved there in 1771, was eager to have Ellis teach him the methods used in the production of Queen's ware, a cream-colored earthenware which Josiah Wedgwood helped popularize in England about ten years earlier. This quality earthenware, also called creamware, was light and delicate, characteristically rococo in design, and borrowed from Chinese motifs. Molds accelerated the bench work involved in applied decoration and were used for forms such as gravy boats.

Aust's apprentice, Rudolf Christ, was so intrigued by this molded ware that he applied to the Collegium to allow him to build his own pottery at Bethabara in 1786 for the production of Queen's ware. Christ simplified the rococo designs to produce a less ornate but fine quality ware and utilized Ellis's technique for making extruded handles and press-molded gravy boats, mechanical procedures English potteries had adopted by the mid-eighteenth century as they moved toward industrialization.

Another journeyman potter, Carl Eisenberg, a German immigrant, visited Christ in 1793 and taught him the technique of tin-glaze or faience pottery, a type of soft-paste earthenware covered with an opaque glaze of tin oxide.[10] Mentioned earlier as Delftware imported to America beginning in the mid-seventeenth century, and originally developed to substitute for expensive oriental porcelain, this cheerful earthenware with its blue-and-white decorations was destined to attract potters anxious to appeal to customers with a taste for finer wares. Christ, possibly the first to imitate Delftware, made it along with all his mugs, bowls, tumblers, and other forms of hollow ware, a simplified version of English prototypes.

SHENANDOAH REDWARE POTTERS IN THE NINETEENTH CENTURY

The folk-pottery roots of American tradition would be incomplete without a discussion of the potters of the Shenandoah Valley who moved south in the late eighteenth century from the northern colonies to an area nestled between the Blue Ridge Mountains on the east and the Allegheny Mountains on the west. Some were farmer-potters attracted by the valley's vast farmlands; others were full-time craftsmen. The Bell family is in the latter category beginning with Peter Bell, Jr., son of a German immigrant, who in 1805 established a pottery in Hagerstown, Maryland, and then moved to Winchester in 1824. Peter and his sons, John, Samuel, and Solomon, set

10. RUDOLF CHRIST
SUGAR BOWL
*Late 18th century. Moravian
earthenware, white, green, and
dark brown slip over a red slip
wash, height 7½". Courtesy
Old Salem Restoration, Winston-Salem, N.C.*

the standard for Shenandoah Valley potters. The Bell brothers established potteries in separate valley towns, selling wares to merchants
who in turn peddled them in wagons to more isolated communities.
Through letters to one another, the Bell brothers solved firing problems, improved their large, beehive-shaped kilns, and refined their
glaze formulas.[11] Although earthenware and stoneware vessels
adorned with tulip leaves and plant forms were the main production
of these potters, Samuel enjoyed making small images of dogs and
cats, and Solomon favored a lion motif on his ware. One of John's
whimsical lions, made as a gift for a niece, displays a sense of humor
and fantasy lacking in the serious lions and dogs produced earlier in
Staffordshire. Although their decorative designs were not as elaborate as those of the Moravians, some late-nineteenth-century Shenandoah Valley potters applied highly original reliefs of seashells and
Shenandoah River fish to their ware.

Stoneware Production in the Eighteenth and Nineteenth Century

Keeping abreast of changes in taste was an important concern for the
eighteenth-century American potter. In Philadelphia in 1730, Anthony Duché, a French Huguenot potter who produced utilitarian

earthenware, applied to the Pennsylvania assembly for a subsidy and a monopoly to manufacture stoneware. Alert potters like Duché realized that even more than tin-glazed earthenware and creamware, stoneware offered qualities earthenware could not match. More durable and less prone to chipping and breakage, stoneware clay bodies fire at a higher temperature and range in color from gray to light beige. Although Duché's application was denied, he began stoneware production anyway, copying English and German models. (Duché may have become familiar with stoneware while living in England in flight from his native France, where Huguenots were being persecuted. Continued religious persecution brought him to Philadelphia.) Another important factor working against earthenware was the discovery that when the lead content in the glaze came into contact with some foods the consequences were fatal. Public attention to the lead problem did not surface until about 1785 when the use of salt-glazed stoneware became a safe alternative.

The discovery of stoneware clays in the Rhineland during the fifteenth century initiated this type of ware and from there it spread to England and other European countries in the centuries that followed. In its early phase, the German ware was utilitarian—sturdy

11. JOHN BELL
PAIR OF SPANIELS
(King Charles type, after Staffordshire mantel figures)
Waynesboro, Pennsylvania. c. 1874. Earthenware, mold-made, height 10". Division of Ceramics and Glass, National Museum of American History, Smithsonian Institution, Washington, D.C.

mugs, tankards, chamber pots, and storage jars. Part of the attraction to stoneware at this period was salt glazing, a method of throwing household salt into the kiln as the ware matured. Salt vaporizes at 2300 degrees Fahrenheit and combines with the high silica content of the clay to form sodium silicate, a hard surface layer that ranges from shiny to dull, from smooth-textured to pockmarked like the skin of an orange. Instead of firing a vessel once to harden the clay and again to melt the glaze, a salt-fired stoneware vessel only needed to be fired once to achieve a glazed surface.

Many earthenware shapes and decorative motifs were transferred to stoneware production. Although there was much variety, stoneware crocks generally were ovoid in shape with turned rims and horizontal loop handles, some flattened against the body of the pot. Jugs were produced in great quantity along with two-handled jars, chamber pots, beer mugs, and kitchen supplies such as bowls, plates, pitchers, bean pots, colanders, and handled cups. Crocks and jars held salted and pickled food; jugs and bottles stored vinegar, whiskey, water, and molasses.

The body shape of jugs and crocks flared out from a small base, curving back to a shoulder and a small neck. Since the accentuated curve presented difficulties in decoration, stamped, stenciled patterns, or painted designs were confined to the upper part of the ware.

12. SOLOMON BELL
LION
c. 1850. Red earthenware, slip decorated, height 11", length 13½". Museum of Early Southern Decorative Arts, Winston-Salem, N.C.

Animals were popular items as toys and, as in the case of this lion, also as doorstops. The animal's whimsical features are a contrast to John Bell's solemn looking molded spaniels from the same period, and which were copies of English Staffordshire mantel figures (fig. 11).

Tools for decorating earthenware, such as coggle wheels and stamps made of fired clay or carved wood, were soon applied on stoneware. Most articles were decorated with incised lines, but unlike earthenware sgraffito, these lines were usually filled in with cobalt slip (the mineral mixed with clay and water) to accentuate the design. Potters continued to use slip-cups, trailing cobalt slip in motifs also used on earlier ware—the coiled spring, a dotted fish scale, plants, flowers (especially the tulip from Pennsylvania German designs), birds perched on a branch, and animals such as deer in a woodland setting.

EARLY VIRGINIA STONEWARE

Although stoneware required learning some new techniques and sustaining a higher temperature in the kiln, men like Duché and William Rogers of Yorktown, Virginia, saw a home market awaiting their ingenuity. A wealthy brewer, surveyor, and merchant, Rogers may have been among the first to attempt stoneware production, according to pottery shards that date from 1720. Seeking to wean American consumers away from imported ware, Rogers copied English stoneware mugs of the same period, an activity usually discouraged by colonial administrators. Apparently, Rogers had a sympathetic ally in William Gooch, the Royal Governor of Virginia, who described Rogers as a "poor potter" in his annual report to the Lords of the Board of Trade in the 1730s. The phrase was calculated to denigrate the potter's industry, and to suggest the poor quality of American-made ware, thus minimizing the perceived threat to English imports.[12]

The English saw the colonies as a market for their products, a notion the colonists did much to counteract and circumvent in subtle ways. Anthony Duché's success with stoneware production reached Isaac Parker of Boston who, in 1742, asked Duché's son James to come north to teach him the technique. Such apprentices were a common method of spreading a new procedure.

EARLY NEW YORK STONEWARE

Initially, deposits of stoneware clay were discovered in Philadelphia, Long Island, and New Jersey, so that potters who were anxious to avoid or reduce shipping costs located nearby. A 1730 map of New York City identifies "pot baker's hill;" on later maps, William Crolius and John Remmey, both German immigrants, were named as potters in that area.[13] Their country of origin suggests they had some experience with stoneware before coming to America as young adults, in the early years of the eighteenth century. Each married sisters, the daughters of a potter, but that circumstance did little to prevent the Crolius and Remmey families from establishing competing stoneware potteries. In succeeding generations, both families produced a prodigious number of children as well as a substantial number of jars, jugs, crocks, and pitchers. John Remmey II operated the pottery during the Revolutionary War and the prosperous years that

13. JOHN REMMEY III
JUG
c. 1815. Stoneware, salt glaze, height 11¹¹/₁₆". Division of Ceramics and Glass, National Museum of American History, Smithsonian Institution, Washington, D.C.

followed. When he died in 1793, his son John III continued the family business. Other Remmey progeny left New York to establish potteries in Philadelphia, South Amboy, New Jersey, and Baltimore in the nineteenth century. John and Clarkson Crolius, William's son and grandson respectively, mixed active participation in New York politics with stoneware pottery production, sustained by the following generations well into the mid-nineteenth century.

New Jersey Stoneware

The banks of Cheesequake Creek (presently in the Madison Township) in New Jersey yielded clay deposits for some of the finest stoneware. By 1750, a third-generation American, James Morgan, the son of a Cheesequake Creek innkeeper with property along the creek (later known as Morgan's Bank), became the area's principal potter. Ultimately, three potteries operated in the Cheesequake area, many, like the Remmey and Crolius families, interconnected by marriage. Reconstructed fragments of late-eighteenth-century ware found on the site of Morgan's pottery are distinguished by geometric designs and spiral motifs in bands of blue. Jugs produced in the early nineteenth century by Morgan's son-in-law, Thomas Warne, with his partner, J. Letts, utilized distinctive, stamped border designs.

Vermont Stoneware

While it may be correct to ascribe Adam States of Greenwich, Connecticut, as having produced the first stoneware in New England

above left:
14. JULIUS AND EDWARD NORTON
BUTTER POT
c. 1850–59. Stoneware, salt glaze, interior brown slip, cobalt blue decoration, height 12", diameter 9". Collection Fran and Doug Faulkner, New Kingston, N.Y.

above right:
15. JAMES MORGAN
JAR
Last quarter of 18th century. Stoneware, salt glaze with "watch spring" design, height 10³⁄₁₆". Division of Ceramics and Glass, National Museum of American History, Smithsonian Institution, Washington, D.C.

after opening his pottery in 1750, another pottery further north gained a greater reputation and enjoyed the longevity afforded the Remmey and Crolius families. In 1793 Captain John Norton established the Norton Pottery in Bennington, Vermont. At first he produced earthenware for New England kitchens. In 1815, he added stoneware when the transportation of clay from New Jersey improved. Salt-glazed stoneware production began in 1823, also the beginning of a period when brushwork replaced incised and impressed decorations. The slip-cup fitted with a goose quill allowed for more complex and calligraphic designs. Ornamental handwriting, popular in the eighteenth and nineteenth centuries, influenced the flourishes and spirals made with cobalt slip. From the 1850s through the 1880s, and under the direction of succeeding generations of Nortons—Julius, Edward, and Edward Lincoln—the slip-trailed decorations on Norton salt-glazed stoneware were particularly well

16. JULIUS AND EDWARD NORTON
12-GALLON WATER COOLER
c. 1850–59. Stoneware, cobalt slip decoration, height 24". Division of Ceramics and Glass, National Museum of American History, Smithsonian Institution, Washington, D.C.

A continuous frieze of an eagle, lion, and deer in a landscape setting runs along the midsection of the vessel. Birds and flowers were more commonly depicted; animals such as these were rare.

executed. Sprightly birds balanced on a tree stump or flowered branch, floral flourishes and deer amid meadows and pine trees distinguish this period. From its earliest years, the Norton Pottery responded to changes in styles; in the mid-nineteenth century the popularity of Rockingham ware and parian statuettes joined stoneware production.

STONEWARE IN THE SOUTH

The Moravians in North Carolina and in particular Rudolf Christ, who had shown his responsiveness to new ideas in the past, also expanded production to include stoneware. Christ perfected the technique about 1795 and added press-molded animal-shaped bottles to his ware. These were decorative as well as practical and were in-

17. ATTRIBUTED TO RUDOLF CHRIST
SQUIRREL BOTTLE AND MOLD
Late 18th century. Moravian earthenware, brown glaze, height 7½". Courtesy Old Salem Restoration, Winston-Salem, N.C.

spired by similar objects made at the Staffordshire potteries in England, and imported to America in large quantities.

Also developing in the South—or where they seemed to derive the most impact—were ceramic face vessels. Familiar to many cultures, and generally less sophisticated than most ceramic sculpture, the face vessel consisted of a jug whose body was carved or sculpted into a face. Their origin in Britain dates from the Roman period, the second and third centuries A.D. By the eighteenth century, the face vessel in England had become a comical figure—the Toby jug. Face vessels have taken many forms, with the earliest examples from Montgomery County, Pennsylvania in 1805.[14] And while they have been found in almost every pottery area in America, the most distinctive pieces from this period were made by the black slave potters of the Edgefield district in South Carolina. Although the origin of

18. FACE JUG
c. 1850–1920. Red earthenware with brown metallic glaze, porcelain teeth, height 10″, base diameter 8″. Private collection

these vessels has not been definitively researched, they suggest comparison with those of Ghana and show a stylistic similarity to Bakongo wood sculpture.[15] Bizarre carved faces on figures were venerated by African households and regarded as powerful objects. In the Edgefield district, faces appeared on earthenware and stoneware on a wide variety of forms—jugs, cups, and bottles—using kaolin (a white clay later used in making porcelain) for eyes and teeth. Arched eyebrows, bulging eyes, long noses, and flaring nostrils give the faces their characteristic grotesque, hypnotic stare.

But face vessels were not the only Afro-American contribution during this period. Over half the labor force in the Edgefield district plus a majority of the artisans were slaves trained by whites. Between 1810 and 1820, Abner Landrum established the first pottery in the area. One of his slaves, known as Dave the Potter, was taught to read and set type for Landrum's newspaper as well as to make pottery. Dave combined these skills to produce a personal, expressive body of ware revealing a sense of humor. Rhymed couplets inscribed on his large, open-mouthed stoneware jars advised, "This noble jar will hold twenty [gallons]/ fill it with silver then you will have plenty." Another comments, "A pretty girl on a virge/ how they burge."[16] His exceptional storage jars required as much as forty pounds of clay, were thrown wide at the shoulders, and fitted with slab handles.

The old Edgefield district was also an early center for producing alkaline-glazed stoneware. Historically of ancient origin—first attributed to the Han Dynasty in China (207 B.C. –A.D. 220)—the basic glaze is a combination of wood ash, clay, and sand and was used in Edgefield by the early nineteenth century, spreading from there to other areas of the South and West. Streaks and rivulets are characteristic features of this glaze, probably the result of imperfect grinding in old stone mills.[17] While some potters used a rib or a comb to draw bands of lines through the glaze, the majority of alkaline-glazed stoneware allowed the beauty of the variegated surface to be the main decoration.

By mid-century, most of the techniques and styles associated with American folk pottery had taken hold. To a large extent stoneware had replaced the crude earthenware characteristic of the eighteenth century. Indeed, the most elaborately decorative stoneware was produced in the 1850s, just prior to the Civil War. When that conflict ended, industrial competition, which had gradually been developing, accelerated. In areas where small pottery workshops, in order to survive, had to substantially increase their output, procedures that could speed production but undercut craftsmanship gradually became the rule. Stencil patterns, a decorative technique requiring a minimum of skill, replaced brush decoration and slip-trailed designs. Then, too, in the postwar period, tin-canned fruits and vegetables and glass canning jars entered the market, offering quality and efficiency beyond the capacity of stoneware jugs and crocks. Hand-thrown, hand-decorated ware that retained a sense of the potter's presence was declining. The evolution from handcrafted to factory-made ware was a response to growing industrialization in America, and charted the future of ceramic production.

Chapter 2

THE INDUSTRIALIZATION OF CLAY

Prototypes for Mechanizing Clay Production

The movement away from the folk-pottery foundation began when potters realized the time-saving value of using molds as they became increasingly pressured to produce more and finer wares. Over time, the industrial practices made small inroads into production methods. Press molds for Pennsylvania German pie plates, molds for Queen's ware brought to America by itinerant English potters, and the use of extruders to form handles were all mechanical aids in the reproduction of vessels that were used in addition to handwork. Another operation which hastened the demise of time-consuming hand-painted ware was the development of transfer printing, invented by John Brooks of Birmingham in 1751 and Sadler and Green of Liverpool, England in 1756. A simple, multi-step process, it involved inking an engraved copper plate, usually with the color blue. Then dampened paper was pressed evenly against the inked surface to pick up the image. While still wet, the paper was applied to the porous pottery surface, transferring the blue-outlined image. Lastly, the vessel was dipped in a clear glaze, dried and fired, thus fixing the image. Prior to the Revolutionary War, one American company successfully used transfer printing on porcelain, making this the earliest attempt to produce a fine china. In the postwar period, Staffordshire potters produced innumerable transfer-printed scenes of American national heroes, or coat of arms of the thirteen states, merchandise developed for export to appeal to the new country's nationalism.

THE EMERGENCE OF AMERICAN PORCELAIN

While late-eighteenth-century earthenware and stoneware began to undergo subtle changes in production, porcelain entered American tradition. Kaolin, the basis for porcelain clay bodies, has fewer impu-

opposite:
19. LYMAN AND FENTON COACHMAN BOTTLE
c. 1849–52. Rockingham-type glaze, height 10⅛". Division of Ceramics and Glass, National Museum of American History, Smithsonian Institution, Washington, D.C.

above:
20. ROCKINGHAM TOBY PITCHERS
(left:) Bennington, Vermont, c. 1870–80. (right:) attributed to United States Pottery Company, c. 1853–58. Yellow earthenware with Rockingham glaze, height 6", diameter 4". Collection Robert and Marie Condon, North Bennington, Vt.

rities than other clays; it is delicate, light in weight, and translucent. A true porcelain body is a mixture of kaolin and feldspar. Soft-paste porcelain is artificial porcelain, a combination of kaolin, flint, and feldspar. With the arrival of Chinese porcelain imports to Europe in the seventeenth century, the pressure to produce porcelain began. The first successful European soft-paste porcelain was made by a Frenchman, M. Chicanneau, working in Saint-Cloud in 1695. Johann Friedrich Böttger's experiments in Dresden in 1709–10 resulted in the establishment of the Meissen factory in Germany in 1713 for porcelain production. The English followed in 1744. Wealthy Americans welcomed the importation of European porcelain in the 1730s, and that of Chinese porcelain tableware direct from Canton to Philadelphia in 1772.

The quest for porcelain in America was initiated by Andrew Duché, son of the Philadelphia merchant-potter Anthony Duché. The younger Duché, equally as enterprising as his father, discovered kaolin deposits about 1741 on Cherokee Indian land near Savannah, Georgia, where he was engaged in making earthenware. Although he was not successful in producing porcelain, reports of the period indicate he sold some of the kaolin to the Bow Pottery in England, which began production in 1744.[1] Perhaps as a result of Duché's sale, Josiah Wedgwood sent his agent to America to purchase kaolin for his factory. He used the clay for plaques, medallions, and seals appliquéd on ware he developed resembling Greek and Etruscan vases.[2]

The first entrepreneurs to successfully manufacture American soft-paste porcelain were Gousse Bonnin and George Anthony Morris, whose porcelain factory opened in Philadelphia in 1770. A year earlier they had advertised in a Philadelphia newspaper their intention to manufacture quality porcelain similar to English Bow china. Kaolin mixed with calcined bones were the ingredients used for the clay body at the London factory and the one Bonnin and Morris followed. At that time, American workers were not trained in porcelain production, so Bonnin and Morris employed skilled workmen from England who produced well-made soft-paste porcelain copies of English Bow and Worcester porcelains—sauceboats, fruit bowls with pierced sides, and sweetmeat dishes. Reverse-curve handles, scallop-shell bowl shapes from molds, and Chinese designs in transfer prints characterize the ware. The rococo style of the porcelain appealed to many wealthy Philadelphia families, but their patronage could not sustain the operation when economic factors became unfavorable to small American businesses. High prices for equipment and raw materials coupled with workers' salaries which were higher than their counterparts in England, lowered profits and caused the Bonnin and Morris enterprise to fold in 1772.

Although their factory was in business for such a short time, the proto-industrial nature of the Bonnin and Morris enterprise was an indication that Americans were knowledgeable about factory methods through the production of quality earthenware. By the early nineteenth century, potteries producing cream-colored earthenware from molds enjoyed more success than porcelain production, even though most were relatively short-lived. David Seixas began a pottery in Trenton, New Jersey in 1812, where he produced a type of

21. GOUSSE BONNIN AND GEORGE ANTHONY MORRIS SWEETMEAT DISH
Pennsylvania 1771–72. Soft-paste porcelain, painted in underglaze blue, height 5¼", diameter 7¼". The Brooklyn Museum (45.174). Museum Purchase Fund

creamware, and also in the more affluent city of Philadelphia in 1817. By limiting his production to pitchers and useful wares similar in style to English Staffordshire, he remained in business until 1822.[3] Alexander Trotter's Columbian Pottery exhibited Queen's ware at Philadelphia's prestigious Peale Museum in 1808, confirming that his ware was of good quality; Trotter retired in 1812, possibly outclassed by American and English competition. Some of that competition may have come from another Philadelphian, Abraham Miller, a second-generation potter. Since few examples of ware remain from this period, information about it has come from records of the Franklin Institute, which was established by Philadelphia businessmen in 1824 to elevate standards for industrial products.[4] Miller's teapots, coffeepots, plates, and vases were commended in the judges' report at the Institute's yearly exhibition, and ranged from common white and yellow to highly decorated tableware adorned with silver luster.[5] The Franklin Institute awarded the Jersey Porcelain and Earthenware Company of Jersey City a silver medal in 1826, only a year after the company began. Unfortunately, no examples have survived to test the Institute's claim that the company produced "the best china from American materials."[6]

Industrial Production for Clay

In spite of recognition by the Franklin Institute, the Jersey Porcelain and Earthenware Company could not solve its serious labor and financial problems. In 1828, the plant was sold to a successful Scots, David Henderson, and his brothers. One hundred years after the Industrial Revolution in England had transformed pottery workshops into factories, David Henderson introduced modern factory methods for the production of American ware, which eased some of the industry's labor problems. The individual craftsman's future was as a member of a group that included a designer and workmen, each trained to perform only one of the many steps involved in the final product.[7]

POPULAR WARE AND DAVID HENDERSON

Henderson's operation was begun four years after the Protective Tariff Act of 1824, which had been enacted to encourage America's industrial progress. In 1833, he incorporated the business as the American Pottery and Manufacturing Company. A circular of the period for the earlier operation, D. and J. Henderson (1828–33), lists items such as coffeepots, teapots, flowerpots, mugs, jars, and pipkins—ware that began winning prizes at the Franklin Institute by 1830. Henderson's styles were derived from popular English pottery: relief figures like those of eighteenth-century Staffordshire were more naively applied on pitchers; hunting scenes adorned molded pitchers. Henderson's Toby jug, a sophisticated face vessel, was a less detailed version of the plump sailor whose humorous visage was popular in eighteenth-century England.

Another ware of English origin which Henderson copied was

22. John B. Caire and Company
PITCHER WITH HOUND HANDLE
c. 1842–52. Stoneware with brown Albany slip, height 10", diameter 7". Collection Robert and Marie Condon, North Bennington, Vt.

Rockingham. Much admired in eighteenth-century rural England, the style was named for the Marquis of Rockingham, at whose pottery located at Swinton in Yorkshire it was thought to have originated in 1757. Characterized by a light-colored or yellow body splotched or mottled by a brown glaze which resembles a tortoise-shell, Rockingham ware became popular in the 1830s when Gothic revival motifs were fashionable in architectural trim, furniture, fabrics, and other decorative accessories. The style lent itself to press-molding and later to casting. Henderson's flint stoneware was similar in composition to Rockingham, capable of being molded into thin-walled containers.

His brown-glazed Rockingham pitchers with realistic rose-vine embossed patterns are distinguished by handles in the shape of a greyhound dog, whose head and forepaws rest against the lip of the pitcher. The design of some of these pitchers has been attributed to Daniel Greatbach, one of the most skillful and prolific modelers of the period. Greatbach had worked in Staffordshire but immigrated to Jersey City in the late 1830s.[8] Although the hound-handled pitchers are English in origin, the Staffordshire modeler also probably owes a debt to books published in England in the late eighteenth century describing the excavations at Pompeii, where pitchers of a similar nature—with dogs as handles—were unearthed. Pre-Columbian and American Indian ware also have examples using similarly shaped handles.

Henderson's wares reflected the taste of the period. A hexagonal spittoon of 1840 places the figure of an Apostle in each facet, framed

23. D. & J. Henderson
PITCHER WITH HOUND HANDLE
c. 1840. Earthenware, height 6", width 6¾", depth 5⅜". The Metropolitan Museum of Art, New York. Gift of John C. Cattus, 1967

Daniel Greatbach, an Englishman who first created the hound handle, came to America in the early 1800s and sold his molds to different American potteries. As a result, variations of the hound-handle pitcher abounded in pottery production in many different states such as New York, New Jersey, Ohio, and Vermont.

24. THREE SPATTERWARE PLATES. *c. 1860–90. New Jersey. Earthenware, diameter 7–10". Collection Bea Cohen, Easton, Penn.*

The spatterware surface was most simply produced by tapping a brush loaded with color against the ware. Later, a sponge dipped in color was patted over a slip-covered white surface and then covered with a transparent glaze. The actual objects were mold-made, even though the surfaces were decorated by hand. In this way, sponge- and spatterware combined folk decoration with an industrial process.

by a Gothic arch similar to prominent architectural details of the time. Henderson's spatterware, a style borrowed from early nineteenth-century English country ware, featured hot milk and chocolate jugs particularly appealing to rural households. Interest in spatterware declined in England in the late eighteenth century, but was eventually revived chiefly for export. The foremost English company associated with this decorative style was W. Adams and Sons of Stoke-on-Trent, operating from 1829 to 1865 and exporting much of their production to America. The eighteenth-century English spatterware surface was made by tapping a brush loaded with color against the damp surface of the ware. Some potteries spattered plates with color just around the inner edge, leaving the center white or with a painted or transfer-printed design. Like Henderson's jugs, other plates, pitchers, and bowls carried an overall pattern of color. The style reached its peak in the mid-1800s, though production continued for several more decades with variations on the process. Associated with spatterware is spongeware, which is similar in appearance but involves a different process. Here, a sponge is dipped in color and patted over a white ground and then covered with transparent glaze.

Transfer-decorated whiteware (or white earthenware) dinner sets titled "Canova" were Henderson's answer to similar ware imported from Staffordshire. Both American and English ware prints featured scenic decorations, typical of the style of painting at that time. American landscape painting expressed the nation's pride in the continent's vast expanse and natural wonders. The Englishman Thomas Cole had founded the Hudson River School of landscape painting in which the timelessness of nature, its grandeur and power, was contrasted with the temporal nature of man. James Fenimore Cooper's novels of the wilderness—*The Last of the Mohicans* (1826), *The Prairie* (1827)—and the nature poetry of William Cullen Bryant further established the landscape as a dominant theme.

Henderson proved it was possible to produce excellent wares that appealed to public taste. Although his leadership was cut short when he suffered an accident resulting in his death in 1845, his company, considered the first successful commercial pottery in America, continued in operation led by several groups of partners until 1892.

WILLIAM TUCKER AND EMPIRE STYLE PORCELAIN

Where David Henderson mechanized the production of earthenware and stoneware, William Tucker applied similar methods to manufacturing porcelain. He used molds and divided among his workmen the tasks of preparing the clay, designing, modeling, and painting the ware, the glazing, and the firing. Tucker's interest in porcelain began when he went to work in his father's Philadelphia china store. As a founding member of the Franklin Institute, the elder Tucker had access to technical books on porcelain that William Tucker consulted when he tried painting on undecorated European ware and firing it in a small kiln behind the store. He soon outgrew his father's backyard workshop. A vase of 1825 commemorates Tucker's decision to manufacture porcelain. A scene painted on the belly of the vase shows a Philadelphia landmark, the old Waterworks, which Tucker and his father leased for their factory. The top of a bottle kiln is visible at the roofline of one building and three small white pitchers sit on a fence, porcelain forms soon to be closely associated with Tucker production.

In order to help finance a manufacturing company, Tucker entered the first of three partnerships by joining with John N. Bird in 1826. Ware for this period was undecorated or minimally decorated with small, romatic, sepia landscapes similar to those on English porcelains. By 1828, Tucker's partner was Thomas Hulme and by this time the quality of the ware had improved, more colors were introduced, and the range of decoration expanded. The company's continually shaky financial condition led to a new change of partners in 1832, Judge Joseph Hemphill. When Hemphill added his financial resources, the company planned to import skilled workmen from France. Bitter anti-British sentiment following the War of 1812 caused Americans to favor French manners and taste. The French Empire Style, the second phase of Neoclassicism (and known as the Federal Style in America), had enveloped American architecture and design in the immediate post–Revolutionary War period. Tucker porcelain designs were based on this shift in taste.

The Tucker and Hemphill factory produced ware which closely resembled French porcelain of the period, although there is no evidence confirming that French workmen were actually employed. Tucker's adaptation of French porcelains included pairs of vases decorated with Grecian garlands, wreaths, gilded ormolu handles, and gold trim. Naturalistic floral and botanical motifs decorated tea and coffee services, compote dishes, beakers, fruit baskets, and scent bottles. Tucker favored pitchers with arched handles, a flaring neck, and a graceful, raised spout. The fluted base on many of the pitchers is original to Tucker porcelain and not traceable to any other European or American factory.[9] Bouquets of roses, tulips, daisies, and other flowers, in compositions often derived from botanical prints, identify the late phase of Tucker porcelain, typical of the romantic naturalism of the Empire Style and the early Rococo Revival.

With his various partners, William Tucker established the first successful porcelain company in America, which received three Franklin Institute awards for its ware. However, because of tariff controversies, which affected porcelain, the company's chances for survival were threatened. As a desperate measure in 1831, Tucker offered to sell President Jackson (who had admired and purchased the ware) the secret of his porcelain production for $20,000, but Jackson was not tempted.[10] Tucker died in 1832, leaving the management of the company to his brother Thomas, who had been the chief designer and decorator. Operating under the name of the American Porcelain Company from 1835 to 1838, the company met its final economic crisis when the financial panic of 1837 ruined Judge Hemphill, forcing the factory to close the following year.

With the demise of Tucker and Hemphill, porcelain was not produced in America again until around 1848, when Charles Cartlidge and Company advertised soft-paste porcelain buttons (less ex-

25. CHARLES CARTLIDGE
PITCHER
1853. Porcelain, cornstalks in relief, highlighted in gold, height 12½". Division of Ceramics and Glass, National Museum of American History, Smithsonian Institution, Washington, D.C.

Cornstalks, such as seen in relief on this pitcher, were used as decoration beginning with the Federal style, the American interpretation of Neoclassicism that began after the Revolutionary War. Corn and tobacco, having become part of an American iconography, were depicted on ceramic pitchers and parian vases.

pensive than pearl) in Greenpoint, New York. A Staffordshire native, Cartlidge produced popular items from dinnerware to bisque porcelain portrait busts and plaques. Especially in demand were pitchers; Cartlidge's designs for this form reflect the rococo style, to which he added symbols distinctly American—the flag, the eagle, and ears of corn. Produced from molds modeled by Josiah Jones, Cartlidge's brother-in-law who was also from Staffordshire, the Cartlidge pitchers, like Tucker's, served both decorative and utilitarian functions. Jones has been credited with producing exceptional busts of prominent Americans such as Daniel Webster, John Marshall, and Henry Clay.[11] Cartlidge's ware was recognized for its high quality at the Crystal Palace in New York in 1853; three years later the factory closed its doors.

Cartlidge's neighbors and competitors in Greenpoint, beginning in 1850, were German immigrants, William Boch and Brothers. Their porcelain clay body was similar to that used by Bonnin and Morris, the English type of soft-paste porcelain referred to as bone china. Boch and Brothers featured Rococo Revival pitchers with ear-shaped handles and leafy scrolls. One particular relief design associated with this pottery was a bacchanalian figure in a grape arbor. The unstable economic situation prior to the Civil War drove Boch to seek a partner in Thomas C. Smith, who invested in the firm in 1857; shortly afterward Smith purchased the company to protect his interests. He renamed the new company the Union Porcelain Works, an enterprise that made its most notable contributions in the post–Civil War period.

THE INNOVATIONS OF CHRISTOPHER FENTON

For a time, the Norton Pottery of Bennington, Vermont, was associated with one of the most innovative potters of this period. Around 1835, Christopher Webber Fenton, the son of a Dorset, Vermont potter, leased an area of the Norton factory to work on his own, where he patented a firebrick in 1837. Julius Norton, the grandson of founder John Norton, became the firm's manager in 1841. While Fenton may have had some earlier association with the factory, at this point his marriage to Julius's sister in the 1830s and his apparent expertise resulted in a partnership with Norton which lasted four years, beginning in 1843. When porcelain clays were discovered in Bennington, Fenton persuaded Norton to hire John Harrison, an English potter from the Copeland factory at Stoke-on-Trent, whose experience with porcelain they hoped would initiate production. Unfortunately, a disastrous factory fire destroyed Harrison's experiments and soon afterward he returned to England.

The Norton-Fenton partnership was dissolved in 1847, perhaps because of a difference of opinion over standard ware. Mold-made Rockingham ware had been part of their output, perhaps at Fenton's insistence, since none had been made previously in New England. Fenton returned to an area of the factory he had leased a decade earlier, and experimented on refining the coloring process for Rockingham ware. He applied a transparent glaze to bisque ware, and then

26. TUCKER AND HEMPHILL PORCELAIN PITCHER
1832–38. *Porcelain, height 9¼", base diameter 7¼". The Brooklyn Museum (47.145). Museum Purchase Fund*

sprinkled the glaze with metallic oxides from a perforated box to obtain tones of blue, yellow, and orange that blended with the brown color of the clay. The resulting glaze, a variation of Rockingham ware, he called flint enamel. In 1849 Fenton patented the process.

Poor Man's Classical Sculpture—Parian Ware

What Fenton learned about porcelain from John Harrison, he applied to a variety of products, including restaurant and hotel china. But his major achievement lay in producing parian ware, a type of porcelain not previously formulated in America. Developed in 1842 at the Copeland factory in England, the porcelain bears a superficial resemblance to marble used for fine statuary. Because of its low plasticity, the clay body is usually cast or press-molded, rather than thrown on the wheel. In 1853, Fenton incorporated his firm as the United States Pottery Company and sent some of his parian wares to the Crystal Palace fair in New York City. He produced parian statuettes that copied English and French tabletop figures in European dress, American marble statues of the period, sentimental angels, cherubs, men of humble occupations, or children at prayer, as well as literary figures such as Milton and Dickens. Extremely popular was a copy of Hiram Powers's *The Greek Slave* (1843). The original white marble sculpture was the embodiment of Neoclassicism's romantic allegories of vice and virtue and marked the high tide of nineteenth-centu-

above left:
27. ATTRIBUTED TO UNITED STATES POTTERY COMPANY
STATUETTES
c. 1848–58. Parian ware, height 9–10", diameter 4–4½". Collection Robert and Marie Condon, Bennington, Vt.

above right:
28. UNITED STATES POTTERY COMPANY
PITCHER
c. 1852–58. Parian ware, height 10", diameter 7⅛". The Metropolitan Museum of Art, New York

During Andrew Jackson's presidency (1829–37), the belief that America was destined for greatness was expressed in paintings of the continent's natural wonders. This pitcher reflects the national feeling of pride in the American landscape.

ry academic sculpture. In contrast to the folk artists who typified America's sculptors in the past, artists like Powers had journeyed to Italy to study and adapt classical and Neoclassical formulas for their own subjects. Thus we have Horatio Greenough's monumental (if not amusing) figure of *George Washington*, draped in classical robes, posed like an "Olympian Zeus."[12]

Lifesize sculpture by these artists were only within the means of the very wealthy and the federal government. But if the originals were beyond the reach of middle-class Americans, they could choose from a variety of parian porcelain copies made by the United States Pottery Company, and other porcelain factories. The favored site for these statuettes was the fireplace mantel, where pairs of small animals or birds flanked the hearth in the manner of ancient, guardian tomb sculptures. Some of these figures, such as a recumbent stag or a pair of poodles holding baskets in their mouths, are attributed to the peripatetic Daniel Greatbach, who became associated with the Norton Pottery in the 1850s. Greatbach sold his molds to any pottery that would purchase them, which accounts for the proliferation of similar objects from many different factories.

Decorative Pitchers

The popularity of figurines was matched by interest in the pitcher—a form with sculptural possibilities that lent itself to the extravagancies of the Rococo Revival and provided a surface for bas relief. A change in social customs, specifically a period of abstinence from alcohol among the upper classes, may account in part for the increased use of pitchers for non-alcoholic beverages such as hot milk and hot chocolate.[13] Besides serving utilitarian needs, decorative pitchers, like Pennsylvania German and Moravian plates, enhanced the open shelves of the mid-nineteenth century sideboard. Henderson's and Fenton's Rockingham pitchers were a popular choice, but foremost among the pitcher designs were Fenton's all-white parian examples, low-relief representations of plants, climbing roses, or cascading water meant to symbolize Niagara Falls. Corn was a popular decorative motif, too, having its first incarnation as an American symbol on the column capitals in the Senate wing of the nation's new legislature designed by Benjamin Henry Latrobe. A Fenton pitcher with a relief design of ears of corn was considered an original American contribution to pottery design. It was eventually copied by many potteries, among them Charles Cartlidge and Company of Greenpoint, New York, who produced pitchers depicting ears of corn unfolding from their husks.

Americans took pride in objects that expressed their nationalism, even though a continuing dependence on European styles remained important, illustrated by the popularity of Fenton's copies of English coachmen bottles, Toby pitchers (see fig. 20), and especially a particular blue-and-white pitcher. This T. J. and J. Mayer English pitcher depicts a romantic, moral tale of two youngsters, Paul and Virginia, who perish for their principles. Rococo in style, the pitcher has a high, arched handle and curved spout; the couple are in high relief surrounded by tropical foliage against a blue, stippled background.

29. CORN VASE
Bennington, Vermont. c. 1847–58. Parian ware, height 6¼". Division of Ceramics and Glass, National Museum of American History, Smithsonian Institution, Washington, D.C.

Like William Tucker, Fenton engaged in several partnerships, and though his production was among the largest in the country, poor marketing procedures, increasing costs, and financial instability caused by the approaching Civil War closed the factory in 1858.

The Rise of American Pottery Centers

The Norton and Fenton establishments in Bennington, Vermont, made the city an important pottery center during the mid-nineteenth century. As mentioned earlier, a large number of potteries opened in New Jersey, especially in Trenton, to take advantage of the state's excellent deposits of clay. The third pottery center established during the mid-nineteenth century was in East Liverpool, Ohio. The geographical location of each center formed a right triangle located in the northeastern section of the country. Although unplanned, this triangular area of pottery production was, in a sense, the Staffordshire of America. East Liverpool offered resources simi-

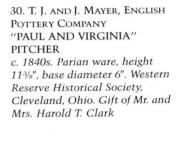

30. T. J. AND J. MAYER, ENGLISH POTTERY COMPANY
"PAUL AND VIRGINIA" PITCHER
c. 1840s. Parian ware, height 11⅜", base diameter 6". Western Reserve Historical Society, Cleveland, Ohio. Gift of Mr. and Mrs. Harold T. Clark

31. KNOWLES, TAYLOR & KNOWLES CO.
TWO VASES
1893. Porcelain. (left:) Height 9¾", base diameter 6⅛"; (right:) height 7½", base diameter 4½". Division of Ceramics and Glass, National Museum of American History, Smithsonian Institution, Washington, D.C.

lar to the other locations—deposits of fine clay and river transportation providing easy access to markets. By 1840 there were more than fifty stoneware potteries in Ohio, earning Akron the tag "Stoneware City."[14] But East Liverpool attracted immigrant English potters, such as James Bennett (who arrived in 1839, having worked for David Henderson), joined in 1841 by his three brothers whose expertise assured a level of quality ware. Bennett's spatterware was considered closer to its English antecedents, although no extant pottery remains. John Hancock, a former Wedgwood apprentice, came to East Liverpool in 1842 from South Amboy, New Jersey, and like the Bennett brothers, began to produce yellowware and Rockingham ware. Isaac Knowles, who started as a salesman for Bennett, left in 1845 to establish a firm with Isaac Harvey. Ohio production consisted of both utilitarian wares and statuettes, with what was perceived as a midwestern preference for plainer surfaces. Seated spaniels, recumbent lions, variations on the hound-handle pitcher, and a Rockingham glaze that more closely resembles a tortoiseshell characterize Ohio wares.

The benefit of transportation along the Ohio River to inland markets was unfortunately accompanied by occasional flooding, which drove some potters to choose other locations. Edward and William Bennett, two of James's brothers, moved to Baltimore in 1846, where they employed Charles Coxon as chief modeler. Coxon produced one of the period's most famous teapots, a biblically inspired design called *Rebecca at the Well*, based on an English design of the same name. Of those designs created by the Bennetts, a blue majolica pitcher featuring reliefs of Chesapeake Bay sea life was exhibited at the Crystal Palace in 1853.

32. HARKER, TAYLOR & CO.
HOUND HANDLE PITCHER
c. 1850. Hunting scene with grapevine pattern around neck of pitcher, height 11". Division of Ceramics and Glass, National Museum of American History, Smithsonian Institution, Washington, D.C.

left:
33. BASKETWEAVE TEAPOT
*c. 1890–1915. Yellowware,
molded, height 7", diameter 9".
Private collection*

below:
34. CUSTARD CUPS
*c. 1880–1930. Yellowware,
height 3–4". Collection Fran and
Doug Faulkner, New Kingston,
N.Y.*

Yellowware is a finer clay body
than redware and more durable.
So-called because of its yellow-
ish color when fired, this type
of clay easily lent itself to slip
casting and mass production
techniques. The raised gridwork
on this teapot and the minimally
decorated custard cups show the
range from simple wheel-thrown
forms to more elaborate molded
forms and surfaces.

Potteries which survived the economic trauma of the Civil War were joined by new establishments as American industry expanded on every front. The factory system for pottery was firmly entrenched. By this time, ceramic design had broadened its range, now drawing on any number of ornamental styles for inspiration. Among the many newly established firms was the Union Porcelain Works of Greenpoint, Long Island (formerly the Boch Brothers pottery), which Thomas Smith purchased from William Boch in 1864. Smith applied the knowledge gained from several years' study of the manufacture of hard-paste porcelain in France and he introduced underglaze decoration. This technique of painting on bisque ware was new to American potters, and it remained unheralded until Limoges underglaze-decorated ware appeared at the Philadelphia Centennial International Exhibition in 1876, where it was noticed and popularized by china painters.

The Philadelphia Centennial International Exhibition, 1876

The industrial momentum that had been building since the early years of the century culminated in the one-hundred-year celebration of the young nation's founding. Proposed in 1869 by the Franklin Institute, the fair was to be an international exposition of fine products, and a landmark opportunity to show the world America's industrial progress. Thirty-five nations accepted America's invitation to participate in the event. To accommodate the huge draw of exhibits, the Centennial planners created over 250 buildings on a 236-acre site; it was to be the largest fair of its kind to date.

The showcasing of ceramics at the Centennial motivated the ceramic industry to form their first national association, the United States Potters, in January 1875. Infected with the spirit of nationalism as were other industries, the seventy representatives of companies from around the country agreed to advance the industry through an exchange of practical information, an unusual step considering the fierce competition between factories. Following the example of the English pottery industry, the association established the Free Evening School of Design at its headquarters in Trenton where workers could advance their skills. Further, the association agreed not to display copies of foreign wares at the Centennial exhibition. Instead, the group encouraged the development of ceramics representing the country's national character.[15]

In response, Thomas Smith hired Karl Müller, a German immigrant considered one of the finest designers in the country, to create a special group of sculptures. Müller utilized easily understood forms and symbols. His bisque figure of a blacksmith in an apron with an upraised, muscular arm holding his pipe appealed to Americans who believed in the nobility of the common man and the dignity of work. Müller's versatility and ability to satisfy a variety of tastes is demonstrated in his Neoclassical parian busts (*Pallas Athena* is one example) and in vases decorated with plant and animal motifs or with designs of oriental extraction. But it was Müller's

Century Vase, designed for the Centennial, that not only distinguished his work, but heralded the art of American ceramics. Considered the finest example of American ceramics at the Centennial, the vase was a twenty-two-inch-high amalgam of American energy, patriotism, and technical achievement in an eclectic, rococo style.

Like Müller, sculptor Isaac Broome, who joined with Ott and Brewer of Trenton, New Jersey (founded in 1873), contributed a landmark piece to the Centennial. Prior to that, his early parian bust of Lincoln (1860) possessed classic dignity and simplicity, while his bust of Cleopatra (1875) was richly colored in black, blue, and gold. His acknowledged masterpiece is his parian *Baseball Vase* (1876), which epitomizes the nation's increasing fixation on an American sport. Here a majestic eagle perches above a baseball supported by a column around which figures of a pitcher, batter, and catcher take their traditional poses, thereby aligning the national symbol with the national pastime.

35. CHARLES COXON (MODELER), FOR EDWARD AND WILLIAM BENNETT
REBECCA AT THE WELL TEAPOT
c. 1860–1900. Yellow earthenware with Rockingham glaze, height 8", diameter 6½". Private collection

THE LEGACY OF INDUSTRIALIZATION

When the Philadelphia Centennial opened its doors on May 10 for six months, visitors were met with a profusion of objects. Besides the display of machinery, industrial arts, and inventions, which included Alexander Graham Bell's embryonic telephone, Americans could revel in paintings portraying historical events and colonial architecture. Ceramics were located in a corner of the Main Exhibition Building, assembled with little regard for an aesthetic arrangement. Ceramics from abroad were in a separate hall. For the first time Americans were exposed to French, German, and Chinese porcelains and the pottery and porcelains of Japan. The display attracted much interest, especially from that part of the public aware of the aesthetic

36. KARL MÜLLER, UNION POR-
CELAIN WORKS
THE CENTURY VASE
*1876. Hard-paste porcelain,
height 22¼", base diameter 10".
The Brooklyn Museum (43.25).
Gift of Carll and Franklin Chace
in memory of Pastora Forest
Smith Chace*

Müller combined American
motifs with scenes attesting to
Yankee ingenuity such as Ful-
ton's steamboat, McCormick's
reaper, Singer's sewing machine.

reform movements in England and Europe. Inspired by exhibitions of
Japanese art in London beginning in the 1860s, European decorative
arts began to emphasize a tasteful simplicity seen in Morris & Company furniture, William DeMorgan ceramics, and Mackintosh interior decoration.

While Americans were justifiably proud of the technical sophistication exemplified by the *Century* and *Baseball* vases, and classic
portraits, it was also obvious that stylistic changes in Europe influenced by exposure to oriental art had outdistanced American design.
In comparison to the uncluttered appearance of hand-decorated Japanese vessels, the eclectic, fussy details in relief of vines, medallions,
and panels applied to Victorian vases seemed overworked. Accustomed to measuring taste by European standards, many artists attending the Philadelphia Centennial were stimulated to reconsider
their ideas of form and surface design. At a time when the examples
of American industrialization at the Centennial raised the self-
esteem of the nation, that same industrialization could no longer
compete effectively with a greater movement afoot in the decorative
arts that favored a return to some aspects of the crafted object left
behind by mechanization.

opposite:
37. ARTUS VAN BRIGGLE
LORELEI
*c. 1902. Stoneware, white glaze,
height 10⅜", diameter 4½".
Everson Museum of Art, Syracuse, N.Y. Gift of Ronald and
Andrew Kuchta in memory of
Clara Mae Kuchta*

The figure as a decorative element on a vase—as a handle or
as surface relief—was the style
in French ceramics of the 1890s.
Van Briggle's use of the head,
arm, and hair to form the lip of a
vase was unusual for an American artist, and is one of five
known figural designs by the
artist.

Part II

The Art Pottery Movement 1876–1918

Chapter 3
THE ARTS AND CRAFTS MOVEMENT

Changes in Victorian Taste—England's Arts and Crafts Movement

To a large extent, nineteenth-century American pottery followed English styles, altered by the processes and techniques of industrialization. Typical of the English factory system was the segmentation of work wherein tasks were divided among several workers. This meant the potter was divorced from the designer, a circumstance that increased quantity at the expense of quality. Additionally, because the designer often lacked direct experience with clay, his designs were not always suitable for ceramic objects, further causing a decline in quality and craftsmanship. The English essayist and historian Thomas Carlyle, troubled by the deterioration of crafts due to the dependence on the machine, warned that the factory system would erode the human spirit. In *Past and Present* (1843), he advocated the revival of the craft guilds of the Middle Ages to solve some of England's social problems resulting from industrialization. Prescribing healthy social conditions combined with education and morality as factors essential to good art, critic John Ruskin, Carlyle's contemporary, attacked mass-produced products in a series of essays published as *Unto This Last* (1862). Drawing from the ideas of Carlyle and Ruskin, poet and designer William Morris sought to revive the art of craftsmanship with the formation of a design firm dedicated to the principles of the medieval craft guilds. By uniting the fine and applied arts, he hoped that the emphasis on the individual craftsman would bring about the reforms necessary to an overly industrialized society. Embracing the beliefs of the Pre-Raphaelites, Morris and his brotherhood of dedicated artisans influenced profoundly the emerging Arts and Crafts Movement in England, and the decorative arts more generally in America.

Through his actions Morris sought to improve the quality of artistic design and raise the level of public taste, a formidable task in the Victorian era. The arbiter of taste at that time was the upper-

opposite:
38. *MARY LOUISE MCLAUGHLIN*
n.d.

above:
39. *BENN PITMAN*, 1889

middle-class Englishwoman, who spent her life in the smothering confines of an amalgam of styles cluttering the late-Victorian household. Attacking this eclectic environment and urging restraint was Charles Locke Eastlake, whose book *Hints on Household Taste* (1862) was one of the first to suggest that one should be surrounded by "objects of beauty to be considered for their artistic merits."[1] Eastlake's influential book reflected both William Morris's philosophy and specifically his own interest in Japanese art, which was destined shortly to have an extensive impact on art in England, the Continent, and America.

WOMEN, CULTURE, AND THE ARTS

Eastlake's book appeared in America in 1877, followed by numerous publications amplifying his ideas and adapting them to American conditions. Since the Civil War, interior decoration had become an increasing preoccupation of affluent Americans. Newly rich bankers, railway barons, and industrialists—all who saw themselves as the American counterpart of European royalty—were as intent on living in an atmosphere of cultured taste as they were in amassing oil pools, trusts, and monopolies. The unrestrained acquisitiveness of the Victorian period suited their life-style, until Eastlake and others demonstrated that the standards for taste in England and Europe were changing.

As the American upper class followed the artistic lead of Europe, so too did the middle classes. The American housewife was particularly receptive to Ruskin's belief that one's surroundings influence moral and ethical values. Eager to raise her family in a proper and tasteful atmosphere, the housewife responded with interest to new publications like *The Art Amateur* ("Devoted to the Cultivation of the Art of the Household"), published in 1879.[2] Within the next ten years, other publications—*The Ladies Home Journal* (1883), *Good Housekeeping* (1885), and *The House Beautiful* (1887)—appeared, satisfying the growing interest in home decoration. Eastlake's book provided the initial impetus for change; combined with industrial advances and affluence it opened new vistas for women seeking to develop their artistic talent.

At the height of the Victorian era, women began to shed some of the restraints imposed by contemporary social mores. Work outside of the home—as teachers, governesses, and domestics—came to be seen as an extension of the woman's broader role in culture, and was therefore acceptable. The invention of the sewing machine in 1851 and the typewriter in 1867 further extended employment possibilities; by 1870, one and one-half million women (or about 3.5 percent of the population) were at work outside of their households, though rarely in positions of authority.[3] Women with artistic talent found few avenues for expression beyond embroidery, crewel, and needlework. Eventually this changed, with the unlikely help of society women who saw themselves as the cultural leaders of their communities.

In 1854, Sara Worthington King Peter of Cincinnati became one of the first women to organize her social equals for the purpose of establishing a Ladies Gallery of Fine Arts; here women learned art and design in an organization whose goal was to raise the city's level of culture. In addition, the school intended to build an art collection that would enhance the city's artistic reputation. With the funds from donors she had solicited, Sara Peter purchased copies of European master paintings and casts of classical sculpture to form the nucleus of Cincinnati's collection.[4] After the Civil War, socially prominent women in other cities who had been influenced by European travel followed Sara Peter's example and initiated fund-raising events for art schools and art museums. The new institutions required experienced teachers.

Cincinnati at that time was fortunate to attract a knowledgeable Englishman, Benn Pitman. A firm believer in the participation of women in the arts, Pitman was sent to America by his brother, Sir Isaac, the inventor of the shorthand method of writing. The younger Pitman taught that skill to American women, but as a disciple of the English Arts and Crafts Movement his sense of public mission was wider than the teaching of secretarial skills. In 1873, Pitman became an instructor in the newly organized Practical Arts Department of the School of Design at the University of Cincinnati, donating his services for the establishment of a department in wood carving, and also presenting Saturday morning lectures on decorative arts. "What a smile is to the human face...true decoration is to human handicraft," Pitman declared. Another of his often-quoted statements synthesized the Victorian attitude toward a woman's place in society: "To whom shall we look for the adornment of our homes? to girls and women most assuredly. Let men construct and women decorate."[5]

In 1874, the art school sponsored an exhibition of student work including examples of china painting done at home by one of the women, Maria Longworth Nichols. Among Pitman's wood-carving students, Mary Louise McLaughlin admired the china-painted pottery and asked Pitman to purchase the mineral colors needed to make it on a forthcoming trip of his to New York.[6] On his return with supplies, Pitman employed a young Cincinnati woman who had learned china painting in her native Berlin to teach a class at the art school. This class became the basis for the china painting movement in America. Thus, Pitman launched the artistic careers of several Cincinnati women and affected the lives of many others.

The China Painting Movement—from England to America

China painting was an appealing medium for women because it allowed for a range of artistic ability on objects—teacups, plates, vases—serving domestic needs. In England, women had become involved in the medium some twenty years earlier as part of the Arts and Crafts Movement. As early as 1852, the National Art Training Schools in South Kensington offered classes for both sexes to prepare students for work at Minton's Kensington Art Pottery Studio. In the uncertain financial climate of mid-nineteenth-century England, china painting offered genteel employment in conditions far better than the regular type of factory work described in the books of Charles Dickens. Following a design drawn in lead pencil, the china painter applied coloring oxides mixed with finely ground glass to the glazed surface of a porcelain form (called a blank), which had been rubbed with turpentine. The technique and the result looked similar to painting with watercolors except that the mineral colors would melt into the transparent glaze surface when fired. Women trained and hired as decorators were usually supervised by a man who provided them with designs. As their skills improved, the more accomplished were allowed to sign their initials or name, which gave the work the status of art in the eyes of its participants and lured a flood of amateurs to the field in the 1870s.

INSPIRATION FROM THE CENTENNIAL

Just as the Centennial International Exhibition inspired a potters association, it also encouraged the formation of committees in many cities to raise funds for exhibitions of local arts and crafts. In 1873, for example, the women of Philadelphia staged a Boston Tea Party. With a lighthearted disregard for historical accuracy, the women hosted the proceedings, each dressed as Martha Washington, and sold commercially made tea cups decorated with patriotic slogans as souvenirs. Not to be outdone, the ladies of Cincinnati staged a Martha Washington tea party in 1874, featuring cups decorated by the art school's china painters, which were auctioned for as much as twenty-five dollars each. More important than the $385 raised, the interest shown by local patrons encouraged the artists.[7] The sweet taste of approval encouraged the china painters of Cincinnati to prepare an exhibit of their work for the Centennial. None of them would have predicted that china painting would be "launched" at the Philadelphia show.

In contrast to the enthusiasm expressed for china painting, factory pottery exhibited in Philadelphia met with harsh criticism, which labeled the ware as inartistic. One reason for this reaction involved the lingering negative sentiments toward American art that stemmed from the pre–Revolutionary War period. As Jennie Young, a writer of the period rather hopelessly observed, "American art may be good, even equal to the best, but unfortunately, it is American."[8] These noble views, however true at the time, could not obscure the fact that American factory pottery was stylistically behind. The nation's pottery companies continued to produce High Victorian shapes and decorations while Europe's designs were based on oriental models, a change that occurred after the first exhibit of Japanese ceramics at the London International Exposition in 1862.

MARY LOUISE MCLAUGHLIN AND CHINA PAINTING

China painting done by women in Cincinnati on exhibit in Philadelphia included the work of Mary Louise McLaughlin, a member of the first china painting class at the School of Design. Given the attention and inquiries from female visitors at the Philadelphia Centennial, McLaughlin was prompted to write a book about the process. In two weeks time she produced the manuscript for *China Painting: A Practical Manual for the Use of Amateurs in the Decoration of Hard Porcelain.* It was first published in 1877 and reissued in several editions, eventually selling 23,000 copies over the next several years. The figures indicate a prompt acceptance by people eager to master the technique. In the book, McLaughlin acknowledges that while china painting can be a delightful leisure activity it is worthy of serious study. Explaining the craft with the care of an art teacher, she urged students to draw, to educate their eye to detect the beauty in nature, and to train their hand to copy these forms. Her advice on purchasing porcelain blanks, china paints, brushes, and procedures reveals a careful analysis of the medium as well as information culled from the Royal Worcester Porcelain Company, Royal Dresden, and M. Lacroix, a writer of the period. Following Charles Eastlake, she stressed the importance of adapting design to the purpose of an object. The china painter's objective, she cautioned, should not be to display work like a painting, but to decorate an object to "bring out the beauty of the form."[9] In contrast to the low and high reliefs of figures, animals, and plants applied to the surface of Victorian pottery which concealed the ceramic form, china painting offered a type of surface enrichment which permitted attention to the vessel's

40. MARY LOUISE MCLAUGHLIN (DECORATOR)
DISH
*c. 1870. Porcelain blank decorated by McLaughlin with china paints, diameter 8¼".
Division of Ceramics and Glass, National Museum of American History, Smithsonian Institution, Washington, D.C.*

shape. Heavy ornamentation was no longer a mask. McLaughlin and the women she influenced decorated imported or American bisque vessels. The return to handcrafted ware showed the influence of the Arts and Crafts Movement; now America was following suit. McLaughlin made esssential information accessible and in doing so laid the technical foundation for the china painting movement.

Underglaze Painting and Asymmetrical Design

Visiting the Centennial in 1876, Mary Louise McLaughlin was attracted to a display of underglaze painting on Haviland ware from Limoges, France. Mentioned earlier in connection with Thomas Smith, underglaze painting—a technique also called barbotine—was perfected by Ernest Chaplet in 1871. It produced a slightly raised surface, much like oil painting on canvas. Slips made from finely pulverized fired clay are painted on a dried, unfired clay body, then covered with a clear, glossy glaze. McLaughlin was intrigued both by the coloring and a painterly approach to pottery decoration that exceeded the effects possible with china paints. Uncertain of how to achieve this surface, and unaware that another American had successfully imitated underglaze painting, she began experimenting with mineral paints. Something she saw on a visit to the Patrick Coultry Pottery of Cincinnati made her decide to combine mineral paints with wet clay slip and apply the mixture to a wet clay body. Generally, pulverized and fired clay slip was applied to a dry clay body. McLaughlin fired her first piece of underglaze painting in October 1877 at the Coultry Pottery. Though it was not a complete success, the results indicated she was moving in the right direction. Because she had no one to consult and had to rely on her own ideas, McLaughlin's method differs from the French process used by Thomas Smith and in the purest sense can be considered an American innovation.

Unlike china painting, underglaze painting brought the artist one step closer to an involvement with clay. The technique required mixing minerals and working on a just-completed damp vessel. Friends of McLaughlin who had worked in china painting urged her to teach a class in the new process. She did so, at the Coultry Pottery, where her first class of men and women approached their work with a seriousness of purpose equal to that of their teacher. Another group of women whose art background stemmed from making antimacassars and afghans also persuaded McLaughlin to instruct them. Working with wet clay vessels was a totally new experience that prompted much experimentation. McLaughlin, who maintained a professional attitude toward her art, viewed the group's unrestrained approach as "a wild ceramic orgy during which much perfectly good clay was spoiled and numerous freaks created."[10]

In response to such undisciplined work, McLaughlin founded and served as president of the Pottery Club, organized in 1879. Through the sixteen years of its existence, the club's twelve participating and three honorary members provided a standard of workmanship for pottery decorators. Maria Longworth Nichols, the china painter whose work on exhibit at the School of Design prompted the

41. *Haviland Faience at the Philadelphia Centennial, 1876*

opposite:
42. THOMAS WHEATLEY
VASE WITH FROG AND CRAYFISH IN RELIEF
c. 1880–82. Earthenware, height 12", diameter 7". Private collection

Following his dispute with Mary Louise McLaughlin over the creation of underglaze painting, Thomas Wheatley went into business for himself in 1880. His choice of marine animals for decoration was influenced by the work of Maria Nichols.

first formal china painting class, was sent an invitation to the start-up meeting of the club but it never arrived. Thinking she had been snubbed, Nichols pursued her interest independent of the club's members, establishing her own pottery, Rookwood, in 1880.

Although china painters could purchase bisque porcelain blanks from a pottery or a china store, underglaze painters had to depend on a commercial pottery for damp, wheel-thrown vessels to decorate. McLaughlin and her friends in the Pottery Club met at the Coultry Pottery until one of the pottery's partners, Thomas Wheatley, claimed he had developed the underglaze painting process. McLaughlin successfully defended her position but decided to move the club meetings to another pottery. Furthermore, the Coultry Pottery yellowware was not the best clay body for their work. Earthenware clays, depending on their origin, fire to many colors—red, yellow, white, brown. Because white is the best color under china paints and underglazes, McLaughlin arranged for a large workroom at the Dallas Pottery where the group could use its whiteware.

As it happened, Maria Nichols and a friend had rented a studio at the Dallas Pottery in 1879, shortly before the Pottery Club arrived.

43. MARY LOUISE McLAUGHLIN (DECORATOR), AT THE COULTRY POTTERY
PILGRIM JAR
1877. Earthenware, "Cincinnati Limoges" height 10¼", width 9½". Cincinnati Art Museum, Ohio. Gift of the Women's Art Museum Association

Both groups discovered the temperature of the Dallas kiln firings too high to preserve china paint colors, which burn out at elevated temperatures. To avoid overfiring, McLaughlin shipped her ware to Union Porcelain Works, operated by Thomas C. Smith and Sons Pottery on Greenpoint, Long Island, while Nichols sent her ware to be fired at Warrin and Lycett's in New York City. Shipping ware out of town proved impractical, so at her own expense McLaughlin had a special kiln built for firing underglaze painting. Nichols soon did the same, building one instead for overglaze firings. Although these firings continued to be handled by trained workmen, both women gained a greater understanding of clay procedures. Nichols regularly enlisted the aid of the pottery's superintendent, Joseph Bailey, Sr., who helped her develop light blue and light green overglaze colors capable of withstanding the kiln's high temperatures.

The growing rivalry between these two women was exacerbated when the Pottery Club held a very well attended first exhibition of two hundred pieces in 1880, representing a year of work at the Dallas Pottery. Members used underglaze and overglaze colors and a variety of techniques. A journalist of the period described incising on a vessel to be as "delicate as a spider's web" and a relief on another container "so bold that one is tempted to reach forth and take the bird from the bough."[11] Other articles in the effusive prose style of the period mistakenly hailed McLaughlin's underglaze painting as a rediscovery of the lost process of Limoges enamel instead of what it was—an American version of French barbotine. However, publicity about the ware reached women living in other areas of the Midwest with the result that many came to Cincinnati for lessons in underglaze and china painting, or also sent their work to be fired. The Pottery Club's members, and those who were inspired by their work, continued the early nineteenth century's fondness for themes in nature expressed in floral motifs. But rather than confine the design to a precise area of the surface by placing it within a border as was characteristic of Victorian ware, these ceramists were influenced instead by new trends in Europe. Their use of decoration was sparing and placed asymmetrically over the shape of the ware, reflecting an oriental aesthetic already present in French Limoges and English pottery. Underglaze painting, McLaughlin emphasized, was well suited to such flowing designs; close to oil painting in appearance, this technique aligned the decorator with the fine artist, widening the gap even further between decorator and potter.

What she had accomplished for china painting, McLaughlin proceeded to do for underglaze painting by publishing her second book, *Pottery Decoration Under the Glaze* (1880). Although at the height of her work in underglaze painting, she decided to leave the field of ceramics for a ten-year hiatus. Frustrated with a dependence on commercial potteries for throwing and firing ware, by 1884 McLaughlin had turned to other art activities.

Through her books on the subject, McLaughlin provided the movement toward painting on clay with a sound technical and philosophical base. She channeled one of the forces set in motion by the Centennial Exhibition, and in so doing established underglaze painting and the oriental aesthetic of asymmetry as the basis for what would become the art pottery movement.

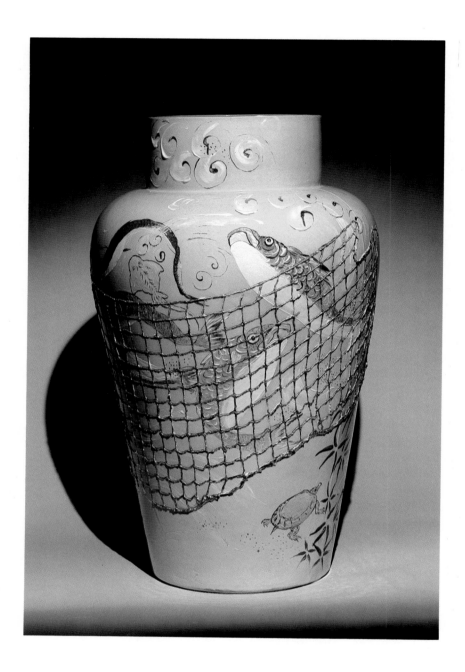

Decorative Art Societies

The Cincinnati Pottery Club which McLaughlin founded became a model for women's clubs and helped to initiate new programs for women in art schools and colleges. Another organization offering support for the arts was the Society of Decorative Art, founded in New York in 1877 by an interested citizen, Candice Wheeler. While visiting the Philadelphia Centennial, Wheeler saw an exhibit of needlework produced by economically depressed women at England's Kensington School. She envisioned an organization aimed at elevating women who could use craft skills to support themselves. To this end she persuaded some of the most prominent artists of the period (including Louis Comfort Tiffany) to teach classes at the society.

44. MARIA LONGWORTH
NICHOLS (DECORATOR)
ALADDIN VASE
*c. 1880–84. Earthenware, height
30", diameter 18". The
Metropolitan Museum of Art,
New York. Gift of William and
Marcia Goodman*

The rivalry between Mary Louise McLaughlin and Maria Longworth Nichols was so great that they even vied with each other over the size of the vases each decorated; the contest over height is evident in this vase and McLaughlin's *Ali Baba* (fig. 45).

The idea captured the imagination of the nation, and a second society was founded in Chicago the following year, with thirty sister societies eventually functioning across the country. In addition to offering classes, many societies filled orders from clubs, businesses, and individuals while providing training and employment for women. By the late 1870s, other institutions, from young ladies' seminaries to established art schools, added china painting classes to their curriculum.

Though it would appear that the Centennial was most beneficial in opening artistic employment opportunities for women, this was not strictly the case. Men, too, profited from the new decorative techniques. During the following twenty years both men and women contributed to broader stylistic visions for American ceramics.

45. MARY LOUISE McLAUGHLIN (DECORATOR), DALLAS POTTERY **ALI BABA VASE** *1880. Earthenware, "Cincinnati Limoges", height 37½", width 16½". Cincinnati Art Museum, Ohio. Gift of Rookwood Pottery*

Because floral motifs were the prevailing decorative motif used by the members of the Pottery Club—especially by McLaughlin—Nichol's work is further distinguished by her choice of fish, birds, and insects.

Chapter 4
THE EARLY ART POTTERIES

The Robertson Family of Potters

While Mary Louise McLaughlin was experimenting with colored slips in Cincinnati, her contemporary, Hugh Cornwall Robertson, working in Chelsea, near Boston, was producing his first pieces of underglaze-painted ware. Given Robertson's family background, nothing could have been more natural. The Robertsons had been potters in Scotland and England for five generations. Hugh Robertson was born in England in 1844. When his father, James Robertson, learned that his livelihood as the head workman in a pottery was threatened by the introduction of machinery, he moved his family to America. By 1859, the Robertsons were settled in East Boston where the elder Robertson managed a pottery.

In 1865, the oldest son, Alexander, set up his own pottery in nearby Chelsea, where a fine red clay was available. Hugh joined him shortly afterward, and they named the pottery A. W. and H. C. Robertson. The Robertson pottery manufactured flowerpots and other utilitarian brown ware, at first plain and unadorned, but later on embellished. In 1872, their father became a partner, at which time they changed the firm's named to Chelsea Keramic Art Works, James Robertson and Sons. Theirs was one of the first American firms to create a line of art pottery separate from their utilitarian pitchers and stew pots, whose unadorned vases and flasks were interpretations of Greek terra-cottas. The ware was hand-thrown and turned, polished with boiled linseed oil, and warmed in the kiln, causing the oil to sink into the earthenware pores and enhance the smooth surface.[1] Shapes reflected the late-nineteenth-century fondness for the Greek Revival style, whose popularity receded with the decade.

Tiles, a common decoration on Victorian fireplaces, were James Robertson's specialty. Low reliefs of stylized fruit, flowers, grasses, and geometric designs were favored motifs. Leaves and grasses were pressed into clay, a technique James Robertson brought from England, and which was still new to America. The Robertson method

opposite:
46. CHELSEA KERAMIC ART WORKS
LAMP BASE
c. 1880. Earthenware, height 8¾", diameter 4⅜". Private collection

Metalwork of the late 1800s was the inspiration for the hammered surface of this lamp. The raised decoration showed Victorian taste for botanical motifs in an asymmetrical placement, influenced by oriental art.

above:
47. LOW ART TILE WORKS
TILE
c. 1885. Earthenware relief panel, 8 x 24". Division of Ceramics and Glass, National Museum of American History, Smithsonian Institution, Washington, D. C.

overleaf:
48. HUGH ROBERTSON, CHELSEA KERAMIC ART WORKS
FOUR VASES AND PITCHER
Earthenware. (left to right:) "Memorial to Garfield". c. 1880. Height 8½", diameter 6⅛"; Vase. c. 1888. Height 8⅛", diameter 4⅛"; Dedham Pottery Vase. c. 1900. Height 10¼", diameter 5¹¹/₁₆"; Vase. c. 1878. Height 5¹¹/₁₆", diameter 3⅛"; Pitcher. c. 1876. Height 6½", diameter 5½". Private collection

became the basis for tile production by other potteries such as Low Art Tile Works, also located in Chelsea.

Other lines characterizing Chelsea pottery were sculptured reliefs modeled on vases by Franz X. Dengler and Hugh Robertson, which continued popular eclectic Victorian styles. A shape much favored between 1875 and 1880 was the flask, whose broad, flat surface could support elaborate scenes or high-relief flowers and birds. Robertson flasks often featured Victorian scroll-shaped feet and ring handles, combined with a hunting scene in low relief. One such tableau, a horseman sounding a trumpet, was probably based on an engraving by James Edward Kelley, a popular illustrator and sculptor of the time.[2] Drawings by well-known artists were frequently reproduced on vases as were themes from literature, such as La Fontaine's fables and characters from Charles Dickens's books. Plaques made by the Robertsons depicted celebrated literary figures, among them Longfellow, Byron, and Dickens.

The Robertsons' subject matter may have been prosaic, but their experiments with technology were not. Before matt glazes were introduced, they developed a dull surface glaze by controlling the kiln heat in a reduction firing rather than by a specific formula.[3] Appealing to the contemporary taste for naturalistic flowers and plants, the Robertsons pressed actual flowers and plants onto the hand-thrown, wet body of a vase or they applied sculptured, floral forms to a vessel surface. A vine of hops sprigged on a beer pitcher was Chelsea Keramic's acknowledgment of Charles Eastlake's philosophy of connecting the vessel's decoration to its purpose.

Much of this ware was produced during a period when Hugh Robertson was also preoccupied with ideas generated after a visit to the Philadelphia Centennial. As significant for him as for McLaughlin, he found the display of Haviland Limoges intriguing and, with his technical background, easy to reproduce. He called his underglaze-painted ware Bourg-la-Reine, after the French town where Ernest Chaplet had revived the art. But for Robertson the process was not the major discovery it had been for McLaughlin; he was much more excited by the display of oriental ceramics, especially the startling glaze colors of Chinese high-fired ware. His fascination with Ming dynasty monochrome glazes soon became a consuming passion.

Several events in the Robertson family history conspired to open the path for extensive glaze experimentation. In 1880 James Robertson died; four years later, Alexander Robertson left for California, where he was certain he could pioneer pottery development. His brother's departure left Hugh Robertson in charge of the company and he began to use company funds to research the formulas for Chinese monochrome glazes.

HUGH ROBERTSON AND THE MONOCHROME GLAZE

Hugh Robertson was the first American potter to consider the overall glaze as the only decoration essential to a vessel. China painting and underglaze painting were procedures which helped diminish

49. Hugh Robertson, Chelsea
Keramic Art Works
TWIN STARS OF CHELSEA
*c. 1845–1908. Earthenware,
height (left) 6¼", (right) 6⅝".
The Museum of Fine Arts, Boston. Gift of Miss Eleanor M.
Hearn*

Victorian excesses in pottery decoration on the one hand while retaining the floral motifs characteristic of the period. The monochrome glaze was a departure that emphasized form, color, and texture in a new relationship. The first results of Hugh Robertson's search were several new glaze colors: deep sea green, apple green, mustard yellow, and turquoise. These shades, highly valued by the Chinese, were only appetizers for Robertson, who longed to rediscover *sang de boeuf* or oxblood, the red color produced and highly prized during the Ming dynasty. After a four-year period of testing glaze formulas, he finally found a red spot the size of a pea on one of his vases and worked from that information until, in 1888, he perfected the clear red color. Removing the first perfect piece from the kiln and remembering the difficulties and frustrations he had encountered, the endless hours of careful kiln watching, of feeding the fire until the last stick of fuel was consumed, he commented that the color should be named "Robertson's Blood."[4] Only the glazes on three hundred pieces met Robertson's high standards; two perfect oxblood vases received the appellation "Twin Stars" of Chelsea. Other successes were two vases whose red glaze was marked with a "pigeon feather" pattern and one peachblow vase whose glaze was a

soft pink-red. Vases displaying examples of Robertson's glaze research were recognized with awards at the Paris Exposition of 1900.

Exhibition judges and connoisseurs of pottery appreciated Hugh
Robertson's outstanding accomplishments but the general public,
accustomed to Rockingham ware or to seeing the ceramic surface
treated as an imperishable "canvas" (as opposed to canvas for oil
painting), was disinterested. Robertson's single-minded devotion to
his glaze experiments so greatly depleted the pottery's capital that
he was forced out of business; in 1889 the pottery closed. A group of
influential Bostonians, familiar with Robertson's work and convinced of his talent, raised the necessary funds for him to reopen a
business in 1891, with dinnerware as the basis of his production. The
new ware required a high firing and a heavy stoneware body, quite
different from the fine red clay in the Chelsea area. One of his bene-
factors owned land near a canal in Dedham, southwest of Boston, a
perfect location for a water-powered factory. Dedham Pottery, the
new company's name, became associated with manufacturing distinctive dinnerware covered with a crackle glaze. Robertson recalled
inadvertently producing this unusual glaze five years earlier, an effect he had seen on Ming dynasty ware. The plates were to have a
hand-painted border—a nod to Arts and Crafts principles—chosen
from a competition held at the Boston Museum of Fine Arts School.
The winning design of plump rabbits running around the rim became the most popular pattern, synonymous with the pottery's
name.

While dinnerware supported the pottery, Robertson experimented with other formulas, including a thickly applied glaze he

50. DEDHAM POTTERY
AZALEA PLATE
*c. 1930. Crackle ware, diameter
6½". Everson Museum of Art,
Syracuse, N.Y. Gift of Albert E.
Simonson in memory of Priscil-
la Lord Simonson.*

Ultimately, over fifty patterns
of conventionalized plants and
animals adorned Dedham
dinnerware.

called "volcanic ware" for its lava-like, pitted surface. Although not commercially viable, this type of glaze was the forerunner of similar glaze experiments achieved in the mid-twentieth century.

When Hugh Robertson died in 1908, the management of the company passed to his son and grandson; when the latter entered the navy in 1943, the pottery closed its doors with an inventory sale at Gimbel's Department Store. Hugh Robertson's appreciation for the simple beauty of Ming dynasty glazes on classical shapes would shortly be shared by a few potters in the early years of the twentieth century, but his achievement in glaze research before the turn of the century was unpresaged.

ALEXANDER ROBERTSON AND NAKED CLAY

Northern California was experiencing the post-gold rush period of expansion when Hugh Robertson's brother, Alexander, arrived in 1884. There is no evidence that the San Francisco Keramic Club, organized in 1888, was aware that the most accomplished ceramic artist of Massachusetts was in its midst. Little is known of Robertson's activities before 1891, the year he met Linna Irelan, a talented artist and wife of a California state mineralogist. Finally in 1898, after several abortive starts, Robertson and Irelan opened the Roblin Art Pottery, beginning with a line of domestic wares, bowls, mugs, and vases from red buff and white California clays and glaze materials. The ware was thrown and fired by Robertson in shapes similar to those produced at Chelsea, much of it left in the bisque state or with

above left:
51. ALEXANDER ROBERTSON, HALCYON POTTERY
VASE WITH LIZARD
*1911. Earthenware, height 3¼".
Oakland Museum, Calif.*

Robertson decorated with lizard and mushroom motifs, comparable in ways to Maria Nichols's choice of marine animals and insects. The unglazed surface he preferred was barely interrupted by beading or a minimally incised border (see fig. 52).

above right:
52. ALEXANDER ROBERTSON, ROBLIN ART POTTERY
VASE
c. 1900. Thrown by Robertson, decorated by Linna Irelan. Earthenware, height 4⅝", diameter 4⅛". Private collection

only the interior glazed. Irelan did the decorating, using a variety of techniques: underglaze slip (she had visited Cincinnati and was familiar with the work of the Pottery Club), incising, modeling, hammering, and slip painting. Her forte was three-dimensional modeling, her favorite motifs mushrooms and lizards. By contrast, Robertson's classical forms were more severe, the only embellishment being a handle or beading. Robertson and Irelan intended to organize a pottery club as the basis for an operation similar to Rookwood Pottery, established in 1880 by Maria L. Nichols, but disaster intervened. The earthquake that destroyed a large part of San Francisco in 1906 also leveled the Roblin Pottery, the new school, and the firm's complete stock.

At the age of sixty-six, Robertson was totally disheartened; he moved to Los Angeles, where his son Fred was working for a brick company. In 1910 he accepted the directorship of Halcyon Pottery, located in a small utopian community near Pismo Beach. Finding it far less placid than its name suggested, Robertson left there in 1912 for a position at Alberhill Coal and Clay Company in southern California, where he developed quality clay bodies. Over a two-year period he produced a group of wheel-thrown, unglazed vases in classical shapes that ranged from terra-cotta red to soft pink and white. At the end of his career, he received a gold medal for his work from the San Diego Exposition of 1915. Robertson, with Linna Irelan, pioneered art pottery in the Far West, with their Roblin Pottery operating for a few years as the only documented art pottery in California.[5] Fortuitously, he had sent several examples of Roblin Pottery to the Smithsonian Institution shortly before 1906. While Irelan's decorative styling was closer to nineteenth-century Romanticism, Robertson's simple shapes, if not as distinguished as his younger brother's, stood apart with quiet assurance against the more flamboyant ware of the period. Along with late-arriving western potteries, the Robertson-Irelan collaboration and Robertson's experimental work with clay bodies provided a basis for the development of the clay industry in California.

Rookwood, The Art Pottery Leader

The Robertson family's expertise in pottery brought innovation and a high standard to American ware. Another pottery, however, went a step further and claimed leadership for the art pottery movement.

China painting and underglaze painting inspired Maria Nichols to establish her own pottery. Before she could realize her plans, several events occurred to shape her aesthetic sensibilities. She had received a book of Japanese woodblock prints and sketches, brought from London by a friend. The designs captured her imagination, and she began copying favorite motifs on porcelain blanks. Visiting the Philadelphia Centennial shortly afterward, Nichols and her husband, George Nichols, were impressed by the Japanese ceramics on view there for the first time in America. Maria Nichols realized later that the sketchbook *Manga*, by Katsushika Hokusai, "prepared me for the wonderful beauty of the Japanese exhibit at the Philadelphia Centennial Exhibition of 1876. It was there that I first felt a desire to

53. *Rookwood Pottery mark on the bottom of a vessel, 1901. Private collection*

In 1887, the only marks on Rookwood Pottery were the initials "RP" (barely distinguishable here), and which were accompanied by the pottery's symbol, one flame. A flame point was added in succeeding years until fourteen of them surrounded the initials. In 1901, Roman numerals were used to signify the years. Arabic numbers identified shapes or patterns and letters indicated size. The letter *z* stood for shapes with a matt glaze finish produced between 1900–04. The monogram "AMV" identifies the decorator, Anna Marie Valentien.

have a place of my own where things could be made."[6] George Nichols, in his book *Art Education Applied to Industry* (1877), accurately predicted that Japanese decorative arts would "exert a wide and positive influence upon American art industries."[7] Maria Nichols's china painting, using designs taken from *Manga*, concentrated on reptiles, insects, and marine creatures, subject matter quite apart from the sprays of dogwood, laurel, and wild roses favored by McLaughlin and the Pottery Club.

As the daughter of wealthy Cincinnati businessman Joseph Longworth, Maria Nichols took every opportunity to suggest to her father that he purchase a pottery for her. He did not indulge her whim to import a Japanese pottery in toto, but when an old schoolhouse became available, Longworth offered it to his daughter. The realization of her dreams required some immediate practical measures. Joseph Bailey, Sr., her friend at the Dallas Pottery, helped purchase equipment, materials, and arrange for an outlet to sell the ware. His son, Joseph, Jr., became her first employee when the transformation from schoolhouse to pottery was completed in September 1880. Nichols named it Rookwood because the last syllable was that of the famous Wedgwood Pottery of England and the first syllable

54. *Art pottery decorating class at the School of Design, Cincinnati Art Museum, 1899*

had pleasant associations with the crows, or rooks, at her father's country estate, her childhood home.[8] The crow became part of the pottery's trademark when the first kiln was drawn that same year on Thanksgiving Day. There is no record of the type of pottery removed from that kiln, but undoubtedly it contained commercial and undecorated ware along with ware fired for amateur decorators, all items Nichols and Bailey decided would sustain the operation.

From the beginning, Rookwood attracted much attention due to its founding by a woman. Promoted as a new art industry which subordinated profit to genuine artistic creation, Rookwood became a popular place to visit for Cincinnati residents and tourists. A few Pottery Club members were among the first to join Nichols at Rookwood. Clara Newton, a girlhood friend, assisted with administrative details, and during the first year local Cincinnati artists functioned rather informally as china decorators. In the autumn of 1881, a decorating department was formally organized when Albert Valentien, a

55. MARIE LONGWORTH STORER (formerly Nichols), ROOKWOOD POTTERY
VASE
c. 1895. Crackle glaze in browns and whites, height 8½". Collection Betty and Robert Hut

56. CLARA CHIPMAN NEWTON (DECORATOR), ROOKWOOD
POTTERY. BARBITONE PAINTED TEAPOT WITH BRONZE
HANDLE. *1882. Earthenware, height (including lid) 5½", width
8". Private collection*

The handle of this teapot bears this inscription: "Made by Clara
Chipman Newton for Maria Longworth Nichols with deepest
appreciation and affection, December 25, 1882." Newton also
taught a decorating class at Rookwood.

57. Kitaro Shirayamadani
(decorator), Rookwood
Pottery
BOWL
*1890. Earthenware, height 5¼",
diameter 10¾". The Metropolitan Museum of Art, New York*

58. Attributed to Albert Valentien (decorator), Rookwood
Pottery
VASE
*1883. Earthenware, height 21",
diameter 12". Everson Museum
of Art, Syracuse, N.Y.*

59. ALBERT P. VALENTIEN (DECO-
RATOR), ROOKWOOD POTTERY
VASE
*1891. Earthenware, cameo
glaze, low relief, height 10½",
diameter 4¾". Collection Flor-
ence Barnes*

former Cincinnati School of Design student, was hired. His training in china and underglaze painting brought a professional approach to Rookwood decoration; he also transferred to Rookwood Benn Pitman's insistence on motifs using American flora and fauna and George Nichols's philosophy based on Ruskin, Morris, and Eastlake, which "laid the theoretical foundation of the Cincinnati decorative arts movement."[9]

To add to the pottery's income and to train future staff, Maria Nichols opened the Rookwood School for Pottery Decoration in 1881 where Laura Fry, a former member of the Pottery Club, served as an instructor. By that time the McLaughlin/Nichols rivalry had lessened somewhat, so with the closing of Dallas Pottery, McLaughlin and the Pottery Club members moved to Rookwood.

A new group of decorators, all School of Design graduates, joined the staff in 1882 even though Rookwood's financial base was less than sound. Joseph Longworth paid the two thousand dollar difference in income and expenses for each year. In 1883, William Watts Taylor, another friend of Nichols, was hired as general business manager. He began by closing all unprofitable operations, which included the decorating school and the Pottery Club. Taylor reorganized the poor arrangement of space, and he began a record book of the 200 existing shapes to determine which ones were most popular.

60. LAURA FRY (DECORATOR), ROOKWOOD POTTERY COVERED CHOCOLATE POT
c. 1884. Earthenware, raised dragon design, spout on opposite side, height 9¼". Private collection

61. WELLER POTTERY
VASE, scene from CANTER-
BURY TALES
*c. 1900. Dickensware, matt and
glossy glazes in browns, whites,
blues, greens, and grays, height
17". Collection Betty and Robert Hut*

62. Albert Valentien (decorator), Rookwood Pottery
HYDRANGEA VASE
*1904. Earthenware, height 14⅝",
diameter 9½". Everson Museum
of Art, Syracuse, N.Y.*

opposite:
63. Frederick H. Rhead,
Roseville Pottery
VASE
*c. 1904. Earthenware, stylized
flowers, squeeze-bag technique,
height 9", diameter 3⅞". Private
collection*

ROOKWOOD STANDARD

Maria Nichols's ambitious plans succeeded because of two fortuitous circumstances. First, Taylor's business acumen steered the pottery toward a sound financial basis. Second, Laura Fry, while a member of the decorating staff, invented a technique, later used to create Rookwood Standard, and which placed the company in the forefront of the art pottery movement. Fry was from an artistic family and had received an extensive art education. Innovative in decoration, she used several methods for applying background color on pottery. In 1884 she approached Valentien with the suggestion that she blow on background color, which he discouraged. But, when he left for vacation, she tried spraying color on vases with the same atomizer she used for applying fixative to charcoal drawings. Not only did this method produce an even ground, but delicate gradations of color could be achieved. Several colors, one applied over the other, gave the background a richness and depth not previously possible. The paintings of flowers with colored slips appeared in spatial relief in relation to the background. As a result, form and decoration worked together, each contributing to and reinforcing the other.[10]

Although Nichols favored insects, fish, and dragons, Rookwood's primary subject matter—plants, flowers, butterflies, grasses, and birds—continued the nineteenth century's preoccupation with assimilated nature. It was a period when botanical gardens, public and private parks, and greenhouses flourished, becoming important parts of culture. William Taylor provided the staff with a library of nature books, and when the pottery moved to the Mt. Adams area in 1890, he constructed a garden for decorators to observe nature at first hand.

In the early years, Taylor faced the formidable technical problem of repeating accidental successes with glazes; to that end he attempted several different solutions. For example, in 1883 an unusual glaze showing streaks of golden crystals appeared accidentally. The staff was not able to duplicate the phenomenon, so Taylor searched for a higher level of technical knowledge. He hired pharmacologist Karl Langenbeck, who became the first American ceramic chemist, and in 1887 he added a Japanese decorator, Kitaro Shirayamadani, to the staff.

At the same time, alert to changes in taste, Taylor answered public demand for lighter colors in pottery and introduced the Cameo line in 1886, which highlighted pastel tones on a dense, white clay body. In the early 1890s, he added shades of blue green and green to Rookwood's palette. Romantic names for new lines, such as Sea Green, which lent itself to depictions of marine life, added to the pottery's charm. To maintain Rookwood's leadership, Taylor sent Valentien and his wife, Anna, to Europe in 1889 to prepare for a Rookwood exhibit in Paris the following year. He sent both Shirayamadani to Japan and a new, young decorator, Artus Van Briggle, to Paris in 1893 to study the latest ceramic styles and procedures respectively in each country. Stanley Burt, a Yale graduate in chemistry, went to Berlin in 1894 and returned with the first Seger cones; these pyromatic cones developed by Herman Seger indicated the heat level inside the kiln by bending at specific temperatures, a more

accurate determination of temperature than the previous method which relied on judging the color of the kiln's interior. By various means, then, Taylor did improve the technology at Rookwood.

Maria Nichols's interest in the pottery diminished when George Nichols died in 1885. By that time, too, Taylor's management skills were effectively guiding the company so that Nichols's presence was no longer essential. A year later she married Bellamy Storer, whose political ambitions kept the couple in Washington, D.C. and Europe more than in Cincinnati. Maria Nichols Storer's final conflict with Mary Louise McLaughlin occurred in 1893 when Taylor rewrote the company's history as part of the publicity for the Rookwood exhibit at the World's Columbian Exposition of 1893 in Chicago. McLaughlin wrote Storer, reminding her that *she* had discovered underglaze painting, the process which later launched Rookwood. Storer replied, claiming that the process had been available in books and used in Limoges porcelains imported to Boston prior to 1874. Although Storer had defended McLaughlin earlier in her contest with Thomas Wheatley, she chose another position at this point, no doubt for the benefit of Rookwood's public image. Storer and Taylor won the battle but McLaughlin won the war when, many years later, the American Ceramic Society acknowledged her method of underglaze painting as the basis for Rookwood's early ware.

64. PAULINE POTTERY PLAQUE
c. 1885. Earthenware, glossy glaze in blue, white, black, and brown; painted and incised decoration, 7 3/16 x 9 13/16".
Private collection

POTTERIES IN THE ROOKWOOD IMAGE

The accomplishments of Mary Louise McLaughlin and Maria Nichols Storer inspired many women of the period. Some began as china painters and remained content with that outlet for their artistic ambitions. Others taught the ceramic process, such as Susan Frackleton, who wrote *Tried by Fire* (1885), a book welcomed by china painters and reprinted several times. The daughter of a Milwaukee banker who owned a brickyard equipped with low-fire kilns, Frackleton opened the Frackleton China Decorating Works in 1883. Trained decorators produced an average of 1,500 to 2,000 pieces a week.[11] Her personal work included experiments with high-fire porcelain and stoneware.

Between 1891 and 1892, Frackleton went beyond McLaughlin's concept of a local club to found an umbrella organization, the National League of Mineral Painters, which united china painting groups in small, rural communities with those in urban areas. In time, the league inspired annual conferences, exhibitions, and publications, among them *Keramic Studio* magazine (1899). Frackleton developed a set of colors known as the Frackleton Dry Watercolors, including gold and bronze for use in china painting, which earned her several medals from a competition held in Belgium in 1894. While she demonstrated the potential for art pottery within the stoneware range, the problem of securing proper equipment proved insurmountable and about 1904 Frackleton gave up the struggle to maintain a viable pottery.

Pauline Jacobus, who had attended the Rookwood School for Pottery Decoration, left in 1882 to organize a small workshop in Chicago, where she exhibited the city's first art pottery. The Pauline Pottery used molds and yellow earthenware clay with underglaze colors, which enjoyed an early success in department stores in Chicago and Boston. The pottery maintained its good fortune for about ten years; rising costs and the death of her husband in 1893, who had supervised production, finally led to bankruptcy and the pottery's demise in 1909.

Frackleton and Jacobus are only two examples of women who were inspired by McLaughlin and Nichols. There were many other women decorators at this time, but equally important during this period were a group of people who saw Rookwood's success as a good business opportunity. W. A. Long, a pharmacist of Steubenville, Ohio, whose knowledge of chemistry probably enabled him to duplicate underglaze painting, has the distinction of being the first to employ large-scale use of the process outside of Cincinnati. The pottery exhibition at the Philadelphia Centennial inspired him to take this direction. In 1889, after nine years of intermittent experimentation, Long produced the prototype for Lonhuda, an artware line which began production in 1892 (the company name combined Long's name with that of two partners). Laura Fry, who had left Rookwood in 1887 for free-lance decorating and a professorship in industrial arts at Purdue University in 1891, joined Lonhuda Pottery. Her method for an even application of background color became the basis for their production, in direct competition with Rookwood. William

65. GRUEBY FAIENCE COMPANY
TILE WITH HORSES FROM
DREAMWOLD
*c. 1900. Earthenware, 6¹/₈ x
6¹/₁₆". Private collection*

66. WILLIAM GRUEBY, GRUEBY
FAIENCE COMPANY
TILE
*c. 1906. Conventionalized trees
with green, blue, lavender,
ocher, and brown matt glazes,
height 13". Division of Ceramics
and Glass, National Museum of
American History, Smithsonian
Institution, Washington, D.C.
Gift of E. Stanley Wires*

Taylor had ignored Fry's earlier application for a patent, so in 1893 she tried to enjoin Rookwood from using the process; the case was not settled until 1898, in Rookwood's favor. The judge ruled that the atomizer was an old tool put to a new use.[12]

Long was not immune from the financial problems endemic to new companies, and in 1895 accepted an offer from Samuel Weller (who had been in the pottery business since 1872) to buy Lonhuda's methods and glazes. Long and his company moved to Weller's Zanesville, Ohio, plant, where Weller began an art pottery line. Weller renamed the ware Louwelsa, a combination of his daughter's name with his. More successful than Long's, Weller's art line soon led the field in mass production of the ware. He imitated Rookwood's many innovations, giving them equally romantic names.

When Long left Weller in 1896, J. B. Owens Company, a pottery in Roseville, Ohio, established in 1885, hired him. Benefiting from Long's expertise, Owens produced Utopia art pottery which resembled Rookwood Standard and Louwelsa. Roseville Pottery, organized in 1890 in Roseville, Ohio, by George F. Young, moved to Zanesville, and in 1900 when Fry's appeal against the verdict to deny her a patent was denied, Roseville entered the art pottery field with ware similar to its competitors. Like Rookwood, Weller, and Owens, Roseville hired many different decorators, whose skills introduced new ideas and new procedures as each vied for the art pottery market. Other potteries, established just prior to or after the Civil War, which had been producing utilitarian wares saw the advantages of adding an art line. Many ambitious men like W. A. Long, working in fields where their scientific knowledge would transfer to pottery production, took the opportunity to enter a growth enterprise, resulting in the proliferation of art potteries around the country.

These companies used mass production methods along with a degree of hand decorating to justify the appellation of art. They kept prices at a moderate level, enabling the growing middle class to acquire art objects previously unattainable. On the other hand, the original intent of the Arts and Crafts Movement to produce handcrafted ware was slowly subverted by the increasing use of mass production methods.

Art Tile and Architectural Ceramics

Art pottery was one direction resulting from the new ideas on home decorating which reached America from England in the 1870s. Another was the incorporation of ceramic tile as part of interior design. The tile-making process James Robertson introduced to America was an English invention of 1840, which by reducing warping and shrinking facilitated mass production. Evidence of the expanded English tile industry appeared in Philadelphia in 1876; the British had sent an elaborate display hoping to generate an American market for their product. Instead, the variety of examples encouraged American manufacturers to develop their own tiles.

Among the many factors contributing to a renewed use of tile was the disastrous Chicago fire of 1871. Because so many of the city's wooden structures were destroyed, the fire-proofing qualities of ceramic tile for public architecture became increasingly attractive; by the end of the century tile decorated the entrances to the Rand McNally building (1890) and the Chicago Stock Exchange (1894), and Chicago architects used it to sheath steel and iron construction.[13]

The Low Art Tile Works, established in 1878 in Chelsea, Massachusetts, was among the first companies to manufacture decorative and plain ceramic tiles for architectural use. Mentioned earlier in connection with the Robertson family, John G. Low built the business on techniques learned during his years as an apprentice with James Robertson. Low's decorative, relief styles were used for panels, dadoes, mantels, hearth facings, and soda fountains.

Another tile manufacturer combined a previous career in archeology with a passion for Pennsylvania German pottery at a time when the latter had diminished in popularity and few people viewed it as an art form. Henry Mercer's aesthetic sensibility for the folk art of the early Moravian settlers prompted him to establish the Moravian Pottery and Tile Works in their name. In 1898, he began manufacturing tiles because the area's red clay was too soft for making pottery. He adapted Pennsylvania stove-plate designs to produce tiles made by hand rather than machines. Mercer's friendship with the British Museum's curator of antiquities enabled him to make pressings and tracings of early English floor tiles from the museum's collection, which he transferred to his tile production.[14]

The heir to the American tile tradition set in motion by the Robertson and Low families was William H. Grueby. Employed in the ceramics industry working mainly with tiles, Grueby began as an apprentice at the age of thirteen. In 1890, after working ten years for the Low Art Tile Works, Grueby went into several different partnerships, including one with Eugene Atwood in 1892 to produce architectural faience; it was an association of short duration which soon led to Grueby's starting his own company. The Grueby Faience Company, established in 1894 and incorporated in 1897, produced a variety of glazed bricks, tiles, and architectural terra-cotta. Architects submitted designs, usually Beaux Arts in character, and the firm followed their specifications. The eclectic architecture of the day required designs in Italian Renaissance or Moorish styles, which Grueby supplied.[15] The company also produced tea tiles and hearth facings with slightly raised surfaces featuring images of pine trees, animals, lily pads, and tulips. Grueby tiles had a handcrafted appearance which resulted in individual differences, at times a source of consternation to purchasers who did not share in the Arts and Crafts Movement's disdain for look-alike, machine-made products.

As the need for architectural tile increased, art pottery companies added a line of tile designs to their offerings. By the turn of the century, many new companies specializing in tiles had entered the field. As one expression of the Arts and Crafts Movement, architectural tile and art pottery maintained the tradition of the individual craftsman. At the same time, a new style—Art Nouveau—and a rich ceramic surface—the matt glaze—were about to make their debut. Both would further enliven and strengthen the art pottery movement set in motion by the celebration of American ingenuity at the Philadelphia Centennial.

Chapter 5

ART NOUVEAU: FORM AND DECORATION UNIFIED

Japonisme in Art Pottery

Through its use of china and underglaze painting the art pottery movement rejected the formalities of Victorian design. The sprigged vines and china-painted dogwood branches on the pottery of the 1880s were applied in an asymmetrical position, quite different from the symmetrical placement of relief work on earlier ware. Asymmetry, characteristic of the Japanese ware exhibited at the Philadelphia Centennial, was a concept applied to pottery decoration by the women ceramists in Cincinnati. Maria Nichols's vases of marine life and dragons in swirling, contorted positions gave movement and energy to the surface. Combined with the shaded, recessive background made possible by Laura Fry's atomizer, Rookwood Standard became a style so distinct from its predecessors that art historian John Marion Nelson labeled it "proto-Art Nouveau."[1] The "new art," which Rookwood Standard anticipated, derived its main characteristics from *japonisme*, a French adaptation of the curvilinear line and flat patterns of nineteenth-century Japanese art. To a greater or lesser degree, almost every American art pottery responded to this new style, the degree often depending upon access to the French model. Six potteries in particular exemplified the assimilation of Art Nouveau into an American variant. The link between French and American Art Nouveau came as a result of the efforts of a Parisian entrepreneur, Siegfried Bing.

A dealer in decorative art objects with a shop in Paris, Bing was one of the first to encourage an interest in Japanese art. In 1875, when *japonisme* was becoming fashionable in France, Bing traveled to China and Japan. When he returned, he opened another gallery, featuring oriental objects. Through articles and catalogue essays, Bing praised the Japanese use of curvilinear forms and a style that emphasized line rather than the Western concern for perspective.

After a government-sponsored art tour of America, Bing realized that the trend in decorative arts was happening on an international

opposite:
67. WILLIAM GRUEBY
FIVE VASES
c. 1900. Earthenware, designed to be used as lamp bases. (left to right:) height 7", diameter 9¹⁄₁₆"; height 4", diameter 9⅝"; height 11½", diameter 7¹¹⁄₁₆"; height 13⅝", diameter 7¹³⁄₁₆"; height 10½", diameter 8¾". Private collection

Grueby's emphasis on decorating along a vertical plane was characteristic of American Art Nouveau, a departure from the swirling lines in French ceramics.

above:
68. *This mark of the Grueby Faience Company shows that the piece is Grueby shape number 161. Private collection*

scale. He christened the movement when he opened his Salon de l'Art Nouveau in December 1895. Convinced that an understanding of the concepts in Japanese design would transform French decorative arts and release it from a repetition of historical styles, Bing searched for designers and craftsmen who would create exclusively for "Art Nouveau Bing."[2]

The Ornamental Glaze

Among the ceramists exhibiting at Bing's salon were Ernest Chaplet and Auguste Delaherche, who, like Hugh Robertson several years earlier, demonstrated a preference for the beauty of flowing glazes on simple forms. A significant departure from china and underglaze painting techniques, the ornamental glaze has its origins in the monochrome glazes of fourteenth- to eighteenth-century Chinese ceramics. The development of sophisticated glaze formulas, first by Robertson and later by William Grueby, Artus Van Briggle, and Louis Comfort Tiffany, was a major advance in the growth of American ceramics. Even so, acceptance by the American public required special circumstances.

GRUEBY FAIENCE, A MATT SURFACE

Pottery by Ernest Chaplet and Auguste Delaherche, both closely identified with Samuel Bing, had an influence on production by William Grueby. At that time, the firm of Atwood and Grueby was producing ceramic tiles. While attending the World's Columbian Exposition of 1893 in Chicago, where Atwood and Grueby had a booth, Grueby spent much of his time admiring an exhibit of French ceramics. Fascinated by the non-shiny surface and stem-like projections on Delaherche's ware, Grueby returned to Boston to experiment with glaze formulas. Later that same year, as the manager of his own firm, Grueby Faience Company, he began making art pottery in order to utilize the space in the center of the kiln which fired at too high a temperature for terra-cotta tiles. His glaze experiments yielded a matt surface. Although not the originator of this type of glaze (the Robertsons had produced it in 1885), Grueby was among the first to achieve a non-shiny surface through a formula rather than sand blasting, acid, or manipulation of the firing. He produced matt yellows, ochers, browns, and occasional reds, blues, and purples, but the color that made Grueby art pottery a household necessity was a cucumber or watermelon shade of dark green.

Grueby's experience with relief sculpture at Low Art Tiles probably influenced his decision to finish each piece by hand. An elderly potter threw each vase, and as demand increased, a decorating staff of young women trained in Boston's art schools was employed. Many of Grueby's vases featured modeled leaves separated by long-stem buds. The latter would either lie flat with edges slightly elevated above the vessel's surface or emerge from the body of the vase, forming four or five handles. The women applied coils of clay to outline leaves and flowers above the vessel's surface. Grueby's monochrome glazes varied slightly by pooling in hollows and thinning on elevations. His pots were heavy because the clay contained grog, essential to manufacturing tiles. In addition to some basic forms—ovoid, conical, spherical—Grueby used pear and single and double gourd shapes. Following general practice, Grueby decorators signed their vases, giving them artistic value in the eyes of the public.

The first international display of Grueby matt-glazed art pottery occurred at the Paris Exposition of 1900 where it caused a sensation and was awarded silver and gold medals. Among the many admirers crowding the Grueby booth was Siegfried Bing, who later became Grueby's European representative. Grueby ware made its American appearance in 1901 at the Pan American Exposition in Buffalo, New York, again winning awards. Grueby Faience shared space at the exposition with Gustav Stickley's Mission furniture, whose straight lines and warm oak finish enhanced the graceful lines and deep colors of the pottery.

Great popularity also had its consequences: the name Grueby became a generic term for a dark green matt glaze, encouraging widespread imitation. Leading the pack was Rookwood, followed by Weller, Owens, and Wheatley. None were quite able to match the quality of Grueby's rich glazes but the result was market saturation. By 1907, handwork could no longer compete with mass production and this along with other financial problems forced Grueby to discontinue making pottery in 1909, though tile production continued. Though his success was relatively short-lived, Grueby directed the art pottery movement away from painted ware toward vessels emphasizing form and ornamental glazes.[3]

69. TECO POTTERY
FOUR VASES
n.d. Earthenware. (left to right:)
Height 13¾"; 10"; 11"; 5½".
Private collection

TECO POTTERY

Like many other entrepreneurs of the period, William Day Gates saw an opportunity to enter a growth business when he discovered clay on an estate he had inherited near Chicago. Aware of the use of ceramics to help fireproof new construction in Chicago, Gates founded the American Terra Cotta and Ceramic Company in Terra Cotta, Illinois in 1886, also known as Gates Pottery. Some years later, Gates's two sons attended Ohio State University's newly inaugurated ceramic engineering program (initiated in 1894), bringing their expertise and that of a fellow graduate chemist to American Terra Cotta.[4] Their experiments with marbled and mottled glaze effects eventually produced a soft, waxy matt glaze in a cool, silvery green that became the hallmark of the pottery. Though Gates was a lawyer by training, he designed some of the pottery's early vases, inspired by classical Greek or oriental shapes, and he produced others for amateur artists to decorate. Many vases were executed by his friends, members of the architectural profession in Chicago whose approval he sought in 1900 when he formally entered the art pottery field.

The artware, named Teco (a contraction of terra-cotta), benefited from the popularity of Grueby's matt green glaze ranging from pale to deep green to tones of weathered bronze. Frederick Moreau, a French sculptor teaching at the School of the Art Institute of Chicago, joined the pottery in 1904 to develop a line of vases in the Art Nouveau style. Shapes distinguished by handles or piers that moved vertically around the form from base to rim, and conventionalized floral motifs—hollyhocks, poppies, thistles—characterized Teco forms and decoration. Teco's unique relationship with Chicago architects gave validity to Gates's claim that his art pottery harmoniously complemented the uncluttered, wood-trimmed interiors and predominantly horizontal lines of the Prairie style of architecture prominent in the Midwest and championed by Frank Lloyd Wright. But Teco suffered a fate similar to Grueby pottery, declining after 1904 when competition with mass production forced Gates to abandon careful finishing and reduce his glaze palette to Teco green.

VAN BRIGGLE POTTERY

The inspiration for Artus Van Briggle's ware was the result of several years of study in Paris, at the apex of the Art Nouveau style. Van Briggle attended the Cincinnati Art Academy in 1886 (formerly the School of Design) and worked at the Avon pottery before joining Rookwood. He advanced to senior decorator within three years and in 1893 was selected to study in Paris at the Académie Julian as part of William Taylor's plan to keep Rookwood in the forefront of changes in style.

Van Briggle arrived in France two years before the opening of Siegfried Bing's Salon de l'Art Nouveau. *Japonisme* was infiltrating all forms of artistic expression—Toulouse Lautrec's lithographs, Pierre Bonnard's posters, Hector Guimard's buildings, and Auguste Rodin's

70. Attributed to RUTH ERICK-
SON, GRUEBY FAIENCE COMPANY
VASE
*c. 1901–07. Glazed earthen-
ware, height 16⅜", diameter
7½". Cooper-Hewitt Museum,
The Smithsonian Institution's
National Museum of Design,
New York. Gift of Marcia and
William Goodman*

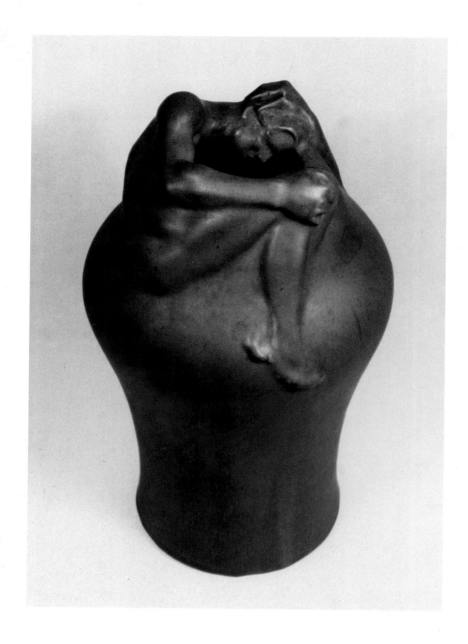

71. ARTUS VAN BRIGGLE
DESPONDENCY VASE
1902. Earthenware, height 13½".
Private collection

sculpture. In ceramics, monochrome glazes dominated, accenting simple shapes. Siegfried Bing's salon featured Delaherche, Emile Gallé, and Pierre Dalpayrat.

Returning to Rookwood in 1896, Van Briggle continued working on Rookwood Standard, but in his free time he experimented with glaze materials in his studio at home. Intrigued by the matt glazes he had seen in Paris, he produced several successful examples which were sent to Paris for the Rookwood display at the Exposition of 1900. Van Briggle's work was interrupted by illness. He had fought tuberculosis for several years; this time, acting on his doctor's advice, Van Briggle resigned from Rookwood and moved to the mountains of Colorado in 1898, where he hoped to recuperate. Although his reasons for leaving Rookwood were certainly due to his poor health, William Taylor and Maria Nichols were hardly sympathetic. They had invested time and expense on Van Briggle; seeing no recovery on their investment in his education, he was never mentioned for his role in developing Rookwood's matt glaze.

As soon as his strength improved, Van Briggle began testing indigenous clay and glaze materials, confident that he could create pottery on the American frontier. Working with a thrower from Rookwood, Van Briggle had five pieces to send to a Paris exposition by 1901 where they were well received, and three hundred pieces for the Christmas season. One of the Paris-bound vases, titled *Despondency*, expressed Van Briggle's feelings about his battle with tuberculosis. A male figure in relief encircles the lip of the vase, head bowed toward the interior void. The figure's position and muscularity suggest Rodin's influence, since Van Briggle probably saw much of his sculpture in Paris. Five vases incorporating figures were part of his pottery at this time.

Encouraged by his Parisian success, Van Briggle and his wife, the former Anne Gregory, formally organized a pottery which they opened in Colorado Springs in 1901. In spite of continuing poor health, Van Briggle developed over three hundred different molds. The staff expanded to fourteen with a division of labor similar to Rookwood. Many of the motifs corresponded to familiar Art Nouveau designs—conventionalized swans heads, dragonflies, narcissus, daffodils—while others were flowers indigenous to Colorado such as anemone, crocus, Aspen leaf, and columbine. Similar to Grueby's ware with its raised edges of leaves and tendrils, Van Briggle's vases more often displayed a higher relief, a free-flowing line that allowed stems and leaves to trail around the surface and embrace the vessel form. His palette of matt glazes included many shades of yellows, greens, blues, and purples, frequently varied by spraying one color over another. The staff used a version of Laura Fry's atomizer, operated by compressed air.

More awards honored Van Briggle pottery, with those from the 1904 Louisiana Purchase Exposition in St. Louis arriving soon after his death. Anne Gregory Van Briggle continued the management of the company using her husband's molds; even following remarriage in 1908 and her withdrawal from the company in 1912, the pottery continued, eventually adding tile production. Van Briggle's Art Nouveau style and his wide range of colors melded form and decoration in an interpretation more organic in feeling than Grueby or Teco.

72. *Mark of Artus Van Briggle. c. 1902. Earthenware. Private collection*

TIFFANY FAVRILE POTTERY

Artus Van Briggle produced his vocabulary of forms at the height of the style's development. Louis Comfort Tiffany entered the art pottery field when the Art Nouveau style peaked. Tiffany had the advantage of observing designs produced by other potteries before deciding on his own direction. Beginning his career as an interior designer in 1879, in the wake of the Centennial, Tiffany, like Samuel Bing, saw himself as a leader in guiding public taste. Then, in 1883, he decided his influence would be more substantial if he established his own workshops producing well-designed decorative objects. Tiffany also opened an art gallery for selling his wares.

overleaf:
73. VAN BRIGGLE POTTERY
SEVEN VASES
*Earthenware. (left to right:)
1902. Height 8", diameter 3¾";
1903. Height 3", diameter 3³/₁₆";
1903; Height 8½", diameter
7⁵/₁₆"; 1902. Height 6", diameter
5⅛"; 1903. Height 13⅝", diameter 6⅞"; 1905. Height 9½",
diameter 4¹³/₁₆"; 1903. Height
4⅞", diameter 4¹¹/₁₆". Private
collection*

Tiffany was interested in establishing himself in glass and interior design. His fascination and success with glass led him to consider producing favrile pottery. The display of ceramics at the Paris Exposition of 1900 finally motivated him to renew experiments with glazes and clay bodies begun a few years earlier. His art gallery exhibitions of Delaherche, Alexander Bigot, Taxile Doat of Sèvres, and his own collection of oriental ceramics influenced his forms.[5] At the Louisiana Purchase Exposition of 1904 in St. Louis, Tiffany displayed three not-for-sale vases he had made before finally presenting favrile pottery at a major sale in September 1905. The son of the founder of a prestigious New York jewelry store, Tiffany had the financial resources to sustain four to six years of research on art pottery. Few others of the period could have invested so much time on experimentation before offering ware for sale. Like the other objects produced by Tiffany Studios, the pottery too would find its audience among the wealthy elite. Showmanship was also involved as Tiffany allowed *Keramic Studio* magazine to report on the progress of his art pottery several years before its public appearance.

Tiffany "favrile" (meaning handmade) was cast from molds, though a small group was thrown by hand. Fern fronds, conventionalized tulips, seed pods, and artichoke blossoms characterized his sculptured vases. His matt glazes, over a semi-porcelaneous clay, were irregularly splotched as though sunlight was dappling the surface. Tiffany was unafraid to mix different glazes on a single form, allowing for chance and a diversity of coloration accented on ridges or pooled in flat areas.

The intricacy and organic quality of twisted stems, interlaced leaves, and vines completely defining the form is a legacy inherited from eighteenth-century English cabbage ware—jugs, bowls, tureens, and teapots molded in the form of cabbages. More sophisticated than these antecedents, Tiffany's vases with their pierced openings and uneven edges are closer to European decorative art. Tiffany, Grueby, Van Briggle, and Teco pottery adhere to an American variant of Art Nouveau that sets them apart from European Art Nouveau. Instead of the exaggerated curvilinear marks characteristic of the French style, the emphasis in American Art Nouveau style was on the vertical lines created by stems, vines, and fern fronds. In this variant on the style that art historian Kirsten Keen labeled "structural naturalism," they were joined by pottery decorator Mary Louise McLaughlin.[6]

Anticipating the Studio Potter—Losanti Ware

China and underglaze painting were the dominant techniques when Mary Louise McLaughlin left the pottery business in 1884. After a ten-year hiatus, she returned to pottery in 1894 when a procedure for decorating with clay inlays captured her imagination. The project was unsuccessful, but the experience prompted her in 1898 to experiment with porcelain clay bodies in a studio at her home, firing a small kiln built for her own use in the backyard.[7]

In doing so, McLaughlin declared her independence from commercial potteries and ventured into a field few had attempted. Un-

74. *Mark of Mary Louise McLaughlin Pottery. Private collection*

sure of how to formulate a porcelain clay body, she hired a potter to follow a Sèvres formula for hard-paste porcelain. After several disasters (the potter had adjusted the formula without her knowledge), she began mixing her own materials. McLaughlin's determination drove her to formulate a large number of clay bodies and glazes. McLaughlin was one of the first women to explore this aspect of pottery, traditionally dominated by men. In 1901, after many disappointments and complaints from neighbors about fire and smoke from the kiln, she finally produced a translucent, cream-colored, hard-paste porcelain ware which she named "Losanti" after Losantiville, the original name for Cincinnati in 1788. In an article discussing her new ware, McLaughlin wrote that she chose to emulate the Chinese, who fired porcelain only once for deeper, richer colors.[8]

Losanti ware reflects the stylistic change from china and underglaze painting to an overall glaze on a sculptured surface. McLaughlin's incised, pierced, and sculptured vases reflect her admiration for pottery by Bing and Grondahl, a Danish porcelain factory whose carved ware was pictured in magazines of the period. McLaughlin transferred her skill at wood carving, practiced earlier in classes at the School of Design, to carving complex relief patterns of twisted vines, leaves, and flowers that flow around her porcelain ware. Losanti ware exhibits a delicacy and lightness possible with porcelain clays, in contrast to the heavier pottery produced by Grueby, Tiffany, and Teco.

There is no evidence that McLaughlin learned to throw on a potter's wheel, the next step in advancing the studio pottery work. But once again her independent spirit—regardless of such lapses—was an inspiration to many women.

75. TIFFANY STUDIO POTTERY
VASE
*c. 1906. Earthenware, height
10⅞", diameter 4½". Courtesy
The Metropolitan Museum of
Art, New York*

The Eccentric Form of George Ohr's Biloxi Pottery

Equally as individualistic as McLaughlin but less sophisticated and well educated, George Ohr followed a circuitous route toward becoming a potter. He began his career as a blacksmith at the family forge in Biloxi, Mississippi. But his discontentment there and his several unsuccessful attempts to find another occupation finally caused his family to ask a potter friend, Joseph Meyer, to accept George as his apprentice. Ohr's first experience with a kick wheel was memorable: "When I found the wheel, I felt it all over like a wild duck in water."[9] This initial excitement never left him, infusing his wheel-thrown ware with a special energy. After learning the basic principles of the craft, he left Meyer to visit potteries around the country, his self-taught approach to an education in clay. Returning to Biloxi in 1883, Ohr built equipment for his first pottery, producing mold-formed pitchers, cooking pots, water coolers, and chimney pots, which he sold at the pottery and at local and regional fairs. Demonstrating prodigious ceramic feats at fairs, Ohr found his flair for showmanship increased sales. His booths became displays of visual and spoken feats: he advertised himself as the "Greatest potter on earth," punning that "The potter said un 2 clay, 'Be Ware' and it was..."[10]

above left:
76. TIFFANY STUDIO POTTERY VASE
c. 1905. Conventionalized tulips, mottled green semigloss glazes, height 11". Private collection

above right:
77. GEORGE OHR VASE
c. 1895. Earthenware, browns, greens, blues, height 13". Collection Betty and Robert A. Hut

78. *Hand-incised George Ohr signature. Private collection*

Nor did George Ohr's flamboyant nature abate when he joined Meyer at the newly formed Newcomb Pottery within a year after it opened in 1895 under the auspices of Newcomb College, an all-women's school in New Orleans. Within a short time his eccentricities caused his dismissal but not before he left behind a muscular plaster cast of his throwing arm for the ladies' drawing classes.

Few of Ohr's pots are dated, thus making chronology difficult, but in the late 1880s he discontinued his molded ware in favor of throwing. Responding to the plasticity of the clay, Ohr ruffled, twisted, creased, pinched, or wrinkled his thinly thrown vessels. While fluting was often used in Victorian glass and in the thrown ware of European potters Emile Gallé and Theobald Bindesboll, Ohr exploited the flexibility of clay for its expressive potential. To these twisted contours he added handles, thin, attenuated strips of clay that curl or ripple down one or two sides of the vessel. Resembling the outline of butterfly wings or the tendril-like forms applied to the surface of Tiffany favrile and Losanti ware, the curved handles reinforced the Art Nouveau character of Ohr's pottery.

More than his shapes, Ohr's glazes were admired in his day, though they were treated with more restraint. Tortoiseshell and mottled glazes (reminiscent of Rockingham ware) suggest his fascination with the surface coloration of the Gulf's marine life. His palette included monochrome or transparent lead and metallic glazes, the latter a pewter color and darker gunmetal, probably one of the earliest examples of this type of glaze.

Although some critics of ceramics appreciated George Ohr's pottery, the general public did not respond to his ware, convincing Ohr that recognition lay beyond his generation. Perhaps for this reason he hated to sell his controversial wheel-thrown ware; if his high prices were not sufficiently discouraging, he would chase after the unsuspecting purchaser, demanding the return of his pottery. In Biloxi, people remarked, "Only the fleet own George Ohr pottery."[11] In 1906, Ohr closed the pottery and began crating six thousand pieces of his work to preserve them for the day when the United States would recognize him as the world's greatest potter. Such acclaim did not occur. Instead, decades later, John Marion Nelson mentioned Ohr's work in a 1963 article which was followed two years later by an exhibit, the first since 1904. Nelson's article and the exhibition attracted the attention of pottery collectors and art historians, but it was not until James W. Carpenter purchased the warehouse of pottery from the Ohr family in 1972 that the extent of his work became public. Ohr's expressive use of clay found enthusiastic support from a generation of American potters engaged in similar pursuits.

Conservative Art Nouveau

By European standards, the American variant of the Art Nouveau style was generally understated, a distillation of the vigorous, swirling movement that animated French ware. Conversely, by American standards Tiffany, Grueby, and Van Briggle's interpretations were at the dynamic end of the spectrum.

A MATT GLAZE WITH SCENIC VISTAS

The typically conservative approach can be seen in Rookwood's rendering of Art Nouveau. While Tiffany was showing his first examples of favrile at the 1904 World's Fair, Rookwood unveiled a vellum glaze, named to suggest the feel of parchment. This transparent matt glaze was particularly effective for pastoral landscapes and other scenic vistas, permitting a greater decorative range. An enthusiasm for landscapes, which released decorators from the limitations of floral designs of the past, imitated American tonalists George Inness and James McNeill Whistler, whose paintings gained prominence beginning in the 1880s through the turn of the century. Rookwood decorator Edward Hurley, who joined the staff in 1896, was a painter, printmaker, and photographer whose paintings on vases and plaques reflected his attraction to the tonalist photographs of Edward Steichen, Alfred Stieglitz, and Clarence White.[12] Hurley's use of trees in silhouette, reflecting poetically painted ponds, and a misty atmosphere depicting a sunrise are close in subject matter and tonality to these early photographs.

Rookwood was not alone in appropriating landscape for subject matter. Newcomb Pottery, mentioned earlier in connection with George Ohr and a latecomer to art pottery, contributed its own interpretation of nature around 1910. New England artist Ellsworth Woodward guided and taught classes at an art league and an art pottery, both operations the forerunners of Newcomb Pottery. Woodward, like Benn Pitman at the School of Design, provided art instruction for upper-class southern women, many of whom were unmarried and had little to occupy their time. When the college pottery opened in 1894, Woodward hired Mary Sheerer, a former Cin-

79. Mary Louise McLaughlin
VASE
*c. 1901. Porcelain Losanti ware,
height 6", diameter 4⅝". Private
collection*

80. GEORGE OHR, BILOXI ART
POTTERY
TEAPOT
*c. 1898–1909. Glazed
earthenware, 4 x 7⅝ x 4⁹/₁₆".
Cooper-Hewitt Museum,
The Smithsonian Institution's
National Museum of Design,
New York. Gift of Marcia and
William Goodman*

cinnati Art Academy student with some experience in china
painting, to work with Joseph Meyer on clay bodies, glazes, and
decorative treatments. The hot, moist climate of New Orleans created problems for underglaze painting. Given the weather and the
quality of the clay, the type of design most effective was a low relief
outlined by deep black lines. Blues, greens, blacks, and yellows
proved the most practical colors, covered with a transparent glaze.
Sheerer's designs frequently featured horizontal bands of color defining areas at the vase's shoulder to support a pattern of wild tomatoes,
chinaberry trees, or narcissus in modified relief. The black outline
connected Newcomb vases to Tiffany stained-glass lamp shades.
Other Newcomb designers favored using the entire vessel for stylized magnolia blossoms or thin stalks of iris. Through its motifs Newcomb Pottery added to the variety within American Art Nouveau.

Woodward went one step further than Pitman in his use of
American flora and fauna; he chose botanical examples indigenous
to the South. As a result, in 1910 when Sadie Irvine graduated from
student to professional decorator and introduced painted landscapes,
her designs had a southern slant. Irvine's vase of a moss-draped oak
tree with the moon appearing behind its branches echoed the
dreamy quality of Edward Hurley's scenic vistas on Rookwood vases
of the same period, but hers exemplified the tropical atmosphere of
New Orleans. Irvine's decorative technique was enhanced by the
work of Paul Cox, whom Woodward hired in 1910. A graduate of Alfred University (whose ceramic department was established in 1900),
Cox was a ceramic chemist. He perfected and extended the range of
Newcomb's glazes and clay bodies, and introduced a matt glaze.

81. *Joseph Meyer, one of the
throwers for Newcomb Pottery*

OTHER INTERPRETATIONS OF ART NOUVEAU

Newcomb Pottery has been termed a provincial Rookwood, yet its contribution to art pottery stands apart for its unique design and as an expression of the South. Other potteries formed in the Rookwood image continued to imitate popular designs while at the same time offering new ideas. For example, Samuel Weller hired Jacques Sicard, who arrived from France in 1902, to develop a metallic lusterware for the pottery. Iridescent glazes had been produced in France as early as 1889, where Sicard learned the technique from Clément Massier, an inspired French potter. Sicardo-ware, as it was called at Weller, used luster colors as the background for French-inspired Art Nouveau motifs such as peacock feathers and snails.

After W. A. Long left Weller, he opened the Clifton Pottery in Newark, New Jersey, in 1905. His low-relief Art Nouveau motifs were inspired by Dalpayrat and Van Briggle's use of the female form. The effusive use of swirling lines surrounding his figures suggests flowing hair or waves of water, a sense of movement closer in feeling to the European style. Albert and Anna Valentien, former associates of Van Briggle's at Rookwood, also used figures on some of their pottery. They had left Rookwood in 1907 for San Diego, where they opened a pottery in 1911. Though of short duration, the Valentien Pottery produced matt-glazed vases with raised flowers, vines, and leaves. Anna Valentien's background in sculpture, combined with her exposure to Rodin earlier in Paris, is apparent in figures less forceful than Van Briggle's; hers lounge around the rim of a vessel or are positioned to dramatically define the edge.

By the turn of the century, the disintegration of the Art Nouveau style had begun, its vitality dissipated by repetition, imitation, and commercialism. In evaluating the importance of Art Nouveau on ceramics, it is clear that the style brought form into alignment with decoration, expanding technique beyond china and underglaze painting and elevating the ornamental glaze to a new position of importance. The introduction of matt glazes opened the field to the use of an allover surface with variations such as Tiffany's mottled surfaces and Ohr's metallic oxides. The ornamental glaze filled the stylistic vacuum left by a fading Art Nouveau.

Siegfried Bing's aspirations were for the development of a mature expression. In some respects, Bing's hopes were realized but in ways he hadn't anticipated. The "structural naturalism" defined by American pottery offered a stylistic identity apart from previous dependence on Europe. Van Briggle's combination of vessel and figure in *Despondency* added a psychological mood not previously found in French ceramics. Only George Ohr threw his own ware, conveying an intimacy with clay and suggesting the vitality possible within a plastic material. Through their affinity for Art Nouveau, potters such as Van Briggle, McLaughlin, and Ohr injected new vigor into the art pottery movement, lengthening its life span. Subsequently, other aspects of this movement—studio pottery and architectural uses for clay—continued to develop momentum.

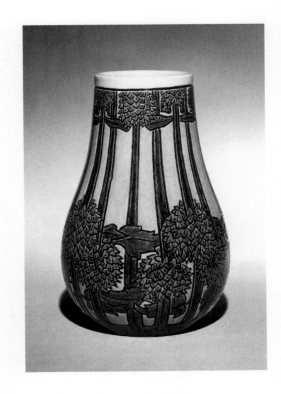

82. LEONA NICHOLSON (DECORATOR), NEWCOMB COLLEGE POTTERY
VASE
c. 1896–1905. Earthenware, carved floral motifs, height 10¼", diameter 6½". Private collection

83. CHARLES SCHMIDT (DECORA-
TOR), ROOKWOOD POTTERY
OVOID VASE WITH PEACOCK
FEATHERS
*1904. Pottery with underglaze
decoration, height 10⅝". Cooper-
Hewitt Museum, The Smith-
sonian Institution's National
Museum of Design, New York*

84. JACQUES SICARD, WELLER
POTTERY
VASE
c. 1903. Iridescent glazed earth-
enware, height 6⅜".
Philadelphia Museum of Art.
Gift of Samuel A. Weller

85. EDWARD T. HURLEY (DECO-
RATOR), ROOKWOOD POTTERY
SCENIC VELLUM VASE
*1909. Earthenware, height 16",
diameter 6¾". Private collection*

Scenic landscapes were Rookwood's conservative interpretation of Art Nouveau. They
evoked a romantic mood and
tied in with the popularity of
landscape painting.

86. NEWCOMB COLLEGE
POTTERY
PLAQUE WITH LILIES
1903. Earthenware, diameter
13". Private collection

Chapter 6

THE CONSEQUENCES OF THE ART POTTERY MOVEMENT

A Continuation of Arts and Crafts Ideals

The momentum generated by the Arts and Crafts Movement continued to express itself through the production of art pottery and decorative tile. Both directions expanded during the early years of the twentieth century; for a short time art pottery served therapeutic needs while architects extended the uses of tile from homes to public buildings.

PAINTING ON POTTERY

As a hobby, a shared social activity, and an economic necessity, pottery decoration continued attracting large numbers of women well into the first decade of the twentieth century. However, in spite of the numbers swelling its ranks, amateur china and underglaze painting as an artistic expression was suffering a loss of prestige. Evidence of this growing disfavor came in part from the jurors for ceramics at the 1901 World's Fair in Paris who were reluctant to consider amateur china-painted ware for awards; they regarded the American designs as derivative, hardly in a class with their notions of original art.[1] Amateur decorators soon found themselves working only with arts and crafts societies and china-painting organizations, their painting having been restricted from participation in art exhibitions.

Recognizing that the advancement of pottery decoration depended on greater professionalism, Adelaide Alsop Robineau and her husband, Samuel, began publication in 1899 of *Keramic Studio*, a magazine specifically for china painters. Robineau, a Syracuse, New York, china painter who at this time made her living selling her ware and teaching, envisioned a magazine that could raise standards by publishing good design. She borrowed liberally from European art publications for the latest ideas and solicited articles from prominent historians, potters, and critics. To counter the loss of artistic

opposite:
87. PEWABIC POTTERY TILES IN CHURCH OF THE MOST HOLY REDEEMER
Detroit, Michigan, 1920.

above:
88. ERNEST BATCHELDER TILES
c. 1909–20. Cast ceramic, 4 x 4".
Collection Elva Meline

89. *A row of five Revelation Kilns, designed by Horace Caulkins*

A technical breakthrough for amateur decorators (and later on, studio potters) was the Revelation Kiln invented by Horace Caulkins, whose principal occupation lay in developing kilns for dentistry. He produced a portable model for china painters in 1892. Larger Revelation Kilns were developed first for Pewabic Pottery and subsequently for other major pottery manufacturers.

recognition for china painting, Robineau advised her readers to become potters and take control over every part of the process. Robineau herself heeded this advice—she became the first woman to learn the potter's wheel and successfully launch a career as a studio potter.

THE BOOM IN TILE PRODUCTION IN THE EARLY TWENTIETH CENTURY

As mentioned earlier, the Arts and Crafts Movement reinforced the aesthetic value of tile in home decoration and public buildings. Tile production expanded further in the early years of the twentieth century; Grueby, Mercer, and Low Art Tile were joined by others, including Van Briggle Pottery and, later, Pewabic Pottery.

Mary Chase Perry, a former china painter, opened the Pewabic Pottery in Detroit in 1903. She took the name Pewabic from the Chippewa Indian word for the color of copper. Perry's partner in the enterprise was Horace Caulkins, a specialist in kilns for firing dental porcelain, and who in 1892 had developed a portable kiln for china painters. The two had become acquainted when Caulkins hired Perry to travel around the country and sell the new kilns. Caulkins's invention, known as the Revelation Kiln, encased the flame—previously potters had to encase their ware in containers called saggers. Something of a technological revolution, this new kiln released china painters from a dependency on commercial potteries. Most of the period's prominent potters used the Revelation Kiln.

At first, Pewabic Pottery primarily produced utilitarian ware and a line of art pottery. Then in 1907 Perry received a commission for architectural tile from Ralph Adams Cram, a prominent Detroit architect whom she met through industrialist Charles Freer. Cram commissioned Pewabic to create the pavement tiles for his design of Detroit's St. Paul's Cathedral. Later, Pewabic Pottery provided the tile panels, borders, and plaques. The project lasted several years and established the pottery's reputation for exceptional tile. Commissions for fireplace tiles for residences and hotels, and decorative tiles for churches in Philadelphia, Washington, D.C., and Pittsburgh soon followed. With a growing reputation for beautiful glazes, Pewabic Pottery became one of the foremost producers of architectural tile in the United States.

Perry purchased equipment for the mechanical production of tiles, although she never used it. She preferred the appearance of hand-pressed tiles. Ironically, while Detroit was becoming the center of the mass-produced automobile, Pewabic Pottery successfully maintained its handwork operation.[2]

Contrary to Pewabic's flat tiles, ceramist Ernest Batchelder was creating tiles with raised designs. Batchelder had gone to the West in 1904 to teach at Throop Polytechnic Institute of Pasadena. His education in England had introduced him to the Arts and Crafts Movement, whose principles he taught to his students at Throop. As the author of several books and articles on design, by 1910 Batchelder decided to put his theories into practice and open a pottery for tile production. He used incised and modeled relief for tiles, hand-pressed in plaster molds, which he would then sun-dry in his backyard among the chickens, cats, and flowers that figured in his designs.

Batchelder's designs had been inspired by Grueby Faience ornamental tiles and those from the Moravian Pottery and Tile Works, whose medieval-based designs matched his aesthetic preferences. His tile production coincided with the arrival in Pasadena of two architects, Charles Sumner Greene and his younger brother, Henry Mather Greene. Their designs for homes had been influenced by the ideas of William Morris and by Japanese architecture; like Frank Lloyd Wright, the Greene brothers believed interior furnishings and landscaping should conform to an overall continuity of design. This concept, along with the use of handcrafted furnishings, identified the Craftsman-style home. The Greene brothers' generous use of tile for their most important commissions, executed between 1907 and 1910, became the standard for other Pasadena architects who emulated the Greene and Greene style.

Batchelder's brown-toned tiles and, later on, those in blues and grays, coordinated well with Craftsman-style homes and furnishings. In his work Batchelder was sensitive to the California landscape as were many of the region's painters of the period. Like them, Batchelder incorporated native flora and fauna into his pottery. The most distinctive design associated with Batchelder tiles was the live oak tree, indigenous to California. While Pewabic tiles reigned in the East and Midwest, ubiquitous Batchelder tiles adorned almost every home constructed in Pasadena between 1910 and 1928.[3]

SOCIAL WELFARE AND CERAMICS

Commercial potteries had many kinds of progenitors. They came into being not only for economic and cultural reasons, but for reasons of social welfare as well. Settlement houses, for example, engendered new interest in pottery making. Originally formed in the late 1800s to acclimate the large influx of immigrants coming to America, settlement houses offered instruction in marketable skills such as ceramics. Greenwich House, founded in 1902 in New York City, began ceramic classes in 1908. Hull House of Chicago, which opened in 1889, sponsored the Chicago Arts and Crafts Society's first organizational meeting in 1897. Initially, instruction was at a very basic level, but in time more experienced teachers guided these programs. Shortly after 1900, art schools such as the School of the Art Institute of Chicago and the Pennsylvania Museum School of Industrial Art also began offering classes in throwing, glazing, and china and underglaze painting.

For the first time pottery was also used as therapy. When Dr. Herbert J. Hall opened a sanatorium in Marblehead, Massachusetts, for women suffering from nervous disorders, he prescribed simple manual tasks, including pottery, as aids to recovery. In 1905, the first year of the sanatorium's pottery's operation, Dr. Hall decided the enterprise needed a professional manager capable of artistic guidance. Arthur Baggs, a student of ceramics at Alfred University, was hired.

As it turned out, Baggs was interested in changing more than a few procedures. He wanted commercial success. As a result, Marble-

head Pottery, as it was named, soon became an independent operation which no longer employed patients as decorators. By 1908, when the ware was introduced to the public, a small staff of three designers, one decorator, a thrower, and a kiln operator produced two hundred pieces a week. Baggs designed much of the ware, which reflected the coastal environment of Marblehead. Restrained shapes with designs confined to a border characterized the vases and bowls. Conventionalized flat patterns of seaweed, fish, gulls, and sea horses decorated Marblehead vases in understated, muted tones of gray, green, blue, and brownish yellow. The satin-like matt texture of the glaze and the colors reflected the town's weathered houses. One bright color, known as Marblehead Blue, blended the shades of sea and sky.

Baggs purchased the pottery in 1915, and went on to develop new glazes and styles. What began as a sociological experiment became a professional enterprise; Marblehead Pottery received numerous awards for its distinctive designs and craftsmanship.

Though Baggs discontinued Dr. Hall's use of clay for therapeutic purposes, the idea inspired a similar experiment on the West Coast. Arequipa Pottery, established in 1911 in Marin County, California, was an outgrowth of Dr. Philip King Brown's sanatorium for working women with tuberculosis. Frederick H. Rhead, an English potter who had previously worked for Weller and had produced Art Nouveau designs for Roseville Pottery, instructed the sanatorium's patients in clay techniques. Under his direction they decorated cast bowls and vases. Rhead's idea of how a pottery should operate brought him into conflict with Brown and he left Arequipa in 1913. Albert L. Solon, also an Englishman and, like Rhead, from a distinguished family of potters, became the new director.

Solon introduced new glazes and expanded Arequipa's market to the East Coast. But the problem of a decorating staff in a constant state of flux mitigated against consistent growth—patients who improved left and untrained women entered. Frustrated, Solon left in 1916 for a teaching position at a new college in San Jose, California.

90. ARTHUR BAGGS
THREE VESSELS
Earthenware. (left to right:) no artist listed, n.d. Height 7⅜"; Arthur Baggs. 1904. Height 4¾"; Arthur Baggs. 1903. Height 3¾". Private collection

Alfred University was one of the first educational institutions having a broad program for training school and university ceramics teachers, studio potters, and pottery managers. Arthur Baggs, whose student work at Alfred is shown here, was trained by Professor Charles Binns. Baggs later became an important university teacher and pottery manager.

overleaf:
91. MARBLEHEAD POTTERY.
SIX VASES
c. 1910. Earthenware. (left to right:) height 4¼", diameter 4¹/₁₆"; height 3⅜", diameter 4 ⁵/₁₆"; height 6⅝", diameter 5³/₁₆"; height 9", diameter 5⁵/₁₆"; height 6¹/₁₆", diameter 3³/₁₆"; height 4½", diameter 4³/₁₆". Private collection

92. FREDERICK H. RHEAD, RHEAD
POTTERY
LOW BOWL
*c. 1915. Glazed earthenware,
diameter 8¾". Oakland Museum, Calif. Gift of the Estate of
Helen Hathaway White*

93. FREDERICK RHEAD, RHEAD
POTTERY
BOWL
*1914–17. Earthenware, height
5". Oakland Museum, Calif.*

Frederick Rhead's peripatetic
career included working at some
of the most important potteries
in Ohio before he came west to
California in 1911. After leaving
Arequipa Pottery, he established
Rhead Pottery in Santa Barbara,
California, where his experiments with inlaid clay
developed into a decorative, incised line filled in with a
contrasting slip.

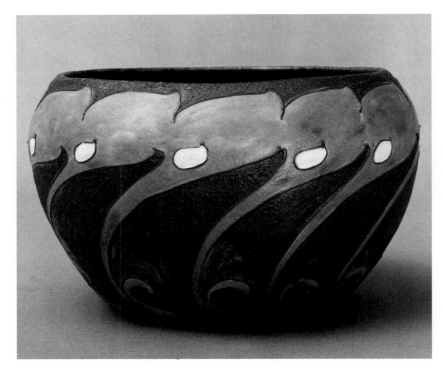

94. *Pottery decorators at the Paul Revere Pottery*

95. PAUL REVERE POTTERY BOWL
1910. Earthenware, diameter 5½". The Newark Museum, N.J.

The next director, Fred H. Wilde, yet another Englishman, initiated tile production at the pottery, using designs that reflected California's Spanish heritage. However, even this could not reverse the pottery's marginal operation and Arequipa was forced to close when America entered World War I. Pottery making for therapeutic purposes had served a valuable function; following the war, the practice was revived for veterans.

Though not strictly therapeutic, pottery making helped acclimate newcomers to Boston. The Saturday Evening Girls, a club for young immigrants, turned to pottery production under the guidance of the group's patron, Mrs. James J. Storrow, a Boston socialite. Storrow purchased a kiln in 1906 for the club's Brookline meeting place, and English ceramist Thomas S. Nickerson taught pottery techniques for a short time. In 1908 the club moved to a building near the Old North Church and the group changed its name to Paul Revere Pottery. Edith Brown, a designer, became the pottery's director and she began by eliminating amateurs in favor of the high school girls whom she herself trained. Brown's decorating techniques resembled those of the Newcomb College Pottery, and the incised and slightly raised designs of Frederick Rhead. Black outlines accented the rabbits and ducks on children's breakfast sets and floral designs on dinnerware in matt shades of yellow, blue, green, gray, and brown.

Paul Revere Pottery lasted twenty-four years, although during that time it was never a commercial success. It survived primarily on Mrs. Storrow's subsidies, which continued until the Depression. Shortly after the subsidies ended, so did the pottery.

The Triumph of the Ornamental Glaze: Matt, Crystalline, and Iridescent

The art pottery movement, on the wane by 1910, had a temporary reprieve with the introduction of the ornamental glaze. The first popular ornamental glaze was the matt surface, an outgrowth of Art Nouveau. Introduced by William Grueby in 1897, the glaze legitimized the use of a rich allover surface and opened the door to other glaze possibilities. Historically, the most prestigious monochrome glazes were those produced in China during the Sung dynasty (A.D. 960–1279), and whose beauty Hugh Robertson was one of the first Americans to appreciate. They were also admired by Charles Binns, the son of the director of the Worcester Porcelain Works of England. In his capacity as the company's sales representative, Binns often visited museum collections of oriental ceramics in London and Paris. They fascinated him—and, in time, inspired him.

After he moved to America in 1897, Binns began to produce his own pottery. In 1900, he accepted the directorship of the newly formed ceramics department of Alfred University, named the New York State School of Clayworking and Ceramics. It was here, in between his lectures on factory technical problems, methods, and decorative techniques, that Binns found the longed-for time to learn the potter's wheel and test his knowledge of glazes on his own ware. He was disciplined in his approach, applying systematic procedures

96. *Charles Binns pottery signature. 1929. Private collection*

97. CHARLES BINNS
VASE
Stoneware, diameter 8½". New York State College of Ceramics Museum, Alfred University

to small bowls and vases of classical shapes. Though he had been trained in porcelain, Binns preferred working with stoneware, making large vessels by throwing and joining several parts. One of his trademarks was a well-trimmed base or foot; while not readily visible, Binns deemed it important because it carried the weight of the vessel.

Like Robertson, Binns was experienced in formulating glazes. However, he went a step further than his predecessor by declaring the glaze to be an expressive aspect of ceramics: "If the artist-potter is to be successful, he must be prepared to compound glazes which are the expression of his own individuality."[4] A Binns matt glaze was either silky like a kid glove or textured like the shell of an egg. His shades of Willow, Moss Green, and Gray Crystal glazes were colors that later became identified with his ware.

Binns was also intrigued by the crystalline glaze, an ornamental glaze in which snowflake or pansy-like formations develop on the surface. The glaze had been developed some twenty years earlier by French potters, who had produced crystals back in the 1880s. Teco

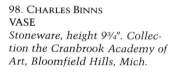

98. CHARLES BINNS
VASE
Stoneware, height 9¾". Collection the Cranbrook Academy of Art, Bloomfield Hills, Mich.

Pottery introduced the first American version of the crystalline glaze at the 1893 World's Fair. Louis Tiffany was also attracted to the crystalline surface; his mottled glazes included tiny crystals of indefinite formation.

Difficult to control in the firing, the crystalline glaze was impressively mastered by Adelaide Robineau. Her interest in porcelain had first been sparked when she published an article in the May 1901 issue of *Keramic Studio* on Royal Copenhagen porcelains which included crystalline glazes. Shortly afterward, she learned about Mary Louise McLaughlin's porcelains. Then, around 1902, Robineau attended a ceramics class at Alfred directed by Charles Binns. He encouraged her to formulate her own glazes; this, in turn, led her to write to the foremost authority on high temperature glazes, Taxile Doat, the director of the ceramics factory at Sèvres. Doat was remarkably generous with details on formulas and techniques, all contained in a manuscript titled "Grand Feu Ceramics." Samuel Robineau translated the material, which was first published as a series of articles for *Keramic Studio*, and later as a book.

99. FULPER POTTERY
RETICULATED VASE WITH
MOLDED MUSHROOM
MOTIF
*c. 1910–12. Earthenware, height
9¾", diameter 4½". Private
collection*

100. Adelaide Alsop Robineau
POPPY VASE
*1910. Porcelain, height 6¼".
Everson Museum of Art, Syracuse, N.Y.*

opposite:
101. Adelaide Alsop Robineau
LANTERN VASE
*1908. Porcelain, height 8⅛".
Everson Museum of Art, Syracuse, N.Y.*

Robineau's first successful crystalline-glazed porcelain vessels appeared in 1904. For a brief period she used this glaze on molded porcelain vases. However, she soon found herself ill-suited to solving the many problems of slip casting and returned to throwing on the wheel. Possessing considerable curiosity and a talent for research and experimentation, Robineau used multiple glazes on porcelains and multiple firings to achieve the colors and crystal patterns she desired. In spite of the heartbreak over the many disastrous firings that often destroyed all her ware, Robineau persevered, producing large crystal clusters, overlapping crystals, crystals completely covering the surface, and crystals in the shape of thin rods or feathery edged ferns. Her interest in unusual crystal formations and colors continued throughout her career, as did her interest in Chinese glazes such as oxblood, flambé, and crackle, and in this field she accomplished a rarity—obtaining crystals over shades of red.[5]

Iridescent glazes, associated with Persian ceramics, had appealed to Mary Chase Perry from her first contact with industrialist Charles Freer's collection of oriental pottery. In 1902, she accidentally produced a small pot bearing a shimmering iridescent surface. Years of experiments followed. By 1909, Perry had developed a full panoply of colors—rose, green, gold, purple, gold-yellow, and copper—a palette she used on tiles and vases throughout Pewabic Pottery's lifetime. A vibrant Egyptian blue which Perry perfected in 1911 was another acclaimed success for the pottery. Less well known were Perry's experiments with crystalline and volcanic or bubbled glazes which, like Robineau's exotic surfaces, required successive firings to achieve their many hues.

The heightened public appeal of unusual glazes wasn't lost on at least one large commercial pottery. In 1909, Fulper Pottery, a firm producing utilitarian ware in Flemington, New Jersey, entered the art pottery field with its "Vasekraft" line, ware decorated exclusively in ornamental glazes. William H. Fulper, Jr., grandson of one of the founders, followed Grueby and Teco potteries in the transition to art pottery. Fulper began experimental glaze research in 1900, persuaded in part by Charles Binns's attitude toward simplicity and the beauty of the monochrome glaze.[6] Impressed by the interest shown in Robineau's glaze developments, Fulper produced crystalline, flambé, luster, matt, monochrome, and polychrome glazes. He borrowed from the Chinese and French in assigning romantic names to glaze colors: Café au Lait, Leopard Skin (a spotted crystalline glaze), Cat's Eye, Blue of the Sky Seen between Clouds after a Rain, Elephant's Breath (a shiny, reflective black). He called his most prestigious and high-priced group of glazes Famille Rose, hues he regarded as a rediscovery of the ancient Chinese formulas for shades of red: deep rose, peach bloom, ashes of roses, and apple blossom.

The rich surface embellishment provided by ornamental glazes satisfied most connoisseurs of pottery decoration. For Adelaide Robineau, however, there remained a lingering attraction for the carved surface beneath an opulent glaze. The class she had attended at Alfred University included incising and excising, and she advanced rapidly from this preliminary instruction to the skillful execution shown in *Viking Ship Vase* (1905): a small boat under full sail bounces on waves that move around the shoulder of the vase, a design repeated in the perforated, separately carved ring base. The Viking ship design, like that of her later work, *Lantern* (1908), was inspired by her reading of European publications and her research into historical forms.[7]

In *Lantern*, Robineau's carving technique expanded from the border and foot areas to the entire surface. Still not satisfied, in 1910 she began planning a monumental vase with an incised pattern just around the time she and her husband joined Doat and Frederick Rhead as faculty at the People's University (founded the previous year in a suburb of St. Louis, Missouri). After numerous experiments with porcelain clay bodies, Robineau designed a symmetrical pattern of lattice work around the motif of the scarab, a beetle revered by the ancient Egyptians as a symbol of rebirth, creative power, patience, and skill. Titled *Apotheosis of the Toiler*, the intricately carved ginger jar required one thousand hours of work.

102. ADELAIDE ALSOP ROBINEAU
VIKING SHIP VASE
1905. Porcelain, height 7¼".
Everson Museum of Art, Syracuse, N.Y.

The Robineaus sent the scarab vase along with a group of porcelains to the International Exposition of Decorative Arts at Turin, Italy, in 1911. There they received the Grand Prize—an astonishing achievement for a studio potter whose career was less than a decade. While carving was frequently a part of her ware in later years, Robineau never again produced a work as elaborate as the scarab vase. Her conservative designs continued to emphasize vertical lines associated with American Art Nouveau; the carved surfaces of her work remained as a carryover of the Victorian style and showed as well an oriental influence in her work.

Industry Initiates Ceramic Education

Classes for the amateur or professional decorator of pottery, beginning in the 1880s and including those initially taught at Alfred University and People's University, emphasized basic decorating techniques. However, more complicated procedures such as the glaze research pursued by McLaughlin, Robineau, Binns, and Perry—required skills and information not taught at any school in the United States before the mid-1890s. (A case in point was William Watts Taylor's decision to send Van Briggle and chemist Stanley Burt to Europe for more information.)

It was a mining engineer who first successfully pushed for professional technical training in clay. Edward Orton, Jr., a graduate of Ohio State University, had entered the clay industry in 1888 and had managed several plants. The experience convinced him that a course in ceramic engineering was essential for understanding the special problems of clay production; to that end he persuaded the National Brick Manufacturers and the Ohio Clay Operators associations to join him in lobbying the Ohio legislature. As a result of their efforts,

opposite:
103. ADELAIDE ALSOP ROBINEAU
APOTHEOSIS OF THE TOILER
[Scarab Vase]
*1910. Porcelain, height 16⅝",
diameter 6". Everson Museum of
Art, Syracuse, N.Y.*

To fashion the minutely detailed lines in her so-called Scarab Vase, Robineau used a crochet needle as a carving tool. During the first firing, a large crack appeared. Undeterred, Robineau filled the area with a paste of ground porcelain, glazed it, and fired it again. That time, no trace of the damage remained.

above left:
104. *Adelaide Alsop Robineau
at work on the Scarab Vase at
People's University in St. Louis,
1910.*

above right:
105. *Mark of Adelaide Alsop
Robineau. This mark also indicates that the vase was made in
1910 at People's University. The
signature is excised in the porcelain. Private collection*

the "Mud Pie" Bill passed in 1894, establishing at Orton's alma mater the first university ceramic engineering program in the country. As program director, Orton supplemented the budget by soliciting gifts of equipment from the ceramics industry, the acknowledged beneficiary of the program.

Other states whose revenues came in part from developing clay industries realized the advantages of professional training. Rutgers, situated in the clayworking center of New Jersey, inaugurated a department in 1902 supported by the New Jersey Clayworkers Association. Within five years, the University of Illinois and Iowa State also offered degrees in ceramic engineering, supported by the clay industry's organizations.

Orton believed that the industry's real competition was Europe, and that America's ceramics industry would prosper only if ideas to solve technical problems were shared for the benefit of all. Not surprisingly, Orton's colleagues in the industry considered such openness alarmingly radical. As a consequence, Orton, along with Theodore Randall, editor and owner of *The Clay Worker*, the first clay trade journal in America, left the National Brick Manufacturers Association in 1899 to launch the American Ceramic Society. The primary objective of the organization, which was incorporated in 1905, was to advance the quality of ceramic production through an exchange of information.

Charles Binns was another outspoken advocate of sharing information, and he became a prominent member of the society, offering his expertise in papers prepared for the society's meetings. Binns also wrote numerous articles for *Keramic Studio* and Gustav Stickley's magazine, *The Craftsman*. Binns's chief purpose was to inform other practicing ceramists, though his many articles did bring Alfred University's ceramics school to the attention of potential students. More than a discussion of technical considerations, Binns also wrote on ceramic history and aesthetics. His books, especially *The Potter's Craft* (1909), constituted a core of literature for ceramics and enabled him to reach an audience quite distant from Alfred University.

Alfred University, or The New York State School of Clayworking and Ceramics, was, like the ceramics departments in other universities, established to bolster the state's brick industry and encourage utilization of the state's raw materials. But unlike the program at Ohio State, ceramic engineering at Alfred was balanced between training decorators and teachers for technical schools. Even though he was unsympathetic to the division of labor in potteries, over time Binns created a curriculum that dealt with factory, laboratory, and studio problems, as well as some classes especially for public school teachers and pottery decorators.

More farsighted than some of his colleagues who concentrated on engineering courses, Binns accurately predicted that Alfred would produce educated men and women who would work in all areas of the country as pottery managers, studio potters, and outstanding teachers. Arthur Baggs, Paul Cox, Elizabeth Overbeck, Mary Chase Perry, and Adelaide Robineau were among the first to fulfill Binns's vision. They were followed by teacher-potters Myrtle French at the School of the Art Institute of Chicago, William Bragdon at the California School of Arts and Crafts, and Frederick Walrath, who served as technical chemist for Newcomb College beginning in 1918. Each helped to circulate Binns's philosophy of ceramics nationwide.

Art and Industry

Charles Binns and others concerned with the arts in the early years of the century attempted to straddle two concurrent movements—the Arts and Crafts rejection of the machine in favor of a return to handcrafts, and an accommodation to the machine for the purpose of advancing design. In the United States, Frank Lloyd Wright championed simplicity in design, in part as a way of bringing the production of handcrafted objects closer to factory procedures. Wright tried to form an association of art and industry in 1893 in Chicago, but the Arts and Crafts Movement, then at its height, made any affiliation with industry unthinkable.

The movement away from static traditionalism and toward maintaining high standards in design found fertile ground in Europe. In England, the search for new directions resulted in the minimal, ornamental style of the Glasgow School led by Charles Rennie Mackintosh and the Guild of Handicrafts formed in 1888 in London by British Socialist Charles Robert Ashbee; both designers' influence extended to Vienna. In 1897, a group of Viennese artists, architects,

106. *A lesson in glaze-making (published in* The Craftsman, *June 1903)*

and designers rebelled against the stifling conservative policies of the Kunstlerhaus Artists' Association, founding a movement known as the Vienna Secession. The revolt rapidly gained public recognition and acceptance through a series of exhibitions that brought the most contemporary examples of European art to Vienna. Articles about Mackintosh, Ashbee, and William Morris in English and German design magazines intrigued Josef Hoffmann, one of the leaders of the Secession; as a result, he arranged to show the work of British craft guilds in a Secession exhibition of 1900. Impressed with the quality of the craftsmanship, Hoffmann arranged to visit Britain in 1902. The following year, he founded the Wiener Werkstätte, modeled on Ashbee's guilds. Like the Arts and Crafts Movement, the Wiener Werkstätte advocated certain craft traditions, along with the caveat that the machine help employ design and production. Exploring this concept more fully was the Deutscher Werkbund (German Work or Craft Alliance), established in 1907. Bringing together architects, craftsmen, industrialists, and teachers, the Werkbund operated on the premise that the machine help ensure the high quality of mass-produced art.

In America, there were those who worked for a more fruitful relationship between art and industry. Wright discussed "The Art and Craft of the Machine" in a lecture delivered at Hull House in 1901. He proposed broadening William Morris's ideas to include an acceptance of the machine. With its straight lines, the furniture Wright designed was more amenable to machine production. Nor was Wright alone in adapting design to the machine. After his visit to Europe in 1898, Gustav Stickley transformed his overall furniture design into one of flat, straight surfaces capable of incorporating certain machine processes.

Still, the American establishment wasn't ready for the workshop setting as a way of merging art and industry. Instead, the museum took on the role of liaison. Nor did this lead to immediate acceptance. The first exhibit of the modern style, as this preference for clean-cut, straight lines was named, was held at the Newark Museum in 1912, one year before the scandalous Armory Show. The objects shown received similar treatment and were labeled "too modern" and "too commercial."[8]

By 1915 attitudes were changing. That year the National Museum of American History and Technology in Washington, D.C., presented an exhibit, "American Industrial Art," featuring a room furnished by a group of manufacturers demonstrating the value of art in design. The Panama Pacific Exposition held that same year in San Francisco exhibited twelve rooms in which interior decoration and accessories conformed to a single motif. Both exhibits were an indication that two of Wright's tenets were beginning to have an impact: coordinating interior design concepts and welcoming the machine as a partner in design. Indeed, Richard Bach, an associate in industrial art at the Metropolitan Museum of Art, while addressing the ninth convention of the American Federation of the Arts in Detroit in 1918, caught the temper of the times by urging his audience to "Harness the machine to the mind."[9] Acceptance of the machine was inevitable—and the craftsman had no alternative but to find a way to coexist.

opposite:
107. Viktor Schreckengost
KERAMOS
c. 1939. Earthenware, height
19¼", width 13". Everson
Museum of Art, Syracuse, N.Y.
Gift of the artist

American Dinnerware

World War I temporarily interrupted the movement toward an aesthetic acceptance of the machine. Imports of ceramics ceased during the war, giving American industry time to consider ways of challenging European competition and appealing to the home market. These circumstances probably contributed to the first American-made dinnerware, Lenox china, which was produced for the White House. In 1917, President Woodrow Wilson ordered a 1,700-piece set of porcelain dinnerware from this Trenton, New Jersey, company. Decorated with the president's seal and a border of stars and stripes in gold, the new tableware represented, in one sense, a coming-of-age for the American dinnerware industry. Past presidents, Theodore Roosevelt in particular, had searched the country for a company able to supply a large quantity of high-quality ware, but without success. Roosevelt had finally settled for English Wedgwood china. President Wilson's choice of Lenox china gave the eleven-year-old company national recognition and may have influenced Franklin Delano Roosevelt, who also purchased Lenox dinnerware during his administration in the 1930s. And it was Roosevelt who suggested the design for the 1,722-piece set, which featured the presidential seal, a gold scroll, and border of gold stars. Roosevelt's successor, Harry Truman, continued the tradition when he placed an order with Lenox for presidential dinnerware during his administration in the late 1940s.

Lack of European competition was just one factor in the choice of Lenox china in 1917. Those dinnerware companies founded in the late 1880s had, by the second decade of the twentieth century, overcome many of the technical and financial problems that prevented earlier companies from producing fine-quality china and staying in business. Lenox, Inc. was in the forefront of these companies. The company's founder, Walter Scott Lenox, and a partner began making fine china in 1889 under the name of the Ceramic Art Company. Lenox's experience in the 1880s as an apprentice and head of the

opposite:
108. VALLY WIESELTHIER
HEAD OF A GIRL
c. 1929. Earthenware, height 6¼". Carlton Atherton Collection, Art Department, Ohio State University, Columbus

Vally Wieselthier's influence extended to Ohio State University when she was invited by Arthur Baggs (then the new ceramics department chairman) to present an art history lecture series in 1929. In between designing pottery at a Sebring, Ohio, factory, she collaborated with Baggs on at least one vase which he threw and she decorated. She made a gift of this sculpture to Baggs.

above:
109. LENOX INC.
WHITE HOUSE CHINA SERVICE, THE WILSON SERVICE
1918. Fine china, cobalt blue with an outer border of etched gold, with the 48 stars shown on an inner etched gold rim; the President's seal is executed in raised 24-karat gold in the center of the plate; dinner plate diameter 10½"; service plate diameter 11". Courtesy Lenox China

decorating department for an older Trenton factory, Ott and Brewer, proved excellent training. By 1906, as the sole owner of Lenox, Inc., he was building a reputation on producing porcelain similar to popular, high-quality Irish Belleek. In time, transfer-printed table services, priced to appeal to moderate incomes, were introduced and became an important part of the company's production. Lenox was noted for the purity of the porcelain paste and for restraint in the handling of design.

Lenox designs were generally conservative alterations of popular European and oriental styles of earlier eras. These designs, along with the prestige of presidential support, met with the approval of the buying public. But discerning critics of American dinnerware had wearied of the repetition of past styles, citing them as outdated and inappropriate for American ware. They blamed the lack of education in design as the reason American manufacturers were unable to respond with fresh ideas. At the same time, the workshop movement in England and Germany and specialized European schools educating craftsmen were hailed as models for bringing the arts into industry, a necessity in developing new styles. It was hoped that American manufacturers, adapting these methods, would thereby develop the potential to capture world markets. Indeed, throughout the war years, articles in a variety of publications stressed the need for a national school of industrial art which would promote a new attitude toward design for the machine age.[1]

Consensus on advancing education in design was lacking. Richard Bach, an associate in industrial arts at the Metropolitan Museum of Art, argued that with its vast collections the museum could act successfully as the "silent partner" and "adjunct of the factory" serving manufacturers and designers.[2] But Bach's proposal implicitly linked design to a revival of historical styles, a questionable solution in the age of automobiles, the moving picture, and airplanes.

Another possible model was the Bauhaus, the successor to the Deutscher Werkbund, which opened in 1919. The Bauhaus philosophy called for functional, rational design based on Cubism; students were taught design for mass production. However, the heavy, somewhat massive style of the Bauhaus had less appeal for the postwar elite of American society than the French decorative arts. It was the French style, not the German, that for the moment would dictate taste.

The Parisian Influence

At the beginning of the twentieth century, Paris was the acknowledged capital of the art world. In the century's early years, Paris experienced a series of aesthetic manifestos which set the artistic tone for the years following the war. In 1907, Picasso's *Les Demoiselles d'Avignon* heralded the advent of Cubism. The Futurist manifesto of 1909 bombastically proclaimed the machine, movement, and speed as the primary sources of inspiration for art. That same year, the Ballets Russes opened their first season in Paris performing *Scheherazade* to an adoring public enchanted by the oriental mood, exotic colors, and luxurious materials. This artistic ferment transformed the French decorative arts, accenting geometric shapes and linear treatments, repetitions of diagonal lines, spirals, zigzags, sun rays, and lightning flashes. Many of these designs, with their roots in ancient art, became the symbols for the machine—speeding cars, fast trains, the propeller airplane. African art, introduced to France by Picasso, satisfied a taste for the exotic first cultivated during the Victorian Age. In 1920, an exhibition in Paris of masks and sculpture from the French Congo led to the use of tropical foliage in French decorative motifs. The discovery of King Tutankhamen's tomb in 1923 and the recently uncovered Mayan temples in Mexico and Central America inspired abstractions of stepped pyramids, which passed from France into the design in America of skyscrapers, furniture, the radio—and eventually, into pottery. Abstractions of machines and geometric forms defined the new or modern style.

The triumph of this emerging style, based largely in France, was the Exposition Internationale des arts décoratifs et industriels modernes held in Paris in 1925. Art Deco, as it was referred to, singularly brought together a wide body of work in architecture and virtually every aspect of the decorative arts. The primary criterion for objects displayed at the Exposition was that they be in the modern style. However, the French government planned the exhibition in honor of France's allies, effectively excluding Germany and the Bauhaus whose products were hotly competitive with those made in France. Several years earlier the United States was invited to participate, but Secretary of Commerce Hoover declined, stating that there was no modern art in America. It is not known how Hoover defined modern art, but a commission appointed to report on the Exposition concluded that America had completely misjudged the French interpretation of "modern."[3]

The confusion about what constituted modern art stirred one museum into action. In 1923, the Metropolitan Museum initiated its own program to define and promote the modern style. Edward C. Moore, Jr., the son of Tiffany and Company's president, underwrote buying trips to Paris for Joseph Breck, curator of the museum's Department of Decorative Arts, and himself. Their purchases of decorative objects would serve as models for American designers. Later, probably at Moore's and Breck's urging, the museum selected a representative group of objects from the French Exposition to travel to New York for a 1926 showing and to tour American museums around the country. Writing in the museum bulletin of that year, Breck anticipated unfriendly public reaction toward the new style but remained optimistic that the exhibit would eventually stimulate new ideas.[4]

At least one American potter, Adelaide Robineau, visiting Paris in 1925, found the Exposition provocative and inspirational. (In some ways Robineau was already a believer; as early as 1917, she had responded to the modern style in *Peruvian Serpent Bowl*, whose parallel lines and intricately carved legs combined the linear and geometric with the exotic.) On her return to Syracuse, where she was now teaching at the university, Robineau began a series of ten articles for her magazine, defining the modern style based on what she'd seen at the exhibition. Because amateur pottery decorating had practically faded into oblivion by the end of the war, the Robineaus had altered the magazine's format to appeal to a new, broader readership. In 1924 *Keramic Studio* was renamed *Design* and geared toward the needs of art teachers and craft hobbyists.

Robineau's influence in promoting the modern style was, of course, in no way equal to the power of the Metropolitan Museum. The museum encouraged Macy's, the New York department store, to follow the lead of Parisian department stores in promoting Art Deco objects. With the help of Richard Bach, now director of industrial relations at the museum, the store sponsored an "Art in Trade" display in 1927. American designers were featured who had adapted the modern style to the needs of American life; and now work in ceramics was included.

The International Exhibition of Ceramic Art

In 1928, the Metropolitan Museum presented its most influential ceramic show of the period. Called the International Exhibition of Ceramic Art, the show presented American ceramics along with a range of European ceramic production, from figurines to tableware. Sponsored by the newly formed Division of Industrial Arts of the American Federation of the Arts, most of the work was assembled by guest-curator Helen Plumb, associated with the Detroit Institute of Arts, who toured Europe and America selecting five hundred objects for the exhibit. The show ultimately toured six cities in the East and Midwest. Plumb chose a wide spectrum of objects ranging from individually crafted, unique ware to pots and jugs produced in quantity or in limited commercial production. Critical response varied. Tableware was given a low artistic rating from critics who noted that traditional styles prevailed. Another criticism was leveled at British potters Bernard Leach and William Staite Murray for not moving beyond an imitation of Chinese Sung dynasty vessels.[5] Ceramics from Austria were singled out as typifying the modern spirit, produced through a collaboration of industrial art schools, government scholarships, excellent teachers, and the activities of the Wiener Werkstätte. The figurative sculptures and busts by Vally Wieselthier, described as "natural, spontaneous, childlike in its gaiety," offered an approach to clay that took advantage of the plastic qualities of the material.[6] Furthermore, Wieselthier's women with their rouged cheeks, bobbed hair, heavy eye makeup, and saucy berets caught the spirit and portrayed with humor that modern woman, the flapper.

In the American section, Robineau's versatility in porcelain and the casually painted utilitarian earthenware of Henry Varnum Poor received special mention, but except for Carl Walters's decorative animal figures the display was hardly exciting. The variety of colored tile, especially examples of Frederick Rhead's glaze research for the American Encaustic Tiling Company, convinced reviewers of tile's increasing popularity. It was an ironic endorsement since two years hence most American tile companies would be facing bankruptcy, casualties of the Great Depression.

The large number of figurines from different countries shown in the International Exhibition indicated their popularity in Europe. In

110. VALLY WIESELTHIER
FAWN'S HEAD
1919. Glazed earthenware, height 12¼". Collection Sammlung Bröhan Museum, West Berlin

America, too, since the nineteenth century, small replicas of large statues, especially those considered morally uplifting, were reproduced for display in the home. When the most distinguished European porcelain factories such as Rosenthal in Germany and Royal Copenhagen in Denmark reestablished figurine production after World War I, Americans were eager customers. One reason for renewed interest in small sculpture was the change in life-styles from large suburban homes to city apartments, smaller living quarters requiring a more efficient use of space. Also, the general affluence of the 1920s created a market for luxury items not tied to utility and necessity.

Art Deco Sculpture at Cowan Pottery

One pottery in particular was preparing to supply decorative sculpture for this growing market. Cowan Pottery Studio of Rocky River, Ohio, was in the forefront of companies able to combine business and art in the production of ceramics—in particular, figurines. R. Guy Cowan, a former student of Binns's at Alfred University, came from a family of potters who had lived and worked in East Liverpool, Ohio, for several generations. Four years after graduating college Cowan opened the Cleveland Pottery and Tile Company in 1912, only to shut its doors in 1917 when he entered service during World War I. Returning to Cleveland in 1919, Cowan decided to reopen the pottery, changing its name to the Cowan Pottery Studio. He moved the pottery to Rocky River and began commercial production in 1921, hiring a national dealer to distribute his ware to department stores.

An inventory of mass-produced ashtrays, desk sets, tea sets, lamp bases, and door knobs subsidized a line of mold-made figurines, produced with care in limited editions. The pottery's most popular decorative item in the mid-twenties was a figurine insert for a dining room table centerpiece with matching candlesticks. Because Japanese-style flower arranging had become part of chic decorating, Cowan's figurines were designed to be used together with flowers or separately as decorative sculptures, art objects displayed on the family radio. The features and body details of these figures were muted with emphasis placed on line and movement. Most were poised in the midst of a vigorous dance and draped romantically in swirls of cloth. Nude figures held flowing scarves, simulating the flames and waves similar to those surrounding women on Art Nouveau pottery.

Cowan, who considered these figures fine-art sculptures, entered them in the May Show, the Cleveland Museum of Art's yearly juried exhibtion of Ohio art (and one of the few competitions admitting ceramics). In 1925, *The Scarf Dancer* was awarded first prize; the following year, *White Swirl Dancer* earned that honor. But the figurines were placed in the category of pottery, a designation unacceptable to Cowan. In response, Cowan began recruiting sculptors from the Cleveland School of Art (now the Cleveland Institute of Art). At Cowan's behest, Alexander Blazys, head of the school's sculpture department, adapted his bronze sculpture of two Russian

111. DREXLER JACOBSEN, COWAN POTTERY STUDIO
ANTINAEUS
*1928. Porcelain, height 13½".
Everson Museum of Art, Syracuse, N.Y. Gift of Justin Beauchat*

112. COWAN POTTERY STUDIO
MOSES
c. 1926–31. Earthenware, matt blue glaze, height 18¾". Western Reserve Historical Society, Cleveland, Ohio

113. R. GUY COWAN, COWAN POTTERY STUDIO
WHITE SWIRL DANCER
1926. Earthenware, height 10". Cowan Pottery Museum at the Rocky River Public Library, Ohio

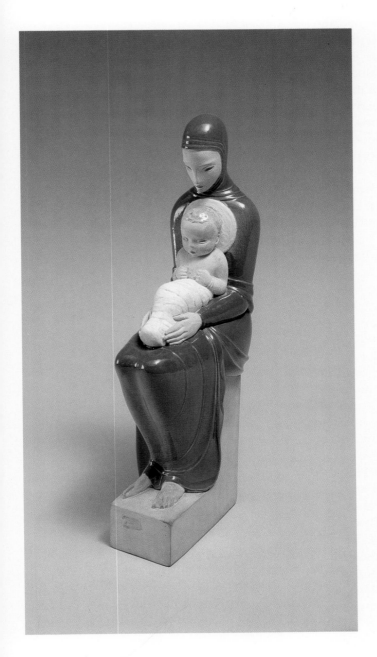

114. Waylande Gregory,
Cowan Pottery Studio
MADONNA AND CHILD
*c. 1928–29. Earthenware, height
15½". Everson Museum of Art,
Syracuse, N.Y.*

115. Waylande Gregory,
Cowan Pottery Studio
SALOME
*c. 1928–29. Earthenware, 19 x
11 x 5". Everson Museum of Art,
Syracuse, N.Y.*

dancers to four figures for clay; in 1927 it received first prize in the May Show's new category of ceramic sculpture. Cowan had achieved his goal, as noted by one critic's comment in *The New York Times*, "The beautiful Cowan pottery rises to successful invasion of the field of sculpture."[7] Cowan Pottery's reputation was further enhanced by its participation that same year in the "Art in Trade" exhibition sponsored by Macy's in New York.

Blazys's association with Cowan Pottery continued periodically over two years. During this time the ties between the museum, the pottery, and the school were strengthened when Cowan began teaching part-time at the school. In the May Show of 1928, Cowan Pottery's *Madonna and Child*, a fifteen-inch-high terra-cotta covered by a soft crackle glaze, captured first prize for clay sculpture and was pictured on the cover of the Cleveland Museum's *Bulletin*. Cowan staff members designed other religious figures incorporating Art Deco's use of flowing lines and step patterns, figures in pairs depicting popular dances, and Pierrot-Pierrette figures (these last derived from eighteenth-century European figurines).

In pursuit of professionally designed sculpture, Cowan used free-lance artists such as Paul Manship and Waylande De Santis Gregory. Gregory joined the Cowan Pottery staff in 1928, producing figurines that illustrated characters from literature, legend, or mythology. *Salome* and *Persephone* are examples of Gregory's lithe, sleek women surrounded by veils or in acrobatic positions. *Torso* is a figure fragment consciously associating the figurine with fine-art subject matter. Plasticity and movement are evident in *Nautch Dancer* (1928); and the popularity of a new form of entertainment probably inspired *Burlesque Dancer* (1929). Angles and planes highlighted by a glossy black glaze and gold and silver lusters mark these statuettes as the essence of Art Deco. Gregory's group of five figures entered in the May Show of 1929 won first prize for clay sculpture.

In 1925 Arthur Baggs, Cowan's fellow student at Alfred University, joined the pottery, dividing his time between Cowan and his own pottery in Marblehead, Massachusetts, to work on glaze research. Cowan's program for building a staff didn't stop with professionals—it included culling talented young artists from the School of Art classes. Thelma Frazier, Edris Eckhardt, Russell Aitken, and Paul Bogatay brought youthful energy to the pottery. Cowan, along with faculty member Julius Mihalik, a former teacher at the Viennese Kunstgewerbeschule (where Vally Wieselthier had been a student), encouraged students to seek further training. Viktor Schreckengost was one student who heeded their advice.[8] Like Wieselthier, in the late 1920s in Vienna he had learned how to build hollow figures. This technique was in contrast to the American method of casting from molds which limited personal expression.

When Schreckengost returned to Cleveland in 1929, he joined Cowan Pottery and began teaching design at the School of Art. One of his first assignments at the pottery was producing twenty punch bowls ordered by Eleanor Roosevelt for the New York State governor's mansion. Schreckengost made each bowl with a separate design using a sgraffito technique he'd invented, a method of underglaze drawing with a wax crayon. Inspired by Cubist and Fu-

turist painting, the style used images and words reflecting the culture of the 1920s—liquor bottles and cocktail glasses, and "jazz,"
"follies," and "dance." Viennese poster art and the lighthearted approach he absorbed in Vienna characterized Schreckengost's designs.

Cowan's effort to elevate clay sculpture to an art form continued to bear fruit, and the pottery received invitations to exhibit in
the most prestigious national shows—the Pennsylvania Academy of
Fine Arts, the National Painting and Sculpture Show, and the Art
Institute of Chicago. But, like many businesses in the late 1920s, the
pottery had overextended its resources; when the crash came in October 1929, Cowan Pottery had to file for bankruptcy. The pottery
managed to retain some of its staff when it was allowed to operate
through 1931, filling orders and selling off the inventory to pay credi-
tors. Schreckengost's designs in these final years include *Leda*, a
highly stylized plaque with an incised design of swans surrounding a
lithesome female nude.

At its height, Cowan Pottery functioned as a training ground for
young artists. In its own way, Cowan's stable of talent was an
American version of the European workshop that brought artists
into industry. It set an example other potteries would follow, al-

above left:
116. VIKTOR SCHRECKENGOST,
COWAN POTTERY STUDIO
THE SEASONS VASE
*1931. White vitrified body, un-
derglaze decoration, height
11⅝", base diameter 8". Cleveland Museum of Art, Ohio. The
Himnam B. Hurlbut Collection*

above right:
117. CHARLES HARDER
VASE
*1931. Earthenware, sgraffito,
slip, transparent glaze, height
6¹¹/₁₆", rim diameter 5". Carlton Atherton Collection, Art
Department, Ohio State
University, Columbus*

Charles Harder, who followed
Charles Binns as the chairman of
ceramics at Alfred University,
employed Art Deco themes.

though more modestly. In Depression America of the thirties, a pottery was a tenuous enterprise at best.

Sculptors and a Painter Boost Clay

The sculptors associated with Cowan Pottery weren't the only ones to breach the barrier of clay in American museum exhibits. Another group of sculptors associated with fine-art materials also worked in clay during the twenties, some of them having been forced to work with a less expensive medium.

Alexander Archipenko came to America in 1923, already an established sculptor and teacher trained in Moscow and Paris. Originally a disciple of Cubism, by 1915 Archipenko began moving toward a more naturalistic yet streamlined treatment of the figure. Clay offered a surface closer to flesh tones and one without the reflections cast by bronze that disrupted the rhythm of line and form. In the past he had cast from clay models, but in 1922, with *Black Ceramic,* a figure fragment, clay became one of his primary materials.

By 1928, Archipenko had defined his ceramic torsos into rhythmic sculptures emphasizing line and form. He taught sculpture in schools around the country, and in 1929 Archipenko opened Arco Studio, a laboratory school for decorative, functional ceramics. Students produced bookends, lamps, ashtrays, bowls, and cigarette boxes in the modern style. Archipenko's timing was unfortunate; like Cowan Pottery, Arco Studio succumbed to the 1929 crash and

118. Viktor Schreckengost, Cowan Pottery Studio
JAZZ BOWL
c. 1929–31. Earthenware, height 8", diameter 14". Private collection

119. VIKTOR SCHRECKENGOST,
COWAN POTTERY STUDIO
LEDA PLAQUE
*1931. White vitrified body, dark
brown engobe, sgraffito design,
diameter 16¾".*

The outstretched wings of the
swans, the figure's billowing
hair, and the linear patterns suggesting both waves and hills
show the influence of the
Futurists on the artist.

120. ALEXANDER ARCHIPENKO
RECLINING TORSO
*1922. Terra-cotta, 21¼ x 8¹⁄₁₆ x
14⁵⁄₁₆". The Brooklyn Museum.
The Woodward Memorial Funds*

soon ceased operations. Archipenko, however, continued using clay in his own work over the next ten years.

Neither as well trained nor as sophisticated as Archipenko, Beniamino Bufano aspired to sculpture as a very young man. He apprenticed himself to Paul Manship while still a teenager, and at the age of eighteen turned to clay as the least expensive material. *Honeymoon*

121. BENIAMINO BENVENUTO BUFANO
CHINESE MAN AND WOMAN
c. 1920s. Stoneware, height 31½", width 17½". The Metropolitan Museum of Art, New York. Gift of George Blumenthal, 1924

Couple (1914) and a 1916 bust of his mother represent early work in a realistic style. A San Francisco patron financed his trip in 1918 to China where, already fascinated by Chinese culture, Bufano studied ceramic technology at potteries in Canton and Ching-tê Chên. On his return to the U.S., he produced a group of busts using Chinese men as models for *Mandarin, Philosopher,* and *Scholar.*

Characteristic of Bufano's work produced in the mid-twenties was the contrast between naturalistic facial representation and a stylized execution of hair and clothing. Later on, work in stone and bronze were commissioned by city parks, museums, and shopping centers in the San Francisco Bay Area. His clay sculptures of this period were admired for their strength and for the rhythmic patterns of lines uniting massed forms.

Commissions for portrait busts kept many sculptors like Bufano and Jo Davidson employed during the twenties. Davidson went to Paris the year Picasso introduced Cubism but, unlike Archipenko, was not impressed, preferring the more traditional modified representational approach of Rodin. He established a reputation for modeling a clay portrait bust in a single sitting. Among the American expatriates in Paris who sat for Davidson was Gertrude Stein. Davidson considered her "a sort of modern Buddha," and posed her seated in a cross-legged position.[9] Although Davidson ventured into refined abstract forms such as in his terra-cotta partial figure *Female Torso* (1927), he became best known for his portraiture which, in later years, included busts of many world leaders.

Archipenko and Davidson's work in clay was accepted as fine art, perhaps because they continued to use traditional materials—bronze, marble, and stone. But it was their acknowledged professionalism that eventually helped change attitudes toward clay sculpture as a whole.

Painters as well as sculptors turned to clay as their primary material. Carl Walters, a painter from the Midwest, had attended the Chase School in New York with Robert Henri. Walters was visiting the Metropolitan Museum of Art in 1919 when some Egyptian blue faience beads caught his attention. The museum loaned him a few fragments which he tried to reproduce; the challenge ultimately led to his abandonment of painting for clay. After firing his first attempt at animal sculpture in 1922, Walters concentrated on the form, taking liberties with realism, anatomy, and proportion in keeping with the decorative spirit of the time. Hide and fur translated into patterns of dots, flower beds, stripes, or abstract contours, a decorative impulse Walters shared with Mexican and Pennsylvania German ceramists. In the late 1920s he attempted a few human figures—*Ella,* a circus fat lady, *Snake Charmer,* and *Before Adam,* an imaginary creature linking man and animal—but these lacked the charm of his animals, which was direct and uncomplicated, humorous and disarming.

The sculpture of the twenties interrupted a long period in which the vessel had occupied center stage. Figurines, however, best suited the mood of the postwar generation and the short-lived prosperity. The momentum generated by the dominance of sculpture carried into the next decade to meet the challenge presented by the flip side of affluence—the Depression of the thirties.

122. CARL WALTERS
STALLION
*1921. Glazed earthenware, 10½
x 10½ x 4¼". Whitney Museum
of American Art, N.Y.*

Chapter 8

D E P R E S S I O N
S C U L P T U R E

The Federal Arts Program

Beginning with the stock market crash in 1929, the Depression ultimately affected all areas of American life. With a faltering economy, unemployment rapidly increased and eventually individual states depleted their relief funds. The only agency capable of employing people was the federal government, and President Roosevelt's New Deal programs were the solution to the crisis. One specific goal of the federal projects was to employ needy artists, whose unemployment rate was higher than that of the general population. George Biddle and Edward Bruce, who implemented the first programs, believed that art should not disappear in a time of crisis. In fact, these men, and others administering the projects, saw an opportunity to make art accessible to all levels of American society. As a result, the documentation of American history in murals for public buildings—hospitals, schools, post offices, and libraries—brought culture to small, distant communities as well as urban centers.

One of the first projects specifically for ceramists was sponsored by the Public Works of Art Program in 1933. Edris Eckhardt, a former Cowan Pottery artist, was selected to direct a five-month pilot project in Cleveland, Ohio. Employing a team of artists, the project produced small ceramic sculptures as part of a children's literature program at the Cleveland Public Library. The success of the pilot program led to a long-term project in 1935 under the Federal Arts Project (FAP), a branch of the Works Progress Administration (WPA). As director, Eckhardt established a unique clay workshop, employing artists from a variety of artistic backgrounds. The project artists were taught to pour molds, assemble parts, and glaze and fire the sculptures, thus rotating jobs so that each member could learn the whole process. Eckhardt also managed to encourage individual creativity through the painting of facial expressions, costumes, and designs.

Capitalizing on the popularity of figurines adapted to children's

opposite:
123. EDRIS ECKHARDT
EARTH
1939. Earthenware, 13 x 8 x 6½".
Everson Museum of Art, Syracuse, N.Y. Gift of Dr. Paul Nelson

above:
124. EDRIS ECKHARDT
TEA PARTY
c. 1935. Earthenware, glazes,
5 x 6". The Cleveland Public Library, Ohio

literature, Eckhardt created such a group based on the characters in *Alice in Wonderland.* The success of the *Alice* series led to the completion of 130 character designs (fifty of them by Eckhardt) over a four-year period—among them characters from Charles Dickens, A. A. Milne, Rudyard Kipling, and from popular nursery rhymes. Team member Grace Luse designed a series of figurines showing the American family in the periods between the Pilgrim era and the Gay Nineties. Alexander Blazys designed masks of famous artists, Ohio-born presidents, and American folk heroes. Libraries and schools across the nation ordered sets of figurines in such large numbers that Eckhardt abandoned the workshop's makeshift firing arrangements with the Board of Education and raised money through the sale of her ware to purchase a kiln for the project.[1] Eventually the workshop's sculptures were exhibited and collected awards at the Cleveland Museum May shows.

In the late thirties, the Cleveland Metropolitan Housing Authority sponsored two art projects in conjunction with the Ohio Art Program, supervised by Eckhardt. At Valleyview Homes Project, Eckhardt's artists produced a project directory that was a massive ceramic map, thirteen by twenty feet, as well as large, figurative tile panels for architectural embellishment. Some of the artwork took inspiration from Cleveland's past, tracing the city's development into an industrial center. This was in keeping with the rediscovery of regionalism, characteristic of art made in the 1930s. A second housing project, Woodhill Homes, utilized folklore and celebrated American farm life in bas relief panels—among them Eckhardt's *Johnny Appleseed* and Louis Regalbuto's *Grain Harvest.*

The large number of projects, both federal and state, involving ceramists in Ohio was probably due to the extensive ceramic industry the state had established. Other states with substantial clay production also had programs, though none was on the level of Ohio's.

Waylande Gregory, also a Cowan alumnus, was the director of one of the arts programs sponsored by the New Jersey Federal Arts Project of the WPA. In 1937 he was assigned to design a monumental fountain for the grounds of the Roosevelt Hospital in New Brunswick, near Thomas Edison's former Menlo Park laboratory. The project, which employed laid-off workmen from a nearby closed terra-cotta factory, provided Gregory with a unique opportunity to enlarge the scale of his work. Homage to the Wizard of Menlo Park was part of Gregory's theme for a fountain titled *Light Dispelling Darkness.* Surrounding the fountain's fifteen-foot-high shaft were terra-cotta figures in relief of men whose inventions advanced technology. In contrast to these noble figures were smaller clay sculptures representing the Four Horsemen of the Apocalypse—Death, War, Famine, and Pestilence—to which Gregory added Greed and Materialism. American achievements, in this case in the area of science, were considered appropriate subject matter for art during a period when public morale needed boosting. Photographs of Gregory's massive sculpture (the original was destroyed by vandals) indicate a sentimental glorification of Western culture offered as an antidote to the sense of distress and shock inflicted by the Depression.

The Cleveland and New Jersey projects were only part of a much larger program of the FAP to keep artists active in such taxing times.

125. GRACE LUSE, VALLEYVIEW HOMES
ACCORDIAN PLAYER (RUSSIAN)
*1939–40. Stoneware, 12 x 15".
Cleveland, Ohio*

126. Louis Regalbuto, Woodhill Homes
GRAIN HARVEST
*1939–1940. Stoneware, 30 x 40".
Cleveland, Ohio*

Many artists considered their assignments as opportunities to revive in broader terms the relationship of the artist to the people.[2] Of course, publicly sponsored art represented only a fraction of the ceramic work produced in the thirties. Those ceramists who were not as fortunate to land federally sponsored jobs had to scramble for the few commissions, teaching positions, or whatever else was available at that time.

The Diversity of 1930s Sculpture

One ceramist who hustled for commissions was Vally Wieselthier, the young Viennese artist whose figures were exhibited at the International Exhibition of Ceramic Art. Following a visit to New York in 1928, Wieselthier set up permanent residence in New York in 1932, and opened a studio. There she produced figures of cosmopolitan women, draped in rustic clothing and usually accompanied by small animals or birds. The lifesize figures were sometimes used as props in department store window displays or as sculptures for garden fountains. Though most of the figures were similar to work she'd produced in Europe, Wieselthier experimented with new ideas. *Bathers* (1930), a tableau of four figures, depicts two couples in bathing suits, holding hands as they brace against oncoming stylized waves. The narrative content was unusual for Wieselthier, who rarely had grouped figures together. Also, the unadorned, rough-textured terra-cotta surface for this group was a departure from the majolica glaze she usually applied as a base for painting facial features.

The unglazed surface also appealed to Waylande Gregory, who had previously met Wieselthier, perhaps when she visited Cowan Pottery. Later, the two became good friends and collaborators. Before Gregory took the FAP directorship in New Jersey, he began a year of teaching at the Cranbrook Academy of Art in Michigan in 1932, organizing the school's first ceramic department. Cranbrook had been established in 1925 by George Booth, who brought Finnish architect Eliel Saarinen to Michigan as director. Together Saarinen and Booth selected well-known artists for the faculty. Stimulated by the ambience of an art school, Gregory's productivity during his Cranbrook tenure was phenomenal, and consciously reflected the aesthetic directions he most admired. The smooth contours of *Girl With Braids* (1932) display the influence of Swedish sculptor Carl Milles, one of Gregory's Cranbrook colleagues, while *Girl with Olive* exhibits an elegance which links it to Brancusi's refined forms. The elongation of hands and neck in these busts parallel the anatomical exaggeration in the sculptures of Wilhelm Lehmbruck, a German contemporary.

Perhaps attracted to the natural finish on Lehmbruck's and Wieselthier's sculptures, Gregory's favored medium became unglazed terra-cotta, and he used it with particular effectiveness in works such as *Ichabod Crane* and *Kansas Madonna* (a mare and nursing colt). Guy Cowan, writing about Gregory, described *Kansas Madonna* as "more American than European, not at all sophisticated and fundamentally human."[3] Another piece, *Horse and Dragon*, won the sculpture award in the annual Exhibition of American Painting and

above left:
127. WAYLANDE GREGORY
Model for "War," one of the six symbolic figures for the fountain LIGHT DISPELLING DARKNESS
1937. Terra-cotta (see also fig. 128)

above right:
128. *The fountain, LIGHT DISPELLING DARKNESS, was commissioned by the WPA/ FAP of New Jersey for Roosevelt Hospital in New Brunswick. As seen here, assistants to Waylande Gregory, the designer of the work, are working on the model for the fountain. It was made of terra-cotta and completed in 1937.*

129. Waylande Gregory
WOMAN'S HEAD
*c. 1933. 24 x 9¾ x 12". Everson
Museum of Art, Syracuse, N.Y.*

Sculpture at the Art Institute of Chicago in 1933. It was the first of
many awards that would recognize Gregory's place in the forefront
of clay sculpture.

Like Wieselthier, and possibly due to her influence, Gregory began producing lifesize figures. Between 1936 and 1939, he created a
series of charming, idealized nudes, young women whose ample
curves were modified versions of Gaston Lachaise's voluptuous
earth goddesses. *Swimmer*, *Bather*, and *Sun Bathers* have a languor-
ous, relaxed air and glossy glazed surfaces which suggest that they,
like representations of Venus, have just emerged from a refreshing
ocean dip. These figures led Gregory to a larger-than-lifesize seated
group, *Mother and Child* (c. 1938). Shrinkage, warping, and sustaining the heaviness of wet clay in a vertical position were just a few of
the technical difficulties Gregory faced in constructing a work of
this scale. One solution was a special cellular or honeycomb interior
structure he devised to support the exterior.[4] While many of Greg-

130. VIKTOR SCHRECKENGOST
THE CREATURES GOD
FORGOT (large and small
giraffe)
1938. Ceramic sculpture, height
(tallest giraffe) 22⁵/₁₆". Special
Award for a Group of Seven in
May Show of 1938. The Cleve-
land Museum of Art, Ohio.
Mary Spedding Milliken Memo-
rial Collection. Gift of William
Mathewson Milliken

ory's idealized figures were critically well received, they were ultimately more important as prototypes for large-scale sculptures in
later commissions.

For a short period in the late 1930s, portraiture became an important part of Gregory's work. Actor Henry Fonda purchased *Child
Diving* (1936), one of Gregory's garden/pool sculptures, and was so
taken with Gregory's work that he subsequently sat for two portraits. The publicity soon brought other actors and well-known figures to Gregory's New Jersey studio; the list of prominent sitters
included Charles Lindbergh and Albert Einstein.

What made the figural sculptures of Gregory and Wieselthier so
unusual for the thirties was their size. More typical were tabletop
sculptures of the kind Cowan Pottery produced. Viktor Schreckengost, a Cowan alumnus, continued to use the hollow form technique

he'd learned in Vienna to create a series of circus figures—acrobats and horseback riders—which express a cheerful exuberance. Another interest of Schreckengost's was black culture. His trips to Europe introduced him to expatriate American blacks, notably Josephine Baker and black ensemble singers, and inspired such subjects as the preacher in *The Baptism* (1937) and the group of women gospel singers in *Glory, Glory* (1938).[5] Although Schreckengost's interpretation of black culture has overtones of cartoon-like simplification (a stereotypical view characteristic of his time), an earthy enthusiasm infuses his figures in contrast to the sterile or purely decorative statuary of the period.

Schreckengost's portrayal of animals conveyed the same spirit. His whimsical animals went beyond the Vienna style to project near-human attributes. He emphasized endearing qualities in animal relationships, such as a mother's affection for her young in *The Creatures God Forgot* (1938). In *Naama, Ship of the Desert* (1939), a camel exhibits the gawkiness of a growing teenager not yet accustomed to long limbs. This empathetic, almost anthropomorphic quality sets Schreckengost's sculptures apart from the more common novelty figures and bric-a-brac figurines.

Like Schreckengost's, the animal sculpture that Carl Walters made stressed human qualities. *Seal* (1931), with its head held high, appears ready to take command while *Walrus* (1933), patterned with floral and marine motifs, projects delightful optimism. *Cat* and *Tiger* (both 1938) sport stripes which become abstract patterns, a use of color that suggests Matisse. Although Walters worked with molds, he never exactly repeated the form. Every piece was individually handled, the stance, glaze, or decorative element altered so that each figure had the suggestion of being handcrafted. The additional attributes of gentle humor and lively gestures separate Walter's figurines from the moldmade stiff, basket-carrying, and glassy-eyed poodles of nineteenth-century Bennington pottery, or of English Staffordshire.

131. CARL WALTERS
WALRUS
1933. Fired ceramic, 7 x 8⅝ x 17¾". National Museum of American Art, Smithsonian Institution, Washington, D.C. Gift of International Business Machines Corporation

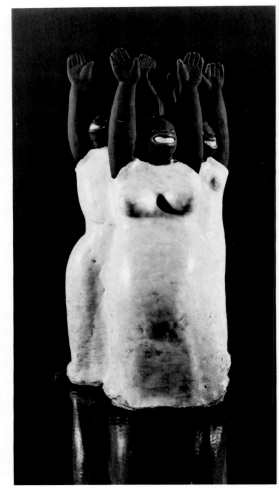

The lively surface embellishment on these animals aligns Walters's work with the decorative qualities in Pennsylvania German ware. But Walters's animals were not genre sculpture as was the work of his contemporary, Pennsylvania-born William Swallow. Born in Scranton, Swallow arrived in Allentown in 1936 as an art supervisor trained at the Philadelphia Museum School of Industrial Art. He had a background in craft materials, but first learned to use clay as part of his program for the Allentown schools. As a result, his approach to clay was like that of a sculptor in wood, carving the exterior surface first, then hollowing out the inside, massing his forms much like Beniamino Bufano and Edris Eckhardt.

Swallow's subjects were the Pennsylvania Germans—women in bonnets and bearded men harvest wheat, ride a buggy to Sunday church, or gather together with their market baskets. *Amish Family* and *Pennsylvania Harvest Family* were both produced in the 1940s and, like most of his groups of figures, have a rough-hewn quality which connotes the hard-working character of Amish life. Curiously, Swallow's animals are more stylized and abstract, similar to Walters's use of patterns, rather than having any representation of fur or hide.

above left:
132. WILLIAM WELDON
SWALLOW
AMISH FAMILY
c. 1940s. Terra-cotta, wood base, 16⅜ x 12¼ x 10½".
National Museum of American Art, Smithsonian Institution, Washington, D.C. Gift of International Business Machines Corporation

above right:
133. VIKTOR SCHRECKENGOST
GLORY, GLORY
1938. Modeled directly in red clay, raw borax glaze, height 19", width 10". Renwick Gallery, National Museum of American Art, Smithsonian Institution, Washington, D.C.

The gangly, awkward but appealing quality of Russell Aitken's small figures imitate his own tall, thin frame and youthfulness. Having worked at Cowan Pottery part-time during his student days, Aitken, like Schreckengost, went to the Kunstgewerbeschule in Vienna after graduation from the Cleveland School of Art. In style, Aitken's work reflects the enormous popularity of cartoon art and that distinctly American form, the comics.[6] Aitken's figures of timid colts, shy fawns, and awkward calves which combined cartoon exaggeration, fantasy, and Viennese whimsy were enormously popular and made his work a constant prizewinner.

In content, Aitken was as eclectic as his interests. He incorporated his admiration for Frederick Remington's sculptures of cowboys and Indians in equestrian figures such as *The Lone Cowboy*, *The Cactus Kid* (both 1932), and *Rodeo Rita* (1937). A trip by Aitken to Africa and exhibits he saw of a private African art collection in Cleveland prompted *Jeddu-Congo Woman* (1932) and *Bini Belle* (c. 1940), subjects treated in a humorous, albeit stereotypical fashion. His travels through Europe in the thirties inspired *Student Singers* (1934), a stylized portrait of three military students in a light mood, with fencing foils and overflowing beer mugs in hand. This was a highly productive period for Aitken, but it came to an end when he entered the service in World War II. After the war he applied his talents to materials other than clay.

EUROPEAN MODERNISM IN AMERICA

Viennese whimsy and the cartoon quality in figurative sculpture served its purpose during the Depression years, and though it would continue into the next decade, declining quality ultimately hastened its demise. New concepts for sculpture were already present. Three artists who had turned to clay in the late twenties or thirties suggested new possibilities to American ceramists: European sculptor Alexander Archipenko, mentioned earlier; Elie Nadelman, who had moved to New York from Paris in 1914; and Isamu Noguchi, American-born but European-trained. During the 1930s, Archipenko's teaching assignments took him to the West Coast, where he taught summer sessions at Mills College in Oakland, California, and at Chouinard Art School in Los Angeles. While in the West, he completed several terra-cotta figures, and on his return to New York in 1937 he finished *Ma Meditation*, a lifesize seated figure in a naturalistic mode. Shortly afterward, he returned to abstraction in *Walking Woman* (1937), seeking textural variations and a greater sense of movement. In many ways, Archipenko continued to serve as a kind of model and mentor for other, younger ceramists. His *Ma Meditation* probably influenced Gregory's larger-than-lifesize terra-cotta seated group *Mother and Child* (c. 1938). Edris Eckhardt, who studied with Archipenko after her graduation from the Cleveland School of Art, credited him with giving her new and fresh insights into form, texture, and movement.[7]

Like Archipenko, Elie Nadelman was attracted to Cubism in his youth, and created Cubist works as early as 1908 in his Paris studio. Once established in New York, Nadelman continued concentrating

134. ISAMU NOGUCHI
THE QUEEN
1931. Terra-cotta, height 45½".
Whitney Museum of American
Art, New York. Gift of the artist

Noguchi was inspired by any number of sources in his work. In this piece, the costume of a Haniwa warrior is seen in the skirted figure, whereas the pawn in a chess game shows in the spherical headpiece.

on the human figure, producing inexpensive, small-scale sculptures in terra-cotta, wood, plaster, and bronze. Nadelman's respect for common materials came from a consuming interest in folk art, and this influenced his use of mass, contour, and the simplification of form. While his work sold well, Nadelman's production methods were not universally admired. His European-style studio practice of employing assistants to turn out up to six editions of each piece met with disapproval from some of his contemporaries.

During the Depression, Nadelman lost much of his wealth, and he turned to clay as a less expensive primary material. Working at the Inwood Potteries of Inwood Park, New York, he formulated his own glazes and fired his own kiln. Between 1933 and 1935, Nadelman produced a series of earthenware figures ranging in size from seven to fourteen inches. These figures were usually grouped in twos having some interaction, such as *One Woman Doing Another's Hair* (1934–35). Like Cowan's dancing women, the curve and counter-curve were important, not the details and features which remained indistinct. A deftly painted line suggesting a cummerbund unifies *Two Seated Women* (c. 1932) and implies the costume of circus performers. *Two Acrobats* (1934) is among many sculptures of circus artists, often grouped for their common contour, the only decorative elements a slight suggestion of costume at the neck, hair, and waist. In contrast to Nadelman's earlier figures whose demeanor conveyed a subtle wit, his circus women are somber. Their muted features and passive stance make them the antithesis of Schreckengost's circus performers cast in mid-act and the lighthearted sculptures of other Cleveland artists.

Some of Nadelman's most private work was the result of an unfortunate accident. In 1935, a workman remodeling Nadelman's studio inadvertently destroyed much of the work in progress. For a time Nadelman retreated into isolation, making small, doll-like figures inspired by the Tanagra statuettes of eastern Mediterranean art dating from the late 4th and 3rd centuries B.C. Plump, dimpled, and gestural, the tiny sculptures suggest a range of associations from ancient fertility goddesses to modern dancers. Undiscovered until his death in 1946, these enigmatic figures were cast posthumously in clay as Nadelman had intended.

Another approach to clay sculpture that combined oriental tradition with European modernism came from Isamu Noguchi. Born in Los Angeles in 1904, Noguchi began his work in sculpture as an apprentice to Gutzon Borglum, the sculptor of Mount Rushmore. His formal studies began at New York's Leonardo da Vinci Art School. In 1927, Noguchi studied with Constantin Brancusi in Paris for two years, where he responded to the sculptor's clean lines and simplified shapes, an appreciation strengthened when he visited Japan in 1931. There, introduced to his ancestral country's sculpture, he felt an immediate affinity for Haniwa figures (A.D. 200–537), literally meaning clay figures. In Kyoto, where he was apprenticed to a potter, Noguchi discovered these ancient grave gods at the Kyoto National Museum. His admiration for these figures, which were quickly executed with a few concise strokes, can be seen in his terra-cotta sculpture *The Queen* (1931), consisting of assembled angular

135. ELIE NADELMAN
FIGURE WITH DOG
1934–35. Glazed earthenware, height 7". Collection Jan Nadelman

136. VALLY WIESELTHIER
EUROPA AND THE BULL
1938. Earthenware, 25 x 20 x 19". Private collection

and circular forms. The smooth texture of the clay and the symmetrical, biomorphic shapes in the form of a totem convey the qualities of goodness and purity associated with Eastern philosophy and realized in Noguchi's work in the modern style.

Of the three artists, Noguchi was the only sculptor who would continue developing his ideas in clay when he returned to Japan twenty years later. His clay sculpture of 1931, along with Archipenko and Nadelman's, was important to American ceramics in the thirties; eminent sculptors were endorsing clay as a suitable medium for artistic expression. Although Archipenko, Nadelman, and Noguchi introduced European modernism to American sculpture, it wasn't adopted until much later by a few artists working in clay. The essentially decorative nature of ceramic sculpture continued to dominate work of this period.

POLITICAL COMMENTARY

In the mythological legend of the rape of Europa, Zeus assumed the shape of a white bull in order to attract the beautiful princess Europa. The legend, which in other times had been an inspiration to artists, could be interpreted in the 1930s as a subtle metaphor for Hitler's aggression since it emerged as a recurring theme in ceramic sculpture. In Schreckengost's *The Abduction* (1938), Europa is African, following one version of the story. Waylande Gregory's *Europa* (1938) is unglazed, colored only with stains. The bull and rider are tilted forward toward highly stylized waves, and which are echoed in the maiden's flowing hair and the curves of modest drapery. Her upraised, bent arm is a languid gesture characteristic of Gregory's fountain maidens and Matisse's nudes, such as *Reclining Nude* (1929). *Europa and the Bull* (1938) by Vally Wieselthier portrays a dreamy maiden and a sweet, almost silly looking bull.

left:
137. VIKTOR SCHRECKENGOST
THE ABDUCTION
1938. Red earthenware, blackbird slip on the figure, borax glaze in brown, white, and turquoise, 14 x 22". Collection the artist

above:
138. RUSSELL BARNETT AITKEN
THE HITCHHIKER
1938. Earthenware, 17 x 13½ x 6½". Whitney Museum of American Art, New York

The choice of mythological characters such as the satyr here, plus the depiction of women as subject matter, continued Art Deco themes. (See also fig. 119).

These figurines were presented as decorations rather than pointed political statements. Yet the fact that the Europa theme surfaced in one particular year is indicative of at least a subtle preoccupation with the bleak politics of the time. But there was nothing subtle about Schreckengost's *The Dictator* (1939), a sculpture prompted by his visit to Europe at the end of the decade. The style is decorative, the figures are rendered as caricatures, but the humor is more satiric than jovial, and the direction of the political commentary easily evident.

Directly to the point, Schreckengost's *Apocalypse* (1942) confronts the war itself. Five years after Gregory's *Light Dispelling Darkness*, Schreckengost depicted a terrified horse carrying the Four Horsemen portrayed as caricatures of Hitler in salutation, Hirohito waving a flag, Death dressed in a German military uniform carrying a bomb, and Mussolini along for the ride on the anxious horse's rear flanks. By this time, the seriousness of a war in progress had banished the earlier frivolity in Schreckengost's work. In contrast, many of Schreckengost's contemporaries continued to deal with the more prosaic, insipid subject matter of the twenties and early thirties, the popularity of which could be attributed to a kind of escapism and desire for less political concerns.

139. WAYLANDE GREGORY
EUROPA
1938. Unglazed earthenware, height 23¾", diameter 27". Everson Museum of Art, Syracuse, N.Y.

MONUMENTAL SCULPTURE

Until 1938, examples of monumental sculpture in clay remained
confined to Archipenko's *Ma Meditation,* Wieselthier's women,
Gregory's New Jersey fountain, and *Mother and Child.* In that year,
Gregory received three commissions for large-scale work, two for
the World's Fair of 1939, and the third for a municipal building in
Washington, D.C. "The World of Tomorrow" theme of the fair gave
Gregory the opportunity to weave ancient and modern theories of
the atom into his *Fountain of the Atom.* Earth, Fire, Air, and Water
assume human form, the first two as women, encircled by the crystalline structure of gems for Earth and flames for Fire. The figure of
Water dives beneath the waves, surrounded by fish and bubbles. Below these sculptures prance eight chubby, childlike figures representing electrons. Playful, exuberant creatures with lightning bolts
and spheres for toys, the electrons convey the innocence of their
time, a time unaware of the destructive potential of the atom. After
the fair, the sculpture was returned to Gregory. It remained in his
Warren, New Jersey, garden until his death in 1971. Gregory's second fair commission came from the General Motors Corporation.
For GMC's display, "American Imports and Exports," Gregory re-

140. VIKTOR SCHRECKENGOST
APOCALYPSE
*1942. Glazed earthenware, 15⅜
x 20⅜ x 8⅞". National Museum
of American Art, Smithsonian
Institution, Washington, D.C.
Gift of the artist*

turned to the style of Social Realism in portraying American farm and factory workers. Idealized and nearly lifesize, the figures of lumbermen, cotton farmers, and mechanics are sober, dignified representatives of American labor.

More energetic and controversial was Gregory's eighty-one-foot-long tile mural for the Municipal Center Building in Washington, D.C., installed in 1941. The mural, *Democracy in Action*, illustrates the activities of the police and fire departments with fifty lifesize figures. Controversy immediately followed over a scene showing the police in conflict with a black lawbreaker; as a result the courtyard displaying the work was closed to the public.

A New Exhibition Structure for Clay

The World's Fair of 1939 was one of those rare exhibition opportunities for ceramic sculpture. In addition to Gregory, Vally Wieselthier and Edris Eckhardt's sculptures were also displayed. Guy Cowan's effort to establish ceramics as a category through the Cleveland Museum May shows did have the effect of opening some national shows to clay sculpture, but generally, work in clay was shown at fairs, industrial art shows, and arts and crafts societies, all places no longer particularly prestigious. The Charles Fergus Binns Medal, instituted in 1925 in honor of Binns's twenty-five years of service to Alfred University, annually recognized outstanding ceramists, but did little to elevate general public awareness of ceramic art.

It was the memory of Adelaide Alsop Robineau that inspired the first annual and national exhibition of ceramics. Anna Olmsted, director of the Syracuse Museum of Fine Arts, conceived the idea of a yearly ceramics exhibit in honor of Robineau, the city's world-renowned ceramist who died in 1929. The exhibition was created with the idea to give ceramic sculpture an equal position with the vessel. The first Robineau Memorial Ceramic Exhibition opened in 1932, with entries limited to New York State. However, in its second year Olmsted opened the show to the entire country. Though entries came from only eleven states, by the third year twenty-one states and over one hundred potters responded. Referred to as the National Ceramic Exhibition or the Ceramic National, the Syracuse-based exhibition was dominated during the thirties by Cleveland artists—Guy Cowan often served as a judge and Gregory and Baggs were repeatedly among the prizewinners. Though Cowan was clearly self-serving in his observation that the exhibits proved "to anyone with an open mind that marble and bronze fall far short of ceramics in interest and decorative possibilities,"[8] he was attempting to dispel the all too frequent and unfair classification of ceramics as industrial arts or bric-a-brac by some critics.

After several years, a national tour was organized to follow the end of each exhibition. Then, in 1937, with financial assistance from the Rockefeller Foundation and under the auspices of the American Ceramic Society, a show assembled from the previous National Ceramic exhibitions left Syracuse to travel the Scandinavian countries at their invitation. This was the first time an exhibition of exclusively American ceramic work traveled beyond the United States. The flow of ideas, if not reversed, was at least moving in both directions.

opposite:
141. MARGUERITE WILDENHAIN
VASE WITH ANGELS AND
DRAGONS
*1952. Stoneware with glazes,
height 8⅞", diameter 7¹¹/₁₆".
Oakland Museum, Calif. Gift of
the artist*

Part IV

The Vessel Revival 1930–1955

Chapter 9
THREE DIRECTIONS FOR THE VESSEL

Folk Pottery

Though the most innovative work during the twenties and thirties occurred in sculpture, vessel making did continue. American folk potters, for whom the vessel was a cultural tradition, were among those keeping the form alive.

There was no folk pottery tradition in America older than that found among the native Americans of the Southwest. While native American crafts had long been ignored and discounted by mainstream American culture, by the early twentieth century there was new appreciation of these crafts, fueled in part, curiously enough, by Art Deco. Because Art Deco exalted geometric design—integral to American Indian design—native American work suddenly had contemporary connotations. Concurrent with this rising interest was the Indians' increasingly skillful decorative ability. Archeologists such as Dr. Edgar Hewett, director of the School of American Archeology in Albuquerque, urged the Pueblo Indians working on digs in New Mexico to examine the shards of ancient pottery and recreate some of the designs.

Examples of traditional black, or smoked, pottery particularly intrigued potters Maria and Julian Martinez of the San Ildefonso Pueblo of New Mexico. Maria Martinezes vessels, decorated with Julian's polychrome designs, were acknowledged as some of the best pottery in the area. The Martinezes studied the black shards to learn the secret of their unusual surface, and in 1918 produced their first decorated black vessels, achieved in part by smothering the flames of their wood firings.[1] Their experiments soon led to a highly burnished ware having an unusual silvery black color. When demand for the ware became greater than their ability to produce it, the Martinezes shared the secret process with other San Ildefonso potters. In 1925 Maria Martinez took a step away from Indian tradition and began signing her work. In time, potters in other pueblos (Santo Domingo, Santa Clara, Acoma) did the same. By dropping their

opposite:
142. MARIA AND JULIAN (MARTINEZ)
VASE
c. 1939. Earthenware, height 5½", diameter 6¼". Maxwell Museum of Anthropology, University of New Mexico, Albuquerque

above:
143. SANTO DOMINGO PUEBLO JAR
c. 1930. Red clay, red-and-cream-colored slip, black paint, 8¾ x 8 x 8". Scripps College, Claremont, Calif. Gift of Mrs. Hartley Burr Alexander, 1940

As a result of the general economic decline in the Southwest between 1850 and 1880, production of Indian pottery diminished. Interest in native American pottery began in the late nineteenth century when the railroad was extended to the Southwest, and passage to Indian life was touted as an exotic travel experience. Tourism, coupled with encouragement from archeologists working in the area in the early 1900s, spurred the Indians to continue the skills their ancestors had achieved in pottery making and decorating.

anonymity and identifying themselves with their work, these native American potters moved a little closer to that of individually signed American art pottery.

By the end of the 1920s, interest in native American ware had begun to spread beyond the confines of the Southwest. Exhibits such as "The Hopi Craftsman," initiated in 1930 at the Museum of Northern Arizona in Flagstaff, became an annual event reviewed in national magazines. At the Chicago World's Fair of 1933, crowds of curious spectators greeted the pottery demonstrations conducted by the Martinezes and other Pueblo Indians. Collecting native American vessels became increasingly popular, although the ware was appreciated less for its origins than for the beauty of its geometric designs and simple shapes.

In the Southeast United States, pottery traditions extended back to the time of the area's first settlers. But by the early twentieth century, the potters there were fighting new technology and losing. New factory jobs and steady wages had attracted potters, while factory-manufactured low-cost china had simultaneously weaned women away from purchasing local handcrafted pottery. Prohibition, enacted in 1919, had practically squelched the flourishing market for clay liquor jugs.

Jacques Busbee and his wife, Julianna, artists and residents of North Carolina, were unwilling to watch this southern ceramic craft die out. In 1921 they formed a cooperative venture called Jugtown and hired a young potter named Ben Owen. Owen was a descendant of a long line of North Carolina potters. Like his predecessors, he used mule power to mix clay dug from nearby pits, and fired individually turned ware in a wood-burning kiln.[2] The first Jugtown ware was traditionally southern: white or brown slip-decorated plates, platters, stew pots, and milk crocks were glazed in Tobacco Spit (a dark brown), buff, or a salt glaze.

Busbee, who handled the marketing, contacted Tiffany Studios of New York City to distribute the ware. Following their suggestion that Jugtown add a more decorative line, Busbee made a study of oriental pottery. He then created a series of Chinese shapes and glazes which Owen integrated into the ware. Mirror Black, Frogskin, and a Chinese blue entered the Jugtown palette of glazes on classical shapes.

In the same way that Rookwood propelled the art pottery movement, Jugtown encouraged the reopening of other North Carolina potteries. Further encouragement of regional crafts came from the federal government. As a spur to the Depression-afflicted economy, Secretary of the Interior Harold Ickes devised a plan for the National Park system that opened up a new retail market for folk pottery. Under a directive from Ickes issued around 1934, all National Park stores operating under a concession from the government were required to sell regional handcrafts.[3] Another boost came from the Smithsonian Institution with a 1933 exhibition of southern crafts (including pottery by the Cherokee Indians) at the Corcoran Gallery of Art in Washington, D.C. The curator of the exhibit, Allen Eaton, supported by the American Federation of the Arts, the Russell Sage Foundation, and the Southern Highlands Handcraft Guild, went on to conduct the first extensive research on southern potteries. *Hand-*

crafts of the Southern Highlands, his landmark study, was published in 1937.

The Eaton book generated interest in the region's folk pottery, but more important to the struggling southern potters was the improved north-south highway which brought tourists traveling between New York and Florida into the southern states. Besides purchasing available local ware, visitors often requested certain shapes and colors. Some potters not only yielded to these demands but aggressively sought the tourist traffic. Jacon Cole, whose ancestors included eighteenth-century North Carolina potters, abandoned salt glazing and the groundhog kiln for bright commercial lead glazes and an upright kiln; in 1932 he issued a catalogue and a road map to his pottery in central North Carolina.[4] The tourist trade also affected the size of traditional ware. Some of the early utilitarian forms such as gallon jugs and churns, no longer essential to a rural kitchen, were miniaturized and sold as souvenir sugar, coffee, or tea containers to tourists.

In the New England states, the handcrafts long associated with the family farm (wood carving, pottery, furniture making) were little in evidence by the second decade of the century. Like Jacques Busbee, who despaired the decline of regional skills, Mrs. J. Randolph

Coolidge of New Hampshire opened a shop in Sandwich, New Hampshire, where tourists could purchase handmade wares. Shortly afterward, craft classes sponsored by the Pottery Club began in neighboring Wolfeboro. With the Depression, crafts became an alternative source of income. The New Hampshire legislature initiated the first state-supported craft program in 1931. Predating the Harold Ickes plan, the League of New Hampshire Arts and Crafts (changed in 1968 to the League of New Hampshire Craftsmen) was formed as a marketing outlet for home industries around the state. In 1934 the first crafts fair, held in a barn at Crawford Notch, was such a success that the fair became an annual event. David Campbell, an architect and interior decorator, assumed the directorship of the league in 1938, expanding classes, relocating sales outlets, and publicizing the program.

Similar groups and programs were organized in other northeastern states. The Depression prompted Aileen Vanderbilt Webb to seek a new source of income for the poor in her area of New York State. She formed Putnam County Products in the 1930s as a marketing outlet for anything anyone wanted to sell in the county's small towns. In 1940, Webb arranged a meeting for representatives of the large number of loosely associated craft groups, north and south. An umbrella organization, the Handcraft Cooperative League of America, elected Webb president and Campbell vice president. The Cooperative League, unlike the earlier urban-based arts and crafts societies, represented rural craftspersons who were supplementing their farm income. With the opening in 1940 of America House in New York City, the league-supported shop gave the rising craft movement a major marketing outlet.

The awareness of handcrafts fostered by Webb, Coolidge, Eaton, and others came during a period when the nation found comfort and strength in its native accomplishments. Not surprisingly, the advent of World War II in no way diminished this need for national pride. While the Ceramic National exhibitions were discontinued during the war, museums began recognizing crafts as a legitimate art form. Allen Eaton's research into New England handcrafts led to an exhibition of contemporary handcrafts at the Worcester Museum in 1943. Shortly thereafter, two major museums opened special galleries for the display of nineteenth-century pottery. Early in the twentieth century, Edwin Barber had amassed a historically significant collection of Pennsylvania German ware for the Philadelphia Museum of Art. But it was not until 1944 that the museum opened a suite of galleries for the Barber acquisitions and a collection of Tucker porcelain. The Metropolitan Museum of Art refurbished and enlarged its American wing with recreations of period rooms featuring Pennsylvania German sgraffito and slipware.

The period's most extensive show of past and present ceramics opened at the Brooklyn Museum in 1944, installed in a permanent gallery by noted ceramics historian Arthur Clements and museum curator John Graham II. The history of the craft's development could be traced from seventeenth-century Jamestown redware and Pennsylvania earthenware, to New England stoneware and the molded ware of the mid-nineteenth century. The most up-to-date ware were dinnerware sets made by Lenox for use in the White House by President Roosevelt. Clements's subsequent book, *Our Pioneer Potters* (1947), along with John Ramsey's *American Potters and Pottery* (1947) and Lura W. Watkins's *Early New England Potters and Their Wares* (1950), added new information, contemporary evaluations, and an impetus to budding collectors. These various activities, programs, and organizations became the basis for an altered attitude toward handcrafts which, as Eaton stated, "can be a very genuine expression of a culture."[5] (It was this same kind of attitude that would be formalized in the 1970s through government-sponsored cultural programs.)

Another development at the time was the establishment of a School for American Craftsmen (now the American Craft Council). The American Craftsmen's Council, organized shortly after America House opened, regarded returning veterans as the ideal student body for a modernized crafts apprentice program, with the G.I. Bill of Rights providing the funds for accredited courses. After several false starts, including one at Alfred University, the ACC school finally found a home in 1950. The five-year-old Rochester Institute of Technology at the University of Rochester accepted the school as part of a university program, thus assuring craftsmen of a college degree.

Industrial Design

Though factory production was at the opposite end of the spectrum from folk pottery, it, too, faced a struggle to survive. The necessity to produce quality products attractive to both world markets and American customers had only been intensified by the Depression. Indeed, the economic crisis of the thirties precipitated an aesthetic crisis. The Art Deco style was viewed by many designers as a kind of betrayal—good design, yes, but affordable only by an elite minority. The Bauhaus in Germany, on the other hand, emphasized design dictated by utilitarian considerations—decorative qualities should derive from the natural properties or texture of the material. Mass production was likewise endorsed because factory products kept costs low, making the goods accessible to a majority of the society. One critic of the period considered the Bauhaus the symbol of a "sound relationship between art and industry based on intelligent use of the machine to beautify man's estate rather than debase it...."[6]

The Bauhaus approach to quality design for industry came at a time when American tableware sales were declining. As early as 1928, critics of the International Exhibition noted that American dinnerware design followed tradition in contrast to the more innovative examples from Europe. After years of devoting innumerable American Ceramic Society meetings to the problem, Ross C. Purdy, the general secretary, suggested establishing a department of ceramic art at Ohio State University; along with the already functioning ceramic engineering department, this program would concentrate on improving and expanding decorative techniques. Ohio State agreed, and in 1928 Arthur Baggs left Cowan Pottery to become the chairman of the new department.

Fresh from his glaze research at Cowan Pottery, Baggs envi-

145. CHARLES TEAGUE, JUGTOWN POTTERY JAR c. 1920s. Salt-glazed stoneware, fired in woodburning groundhog kiln to 2300°F, height 13", diameter 9". Private collection

146. *Charles Harder in the classroom. College Archives, New York State College of Ceramics at Alfred University*

sioned the new department as an experimental workshop where beautiful and commercially dependable glazes could be developed. Aided by an $8,000 grant from the Rockefeller Foundation, Baggs went to work. One of the first projects he pursued was the technical problem of obtaining a reliable copper red glaze in a reducing kiln. Here he met with success. In the early 1930s, he and Edgar Littlefield discovered that using silicon carbide as a reducing agent in an oxidizing atmosphere made the elusive copper red glaze more dependable for industrial use.

The research at Ohio State covered a variety of glazing techniques. Work on different clay bodies ultimately yielded a low-fire, high-talc body capable of sustaining underglaze decorations in bright colors. Before the grant was depleted in 1933, Baggs and his staff completed experiments on high-fire copper blue glazes, and explored the decorative possibilities in the use of stencils and the air brush. Then around 1936, Baggs became interested in salt glazing. In fact, it was his prizewinning salt-glazed cookie jar at the 1938 Ceramic National that became the one piece closely associated with his work. Baggs, however, felt the jar's handles and knobs were overly flamboyant and he considered other examples of his work as more representative.[7]

Baggs's commitment to industry, upon which he depended for equipment and research funds, did not impress the majority of his students; they were more interested in teaching ceramics in expanded high school and college programs. What his department needed, Baggs decided, was a "pilot plant" to smooth the path from classroom to factory. His plans for such a plant were delayed in part by World War II and then, in 1947, left to others when injuries from a car accident resulted in his death.

Baggs's experiments with glazes and clay bodies solved some important technical problems for industrial ceramics. Charles Harder, a former Alfred student and Binns's successor at Alfred University, was much more successful in educating students for industry. In 1935, Harder began a reorganization of the department that shifted the emphasis from applied arts toward industrial ceramic design. Harder deemed the machine as having the potential to fulfill the goals of a democracy by providing quality ware at prices the masses could afford. Harder's heroes were Bernard de Voto, Lewis Mumford, and Alexis de Tocqueville, careful observers of American democracy (and required reading for his students).[8] American culture, not European, should be studied, he believed, because a nation's objects reflect its culture. Harder championed the Bauhaus aesthetic of working directly with the material, and under his leadership the ceramics department at Alfred gained a reputation for transforming the technical aspects of ceramics into a sophisticated science.[9]

The programs at Ohio and Alfred reflected the upheaval in the pottery industry during the thirties. Tile companies whose business depended on the building industry were faced with bankruptcy when construction declined. Some, like Pewabic Pottery, survived by shifting from tile to tableware. In addition, owner Mary Chase Perry supplemented Pewabic's income by teaching at local colleges. Even those potteries not in the business of producing tile felt the economic squeeze.

147. J. A. BAUER POTTERY COMPANY
"RING" PATTERN WARE
1932. Earthenware. Dinner plate, diameter 10½"; Footed sherbet cup, diameter 2¾"; Footed goblet, height 4½"; Sherbet liner, diameter 4"; Egg cup, height 3½". Collection Buddy Wilson, Santa Monica, Calif.

opposite above:
148. HOMER LAUGHLIN COMPANY
FIESTAWARE
1936. Earthenware. Carafe, height 9"; Dinner plate, diameter 10"; Cup, diameter 3¼"; Saucer, diameter 6". Collection Buddy Wilson, Santa Monica, Calif.

opposite below:
149. RUSSEL WRIGHT (DESIGNER)
IROQUOIS "CASUAL CHINA"
All pieces earthenware. (clockwise from top:) Salad bowl, 1⅞ x 7¼ x 10". Gift of Courtney A. Spore. Carafe, height 10", diameter 4½"; Creamer, c. 1946–51. 2½ x 4¾ x 4". Gift of Mr. and Mrs. Victor Cole. Party plate with cup, plate diameter 10½"; cup height 2", diameter 3¾". Gift of Courtney A. Spore. Steubenville Pottery "Modern Living" Pitcher. c. 1939–59. 10½ x 8½ x 6¾". Everson Museum of Art, Syracuse, N.Y.

The J. A. Bauer Pottery of Los Angeles attracted customers by offering a product new to their production—dinnerware—along with their line of flowerpots. The initial design of the dishes resembled flowerpot saucers. Victor Houser, Bauer's ceramic engineer who had trained at the University of Illinois, had developed a group of opaque colored glazes which brightened the dishes. The Bauer plain service, launched in 1930 in solid shades of green, light blue, and yellow, was an immediate success. "Ringware," the next line in a new spectrum of colors, appeared after Bauer purchased the Batchelder tile plant in 1932. The concentric circles on this ware were muted indentations of a potter's finger ridges, and the colors a reflection of California's Spanish-Mexican heritage. With less money to spend, the public embraced an informal life-style more accepting of casual ware. Entertainment in a home without servants was the rule; simple, inexpensive dinnerware in a Depression society was the accepted norm.

Bauer's success stimulated other California companies—Gladding, McBean, Catalina, and Metlox—to produce dinnerware decorated in bright colors. This path to profits didn't go unnoticed in the East. Frederick Rhead's experiences at Arequipa and in Santa Barbara (which holds an annual fiesta to celebrate its Spanish heritage) may have contributed to his creation of Fiestaware. As art director for Homer Laughlin China Company of East Liverpool, Ohio, Rhead designed this colorful dinnerware, which was first retailed in 1936. It was originally produced in five deep colors, the result of Rhead's market research—orange red, deep blue, cucumber green, egg yellow, and vellum ivory—and was promoted by posters showing a Mexican fiesta.[10] Rhead's research also persuaded him to price Fiesta very low, selling it through stores such as F. W. Woolworth. His public, one he had not previously targeted, was the working class which during the Depression, he estimated constituted forty percent of the population.[11] No doubt contributing to the popularity of the ware was Rhead's idea of mix-and-match table settings. Fiesta's success was follow by variations such as Harlequin, which was sold exclusively at Woolworth's. Fiesta colors were used on kitchen accesso-

150. RUSSEL WRIGHT (DESIGNER), HARKER POTTERY COMPANY
BOWL, SALT, AND PEPPER
1951. Earthenware, "White Clover" pattern. (left to right:) Bowl, height 4½", diameter 8½"; Salt Shaker, height 3¾", diameter 2"; Pepper, height 2¼", diameter 2". Private collection

ries—mixing bowls, cake servers, and other utensils—when Rhead introduced Kitchen Kraft in 1939.

In the 1920s, Hall China Company of Ohio expanded its production of hotel and restaurant tableware to include a line of teapots. In the thirties, its designs included novel teapots in the shapes of automobiles, footballs, and seashells. These wares were the precursors of 1960s Pop Art teapots.

Another influential tableware style was produced by industrial designer Russel Wright. In 1937 Wright completed his designs for "American Modern." More organic than geometric, the flowing lines and exaggerated lips of Wright's pitchers and platters suggested the influence of Surrealism. Asymmetrical serving dishes and the soft contours of salt and pepper shakers and gravy boats recall Salvador Dalí paintings in which hard objects appear pliable. Wright's color combinations were rich, though muted and restrained. Wright developed harmonious glaze color relationships in collaboration with the ceramics department at Alfred University. But because his designs and colors were so unusual, Wright had trouble finding a factory willing to risk production. The bankrupt Steubenville Pottery of East Liverpool, Ohio, agreed to revive its operation; by 1939 the dinnerware was available to the public.[12] A determined publicity campaign by Wright introduced the concept of a "starter set," and was responsible for making "American Modern" the most popular dinnerware ever sold.

The Expressive Vessel

"American Modern" came close to expressing one of the basic qualities of clay—its plasticity. Nor was it the first to do so. Arthur Baggs's cookie jar, with its finger ridges, pulled handles, and knobs, conveyed the softness of leather-hard, unfired clay. Indeed, for some potters and designers, calling attention to the material was becoming a function of their style.

This sensitivity to the clay itself characterized ware made by Glen Lukens. Largely self-taught and without technical expertise, Lukens nevertheless was made chairman of a new ceramics department at the University of Southern California in Los Angeles in 1933. Unlike other college ceramics departments, the USC program was part of the School of Architecture. For Lukens, teaching at a private college in the depths of the Depression meant attracting non-art students from other departments and devising simple methods for them to achieve a measure of success.

Lukens preferred press-molding his bowls and plates, a technique that could be managed by the dentistry, architecture, and art education majors in his classes. His glazes were equally simple—transparent turquoise blues and yellows and later a uranium orange. He used these glazes over a white earthenware clay body (similar to the one perfected by Baggs at Ohio State), which kept the colors clear and bright but caused the glaze to crackle. Lukens emphasized the lines created by this phenomenon by rubbing dark oxides into the cracks. Though not a scholar, Lukens was interested in historical ware when such knowledge served his needs. While he may have

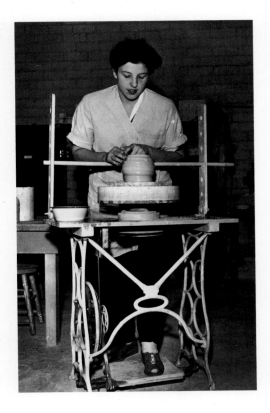

151. *Treadle wheel with sewing machine base used at the University of Southern California during the 1930s and 1940s.*

College budgets were not exempt from shortage of funds during the Depression years. An inexpensive method of making potter's wheels incorporated the bases of old Singer sewing machines. This confined the potter to making small vessels. It was effective, however, for trimming press-molded ware.

above left:
152. GLEN LUKENS
PLATE
c. 1940s. Earthenware, height 2",
diameter 17¾", The Oakland
Museum, Calif.

above:
153. GLEN LUKENS
BOWL
1936. Earthenware, height 3⅛",
diameter 6⅛". Everson Museum
of Art, Syracuse, N.Y. Gift of
the artist

been aware of Chinese crackle glazes, duplication of an ancient technique was of less importance to him than fully exploiting the natural tendencies of a glaze.

The bright glaze colors of Lukens's early ware attracted critical attention, and in 1936 the jurors of the Fifth National Ceramic Exhibition awarded Lukens first prize for several large platters decorated with a yellow crackle glaze. This marked the first time a California ceramist had been honored in any national exhibit. Lukens used the award to promote the first all-California ceramic exhibitions which opened in 1938 at the Fine Arts Gallery of San Diego. Considering the over one hundred objects on exhibit, one reviewer wrote, "This exhibition means that the Pacific Coast ceramic child is able to walk alone."[13]

By the late thirties, Lukens was experimenting with glazes which flowed over square and rectangular forms and pooled in the center of a bowl. Long before other potters saw the beauty in a glaze that dripped or pooled, Lukens reveled in it, comparing it to phenomena in nature—"I used to watch lightning across the sky and think, if we could control that lightning, it wouldn't be beautiful anymore."[14]

Faced with a scarcity of college funding for glaze materials, the inventive Lukens made numerous visits to Death Valley, just northeast of Los Angeles, known for deposits of minerals. How lucrative these trips were is unclear but the desert scenery and the unusual colors of the bare hills impressed the Missouri native. Always a romantic, Lukens's love of the desert was evident in the names he gave his favorite glazes: Death Valley Yellow, Mesa Blue, Mojave Golden Amber. Other travels around the Southwest also shaped his vision of pottery. On vacation in Santa Fe, New Mexico, to see Indi-

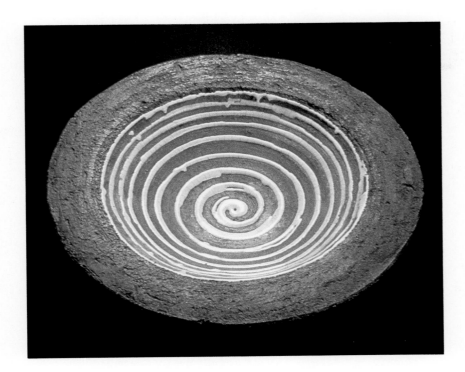

154. GLEN LUKENS.
PLATE WITH SPIRAL GLAZE
DESIGN.
*c. 1940s. Earthenware, height 3",
diameter 18¾". Private
collection*

Many viewers of Lukens's large, rough surfaces and "juicy" glazes considered the ware too unsophisticated for contemporary taste. But critics of ceramics and design honored him for expressing the ambience of the Southwest in his use of contrasting bare, textured clay with smooth, crackled glazes.

an ware, Lukens met essayist and poet Mary Austin. Her belief that Indian cultural values emphasized sincerity, naturalness, and honesty was one that Lukens would adopt. It also served to reinforce his attraction to Indian ceramics. While in New Mexico, Lukens purchased Maria Martinezes pottery, and upon his return to Los Angeles he experimented with reducing oxygen in his firings to duplicate the black pottery. Though his first step was a technical one, he soon went beyond imitation to an understanding of the beauty in that unsophisticated black ware.

Lukens's exposure to native American ware brought a realization of how expressive the unglazed clay surface could be. He began confining glaze areas to grooves cut into the broad rim of plates, creating concentric circles or spirals. To emphasize the contrast between a smooth glaze and the unglazed clay body, Lukens scored the clay or exposed grogged areas. Before the term organic entered the ceramic vocabulary, Lukens's ware defined the word. As a result, his vessels balanced on the boundary line of utility and art object. His forms never quite abandoned the realm of containers, but some features—dark clay that looked like freshly dug earth, unexpected colors beneath a pool of glaze—had much more to do with aesthetics than function.

Lukens was honored with many awards, including the Charles Fergus Binns Medal presented to him in 1949. He was considered the leading ceramist in the West and commended for his postwar, government-sponsored work developing a ceramics industry in Haiti. However, despite the national acclaim, Lukens's aesthetic attitudes remained ahead of his time; most potters were not yet prepared for an approach to pottery that advocated spontaneity, intuition, and the free expression of clay and glazes.

Chapter 10
DEFINING A VESSEL AESTHETIC

European Potters in America

The political tensions that erupted into World War II drove many European artists into exile. Throughout the 1930s, numerous painters and sculptors arrived in America, the majority making New York City their home. A similar emigration of European ceramists occurred about the same time, but unlike so many of their artistic colleagues, the members of this small group did not settle on the East Coast. Instead they scattered around the country. However, in spite of their geographic dispersal and few numbers, their presence helped shape the thinking of a generation of American potters.

Among the first to establish themselves in the United States were Gertrud and Otto Natzler of Vienna. Gertrud's exceptional ability on the potter's wheel and Otto's glaze technology had already earned them a silver medal in the 1937 World's Exposition in Paris. This honor opened doors to the southern California ceramic community when the Natzlers arrived in October 1938, and they quickly met the ceramists teaching at the local colleges—Glen Lukens at the University of Southern California, Laura Andreson at University of California in Los Angeles, and William Manker at Scripps College.

Gertrud Natzler's fly wheel and her method of throwing attracted the southern California ceramists. Hand-building was the main procedure for forming clay in Los Angeles classes, in part because the only type of wheel then available had a sewing machine treadle base. The potter stood on one foot, pedaled with the other, and braced his arms against a bar as his hands centered the clay—an awkward balancing act at best. In contrast, Gertrud Natzler's wheel allowed her to sit; after her foot rotated the wheel, her body position helped her hands center the clay. The obvious substantial difference in control with the Natzler wheel soon made it the prototype for classrooms in southern California. Laura Andreson took lessons on throwing from Gertrud, but found her method of holding a chamois in her hand as she pulled up the clay too difficult to master.

opposite:
155. GERTRUD AND OTTO NATZLER
BOWL
1969. Earthenware, crater glaze, 10 x 14". Private collection

above:
156. RUDOLF STAFFEL
OVAL VASE
c. 1955. Stoneware, height 7½", diameter 6⅞". Courtesy Helen Drutt Gallery, Philadelphia

157. GERTRUD AND OTTO
NATZLER
BOTTLE (detail)
*1974. Earthenware, green and
black glaze with iridescent crystals. Private collection*

158. GERTRUD AND OTTO
NATZLER
THREE BOTTLES (detail)
*Earthenware. (left:) 1974. Verdi-
gris crater glaze; (center:) 1974.
Green and black glaze with
iridescent crystals; (right:)
1960. Turquoise lava glaze.
Private collection*

The Natzlers demonstrated the utility of something else to the Californians—California clay. Instead of importing clay from other states, as did many local potters, Otto tested local clay and glaze materials until he found a fine-quality earthenware. The indigenous clay proved workable, and recognition from their new American peers came early. In 1939 the Natzlers' entries received first prize at the Ceramic National Exhibition.

While still in Vienna, the Natzlers identified with Viennese designer Adolf Loos in rejecting the prevailing taste for the ornate, excessive decoration characteristic of the Wiener Werkstätte. Instead they produced ware much more simple in color and form. However, Otto had become intrigued by the crevices and pitting he accidentally produced while learning to formulate glazes. After settling in California, he began capitalizing on what others considered glaze defects. A phenomenon he eventually labeled a "melt fissure," where the top glaze separates to reveal the first layer of glaze, appeared in 1942. (It was only some time later that Otto realized that a "melt fissure" was the result of a draft he'd inadvertently caused during the firing.[1]) Opaque glazes he named Crater, Pompei, and Lava, formulated during the first years in America, incorporated blisters and depressions on rough, porous, lava-like surfaces. Experiments with reduction firings yielded a variety of effects: iridescence, smoked areas, and glazes that appeared shriveled. Highly textured Crater glazes of a more intense color (developed in 1948) resembled the pockmarked appearance of the moon. The appeal of this rough, irregular surface recalls the height of the ornamental glaze period, and the experiments of Hugh Robertson, Adelaide Robineau, and Mary Chase Perry who produced variations of what they termed Volcanic glaze.

By the time cystalline glazes became a part of the Natzler repertoire in 1956, Otto was able to orchestrate a variety of surface effects in the kiln through the reducing agent he chose or by using a draft, ashes, or inducing smoke. Over the years the glaze formula grew less important than the manipulation of the firing. For Otto, the kiln became a major instrument of creation.

Otto's concentration on a rich surface always addressed Gertrud's forms. From their earliest collaborations, Gertrud sensitively worked the clay, with the result that a pleasing form remained in her hands until it achieved the proportions she considered ideal. As she expressed it, "In pottery, form is content."[2] During the early years, family economics demanded that Gertrud produce more bowls than bottles because wide-rimmed bowls, which served as containers for flower arrangements, sold better. Later, enjoying a more secure reputation, she explored closed forms: ovoids, bottles, double gourds, teardrop shapes. Objects found in nature—seed pods, pine cones, shells—and the classic periods of ceramic tradition (Chinese Sung and Korean Yi dynasties) also inspired shapes. Throughout, Gertrud strived for greater simplicity and purity of line.

The European aesthetic brought by the Natzlers to southern California was matched in the northern part of the state by the arrival of German potter Marguerite Wildenhain in 1940. Well trained by the best artists the Bauhaus had to offer, Wildenhain, like the Natzlers, at first confronted a society unreceptive to their pottery.

159. MARGUERITE WILDENHAIN
TEA SET
1946. Stoneware. Pot, height 5",
width 10"; Creamer, height 3",
width 5½"; Sugar, height 2½",
diameter 4½"; 5 cups, height
2¼", diameter 3¾". Everson
Museum of Art, Syracuse, N.Y.

For financial reasons, they all initially resorted to teaching; the Natzlers held classes in their Hollywood studio, stopping just as soon as they could afford it. Wildenhain taught at the California College of Arts and Crafts in Oakland for two years, and then quit. As she put it, "I'd rather starve in my own way than go on trying to teach those kids who don't want to learn."[3] She moved north to Guerneville, where friends had purchased some land that Wildenhain named Pond Farm. Together they constructed a pottery workshop and a small cabin. Limiting her teaching to summer months and to applicants with a high level of dedication, Wildenhain returned to a schedule of production similar to her post-Bauhaus years. (In 1947, when her husband, Frans Wildenhain, was able to leave Europe, he also taught classes at Pond Farm. In 1950 he left to teach in Rochester, New York, at the School for American Craftsmen.) Managing her own pottery, she sold her ware through stores in San Francisco, Chicago, and Dallas and earned awards regularly from the Ceramic National exhibits.

Like the Natzlers, Wildenhain believed that ceramics was a fine art, and she became an outspoken advocate for the Bauhaus concept that no boundary exists between art and craft. Her choice of a rural life dedicated to pottery strongly impressed the Pond Farm summer students, especially veterans returning from World War II, and her skill on the kick wheel was as fascinating to ceramists in the Bay Area as was Gertrud Natzler's in Los Angeles. In 1952 Richard Petterson, chairman of the ceramics department at Scripps College, invited her to conduct a workshop for his students. Soon Wildenhain, in faded blue jeans with her pottery tools in her back pocket, was traveling around the country several times a year conducting college workshops. She displayed no reticence in telling students of the importance of a disciplined life, and of devotion to one's art through intense training. "To be a craftsman," she cautioned, "is also a way of life."[4]

The ambience of Pond Farm contributed to Wildenhain's interest in textures. She was attracted not to glazes, as was Otto Natzler, but to abstract, tactile patterns often inspired by pine cones and tree bark. In the 1940s, she favored tooled or combed surfaces. Beginning

160. SUSI SINGER
ADAM AND EVE
c. 1947. Earthenware, height
29". Scripps College, Claremont,
Calif. Gift of Benjamin Kirby,
the Fine Arts Foundation, and
an anonymous donor, 1946–47

A compatriot of the Natzlers, Susi Singer arrived in Pasadena, California, in 1939 just as the influence of Viennese sculpture was on the wane. But her subject matter—mythological figures and humorous tableaux of daily life—were later echoed in sculpture of the 1970s.

in the 1950s, figures enlivened her tall, footed vessels. *Murder in the Cathedral* (1935) portrayed scenes from T. S. Eliot's play. Other vessels pictured characters from Bible stories or friends whose visits to Pond Farm included farm activities such as picking peaches or hoeing in the garden.

Like Wildenhain, Swiss-born potter Paul Bonifas was well trained, but in the European system which divided studio procedures like a factory. For eighteen years Bonifas had studio assistants who prepared the molded and thrown ware he designed; European glazes modeled after ancient Chinese pottery marked his studio's standards. Arriving to teach at the University of Washington in Seattle in 1946, Bonifas confronted a system and a technology quite different from that in Europe. Although his wife helped him with glazing, the loss of a technical staff made Bonifas realize the importance of learning each step of the process. It required discipline and hard work on his part to adjust—and he required the same discipline from his students. Bonifas was primarily vessel-oriented, producing precise wheel-thrown and handbuilt bowls, dishes, and jars, classical in form. In the late 1950s, a few years before his retirement, Bonifas used relief figures on vessel surfaces, and faces on jugs.

Not all of the emigré ceramists had begun as potters. Thomas Samuel Haile, an Englishman, was an avant-garde painter in the thirties with a great appetite for the newest ideas in politics, music, and literature as well as in art. In 1931, his surrealist tendencies jeopardized his scholarship at the conservative Royal College of Art in London. In order to remain at the college, he transferred to pottery under William Staite Murray, a compromise that allowed him to stay without forgoing his principles. Murray's interest in Chinese and Korean pottery and in Zen Buddhism introduced Haile to the oriental view of the potter as an artist.

Haile was a conscientious objector. When World War II began in Europe, he emigrated to New York. There he held a variety of jobs until an exhibition of his pottery attracted the attention of Charles Harder. Even though Harder's ceramics department at Alfred University emphasized technical procedures over personal expression, Harder found Haile's pottery much to his liking; in 1940 he invited him to teach at Alfred. Unconventional in terms of Alfred's orientation, Haile was never a good technician. Alfred glaze formulas were extremely complex. Haile's glazes were simple, but quite effective for his needs. His large jars with a slip-trailed, seemingly casual, spontaneous depiction of figures conveyed a remarkable vitality that Harder was among the first to recognize.

Harder's budget only allowed Haile one year at Alfred. In 1942, he taught at the University of Michigan in the College of Architecture; there he produced rough, coarse, stoneware vases, some oddly shaped and attenuated. Two strong tendencies were becoming more apparent: humorous slipware figures echoing Picasso's style of painting, and an affinity for pre-Columbian art as exemplified in his *Chichén Itzá* vase (1942). Haile's work of this period demonstrates his sustained interest in surrealist fantasy and his openness to pottery from different cultures.

By 1943, Haile was serving as a non-combatant in the war, first with the U.S. Army, then with the British Army. After the war, he

161. SAMUEL HAILE
PLATE
n.d. Earthenware with under-glaze and sgraffito figural decoration, diameter 14⅝", height 2¾". The University of Michigan Museum of Art, Ann Arbor. Gift of Miss Catherine B. Heller

settled in Dartington, England, intending to establish a pottery workshop. Before his plans could mature, however, he was in a fatal car accident in 1948. Haile's career had been a promising one, and a career that tested traditional limits. His distorted shapes and casual decoration presented a vision of the vessel in opposition to the precise and more austere forms of Wildenhain and Gertrud Natzler.

Maija Grotell did not leave her native Finland in 1927 because of the imminence of war; it was the expectation of opportunities that motivated her move to America. Shortly after her arrival, she attended a summer-school class at Alfred taught by Charles Binns. Then, residing first in New York City, Grotell was hired to teach at the Henry Street Crafts School (an adjunct of the Henry Street Settlement House). Using the school as her base, she pursued research on glazes and Art Deco patterns, earning prizes in a Ceramic National exhibition, a Paris exhibition, and in 1938, the title of Master Craftsman from the Boston Arts and Crafts Society.

That same year, Eliel Saarinen, director of the Cranbrook Academy of Art, invited her to join the faculty. With the departure of Waylande Gregory in 1933, ceramics at Cranbrook had floundered. Grotell had the opportunity to mold it to her philosophy and she took it. She was a conscientious teacher with high standards, expecting her advanced students to do research and to learn as much from their own experiments as from her.

Grotell generally favored two forms, the cylinder and the sphere. She abandoned the Art Deco geometric designs on her ware of the 1930s for more textured surfaces with linear accents. During the 1940s, along with Glen Lukens, Marguerite Wildenhain, and Laura Andreson, Grotell explored the unglazed, tooled, or textured surface, using color in clay bodies. At the same time, certain glaze problems—formulas for copper red, ash glazes, intense blues, and crackle patterns in alkaline glazes—kept her experimenting. A Bristol-type glaze over Albany slip, she discovered, produced pits and pinholes that did not "heal" during the firing. After years of working to control the size and placement of these rings she succeeded. Her *Leopard Skin* vase (1949), the result of her labors, received an award at the Fourteenth Ceramic National Exhibition in 1950.

During the fifties, Grotell combined the bubbled glaze with linear accents in rhythmic patterns around the vessel's surface. By cutting through the glaze to bright colored layers of slip below, she interrupted the textured surface to lend a sense of movement and grace to her large, heavy containers.[5]

Long before retirement in 1966, Grotell's efforts had served to place Cranbrook high on the list of schools essential to an education in ceramics. She had also advanced respect for the form. Neither as vocal as Wildenhain nor given to writing like Otto Natzler, Grotell depended primarily on her handsome vessels to convey her conviction that ceramics were art.

As propounded by the European emigrés, Modernism had its greatest influence in the years between 1940 and 1960. The Europeans' strong convictions, expressed in articles, teaching, and pottery, defined a vessel aesthetic of classic shapes clothed in rich surfaces. In so doing, they challenged the American Craft Council's folk pottery orientation as the main direction for American ceramics.

162. MAIJA GROTELL
VASE
c. 1938–40. Stoneware, height 15". Private collection

University Teacher-Potters

The European ceramists were joined and supported philosophically by the next generation of American teacher-potters. The students of Arthur Baggs and Glen Lukens, along with a group of self-taught potters, filled the available positions for pottery teachers in universities across the country during the 1940s. The need for a higher level of craftsmanship differed geographically, depending on the nature of pottery development in each area of the country. In New England, David Campbell, director of the League of New Hampshire Arts and Crafts, was anxious to upgrade folk pottery. He proposed hiring professional potters to teach ceramics classes at the University of New Hampshire. By combining resources, a small teaching staff could serve the league and the university.

In 1940, Edwin and Mary Scheier arrived to teach at both institutions and to produce ware for the league shops. Largely self-taught, the Scheiers had learned pottery techniques together in the thirties while Edwin directed an art center in Tennessee.

The Scheiers' uncluttered shapes and soft glaze colors on early ware reflected their affection for the pottery of their neighbors, Appalachian folk potters. This style, which aligned form with function, was appropriate for the league's shops as well. Though they each made their own ware, they also collaborated on vessels—Mary threw the vessels and Edwin decorated and glazed them.

When army service interrupted Edwin's university teaching, Mary ran the department until Edwin's return in 1945. The following year the Scheiers took a year's leave of absence to train workers

above left:
163. MAIJA GROTELL
VASE
*1946. Stoneware, height 17",
diameter 9⅞". Everson Museum
of Art, Syracuse, N. Y.*

Birds in flight, the movement of clouds, or the shape of lightning are suggested by Maija Grotell's use of V-shaped lines.

above right:
164. MAIJA GROTELL
VASE
*1949. Stoneware, height 12⅝",
diameter 10⅜". Private
collection*

165. EDWIN AND MARY SCHEIER
"DEVIL AND DANIEL
WEBSTER" PLATE
c. 1948. Earthenware, diameter
14". Collection Container Corporation of America

for a ceramics industry in Puerto Rico. Like Glen Lukens in Haiti, they confronted the problem of a poor country with no ceramic tradition. In the process of locating native materials for small-scale production, the Scheiers grew to appreciate Puerto Rican art and its African undertones, an appreciation that lingered long after their return to New Hampshire.

While the postwar influx of veterans taking advantage of the G.I. Bill expanded the department and increased the teaching load, the Scheiers maintained their own personal explorations of form and design. Mary's coffeepots and matching cups of the late 1940s displayed techniques similar to Marguerite Wildenhain's sparing use of glaze to contrast with an exposed, textured clay body. Edwin's large stoneware platters and bowls combined sgraffito and relief decorations; incised drawings of male figures in profile suggested the ceremonial ware of primitive cultures. The Adam and Eve legend and other myths depicting generation and regeneration were main themes of his.

The Scheiers' interest in anthropology and archeology intensified with trips made to Mexico during the 1950s. Such subject matter was certainly unusual for the 1950s, but consistent with Edwin's view of the vessel as capable of expressing "some aspect of the human spirit."[6] Before his retirement from teaching in 1960, Edwin Scheier saw his philosophy embraced by yet another generation of teacher-potters.

Like the Scheiers and many others who had no formal training in ceramics, Rudolf Staffel's route to teaching was circuitous. Educated as a painter at the School of the Art Institute of Chicago, Staffel studied pottery first in Mexico, then in New Orleans where he

166. EDWIN SCHEIER
BOWL
c. 1958. Stoneware, height 9½",
diameter 10". Everson Museum
of Art, Syracuse, N.Y.

Pre-Columbian pottery had a refining effect on Edwin Scheier's concept of surface decoration. A repeat pattern of interlocking figures acted like an incantation; suggestions of body features resembled the Chinesco style of Nayarit (Mexico) mortuary figures.

opened a studio. During his years in New Orleans, Staffel's surface decoration developed partly in response to the blue-green color scheme of early Newcomb College pottery. Drawings of people and vehicles that decorated his vessels resembled those in his paintings; though reminiscent of Social Realism, these drawings were, in fact, closer to a form of genre painting. In 1940, he joined the faculty of the Tyler School of Art at Temple University in Philadelphia. The school had an open, interdisciplinary approach in which all the arts were equal. Sixty students, the total student body, were allowed to proceed at their own pace, an atmosphere Staffel found productive for his own work as well.

Staffel's continuing attachment to painting led him into classes with European emigré painter Hans Hofmann, then living in New York. Commuting there from Tyler in the late forties, Staffel found himself in the midst of the community of Action painters, an experience that jolted him. He felt his basic philosophy was contradicted—the Bauhaus concept of beauty and utility—"prejudices I didn't know I had."[7] Staffel was among the first to sense the need for a response in clay to the new concepts in painting. The sense of crisis he felt in the late 1940s anticipated the reaction of most other ceramists a decade later.

Daniel Rhodes was another ceramist who began his career as a painter. He was also part of the second generation to inherit the Binns tradition, having attended Alfred in 1941–42 during Harder's tenure and Sam Haile's brief career. After graduation and five years spent on the West Coast producing cast and thrown ware for Gumps Department Store of San Francisco, Rhodes returned to Alfred as an instructor. There he concentrated on high-fired stoneware clay, glazing bottles and vases so that the iron in the clay was exposed. Areas of unglazed clay, deeply scratched, contrasted with a lip or bowl interior in a dark, matt glaze. Rhodes's style evolved partly from reading *A Potter's Book* (1940) by Englishman Bernard Leach. Leach advocated personal expression, which combined with Rhodes's fascination with the new Abstract Expressionist painting, encouraged Rhodes to explore the effects of overlapped, splashed, poured, dripped, and dipped glazes on tall, footed goblets and wheel-thrown vessels.

Rhodes's free-wheeling glaze applications no doubt impressed his students, but his greater contribution to ceramics education came about ten years later with the publication of his book, *Clay and Glazes for the Potter* (1957). This compilation of material from the Alfred curriculum arrived at a time when Charles Binns's book had grown inadequate and some of Leach's techniques outdated. Rhodes offered enough technical detail to make the process understandable but not overwhelming. His writing fit his view of ceramics in the 1950s:

> We saw it as a modest craft without any thought of fame or fortune because there was no mechanism to advance one's work—few opportunities to exhibit beyond the Ceramic Nationals in Syracuse.[8]

On the West Coast, academic education in ceramics began in the 1930s, first with Glen Lukens at the University of Southern California. USC's across-town rival in football was the University of

167. Laura Andreson
BOWL
*1945. Earthenware, height 5½",
diameter 8½". Collection the
artist*

Before stoneware and porcelain
clays were available on the
West Coast, Laura Andreson
succeeded in making earthenware appear as refined as high-
fired clay bodies. Her work here
also reflects the period's affinity
for bright colors associated
with California.

California, and it became a rival in ceramics as well. The head of the
department there was Laura Andreson, who had received her degree
from UCLA in 1933 when it was primarily a teacher's college. Following graduation, Andreson remained at UCLA teaching a variety
of art education courses. Then in 1936, after earning a master's degree from Columbia University, she added ceramics classes to her
schedule. Her experience with clay, however, had been minimal; an
evening class with Glen Lukens and a short period of study with
Gertrud Natzler added technical information, but she was largely
self-taught.

For Andreson, teaching included working along with her students and producing her own work.[9] Her low-fire, handbuilt earthenware plates and bowls were glazed in bright, glossy colors similar to
Lukens's ware of the thirties. Bernard Leach's book influenced her in
much the same way it affected Daniel Rhodes, but stoneware clays
were not yet available in California. To make do, Andreson resorted
to making earthenware look like high-fired clay.

In the early 1940s, Andreson heard that Carlton Ball, a former
student of Lukens, had mastered the wheel by watching Marguerite
Wildenhain at local Bay Area demonstrations. Andreson sent several
students north to take lessons from Ball, and when they returned
they taught her how to throw on the wheel. Once she learned, the
wheel became Andreson's primary tool.

When stoneware clays were discovered in California in 1948,
Andreson was among the first to use them. She gave increasing time
to research, and paid more and more attention to a form that would
best display the glaze. Andreson favored the Bauhaus aesthetic of
simplicity of form. She combined this with an affinity for Scandinavian design she'd encountered on visits to Europe. During trips
abroad, she collected examples of historical ware to show her
students.

In the 1950s Albert King, whose local pottery Lotus and
Acanthus Studios produced molded porcelain wares, encouraged An-

168. Daniel Rhodes
UNTITLED
*1960. Stoneware, height 12",
width 10". Private collection*

169. LAURA ANDRESON
UNTITLED
1969. Luster glaze. 7½ x 7". Collection Regina Roditi

170. HERBERT SANDERS
TWO VASES
c. 1970. Porcelain, crystalline glazes, (left:) height 8¼"; (right:) height 5". Collection the artist

dreson to throw porcelain. At the time, this clay body was considered the exclusive province of commercial potteries. Captivated by the idea, Andreson submerged herself in experiments on porcelain bodies and glazes—crystals, celadons, ash glazes, and copper reds. She was one of the first studio potters in the West to work in porcelain; her enthusiasm for the medium grew to the point that by the end of the decade Andreson had become *the* western expert on porcelain clays and glazes.

UCLA and USC weren't the only southern California schools during the thirties to offer an education in ceramics. In 1934, William Manker, formerly a designer for Ernest Batchelder's tile company in Pasadena, brought ceramics to Scripps College in Claremont, east of Los Angeles. Manker's years with Batchelder had wedded him to the principles of the Arts and Crafts Movement, principles that he transmitted to his students. Handbuilding and casting were the most widely used techniques at Scripps until Manker took a series of classes with Gertrud Natzler. After that he began using a wheel. His admiration for oriental ceramics led to his refinement of copper-red reduction glazes; however, his more enduring contribution to the area's ceramists was the Scripps Invitational exhibitions which he initiated in 1945. These shows were the first annual exhibitions in the West for fine-art ceramics, and are continued by Manker's successors to this day.

The growth of ceramics education in southern California was paralleled in the north. Herbert Sanders, an Ohio State University graduate with a master's degree in ceramics, came West in the late 1930s to teach at San Jose State College. Like Rhodes, he was a member of the second generation of ceramists, carrying the Binns/Baggs tradition to another part of the country. In the rich agricultural area of the Santa Clara Valley, Sanders found raw materials for experimenting with ash glazes; his guide in this research was Bernard Leach's *A Potter's Book*. His teaching career was interrupted by the war in the early 1940s; but in 1947 he became director of the School for American Craftsmen, then at Alfred University. He re-enrolled at Ohio State in 1949 to work on a doctorate in ceramics.[10] Then in 1951 Sanders returned to San Jose, having become at the age of forty-two the first person in the United States granted a Ph.D. in ceramics.

Sharing what he had learned with others became the cornerstone of Sanders's career; his articles and books were read by a wide audience far beyond San Jose State. In 1958, his own education took a new turn when he received a Fulbright Fellowship to study in Japan. The result of that experience, *The World of Japanese Ceramics*, appeared ten years later, just at the moment when American interest in Japanese ceramics was at its zenith.

Sanders's northern California colleague in the late thirties and forties was Carlton Ball, who began his teaching career at the California College of Arts and Crafts. When Ball left in 1940 for a position at nearby Mills College, Marguerite Wildenhain arrived to take his position. Unaccustomed to earthenware clays and glazes, she overfired the kiln; afterward she adjusted the clay body but continued to overfire the cone 08 glaze. For Ball, the results were an important lesson: "Overfired, that glaze allowed the quality of the clay to come through and that was the beauty of her pots."[11]

171. *Carlton Ball working on the wheel at the University of Southern California, 1956*

On his return to southern California from teaching in the Midwest, Ball reflected the local spirit for throwing ever larger vessels. By the 1960s, the slogan at the university was, "Throw 'em big, throw 'em tall, throw 'em just like Carlton Ball"

As an associate professor at Mills College in the early 1940s, Ball demonstrated a resourcefulness comparable to that of his former teacher, Glen Lukens. He organized a guild for non-college ceramics classes, the Mills College Guild, which helped finance equipment for all his students. He also persuaded a local doll factory, the only source of porcelain, to sell him some clay which he used for a short period. Bernard Leach's book led him to experiment with reduction firing in the college's first cone 10 kiln. (In contrast, Laura Andreson learned reduction firing in a more serendipitous fashion—the roof of her department's old kiln caved in, smoking the kilns contents.) Leach's description of raku firing motivated Ball in 1947 to try the process, but he didn't pursue it very far.

The success of the Mills College Guild prompted Ball to found the Association of San Francisco Potters in 1945. The annual exhibits served to promote the work of association members. The Ceramic National exhibitions created a certain amount of rivalry between potters north and south, which prompted Ball to lobby for a regional jury to judge work in order to have fairer representation from California. Thereafter he frequently served as a juror, often with Wildenhain.

One of Ball's most influential acts was inviting Bernard Leach to Mills. Leach, who'd been lecturing at Alfred in 1950, came for a two-week workshop. Because of the popularity of his book, Leach drew tremendous crowds. However, Leach made enemies when he commented on the lack of any American tradition in pottery, with the exception of American Indian ware. This lack of a "tap root," as he termed it, stirred strong emotions and provoked many responses—Marguerite Wildenhain's among them—in the following months and years. In an open letter to *Craft Horizons* Wildenhain commented:

> Tradition is only good when it is alive, when no one is conscious of it, when it needs no praise. [One has to] search honestly for those forms that are related to us, that express what we feel, think, and believe.... Roots grow when [we] are deeply related...closely connected with the country, the society, the ideas of the people around one.[12]

The dispute had been one long in brewing. Leach's pottery, glazed in earth tones, represented a rejection of earthenware's bright colors. For a time, Leach's philosophy divided potters into two camps: those who championed his expressive, emotional, antimechanical approach to clay, and those who considered such ideas an anathema to the tenets of the Bauhaus. The controversy continued over the following years, stirred by Leach's visits to America.

Meanwhile, Ball left for teaching positions in the Midwest, where he found time to begin a writing career. In articles for *Ceramic Industry* and *Ceramics Monthly* (the latter began publication in 1953), Ball described a range of technical procedures, illustrated by his own work. Many years later, he commented on the energy of that early period and his position in it:

> The new and different seemed like progress...I found it more exciting to explore new techniques, a new glaze. I guess I didn't go back to refine anything very much.[13]

172. CARLTON BALL
JAR
1967. Stoneware, press-mold design, height 12½". American Craft Museum, New York

173. FRANCES SENSKA
SOUP TUREEN
*1976. Stoneware, height 8",
width 9". Private collection*

In 1946, about the same time that Paul Bonifas brought a European sensibility to the University of Washington, African-born Frances Senska began teaching in Montana. Senska, the daughter of missionaries to the Cameroon where she was born in 1914, attended the University of Iowa, the School of Design in Chicago (directed by former Bauhaus teacher Laszlo Moholy-Nagy), and took ceramics classes from Edith Heath, who later founded a successful dinnerware company in San Francisco. Senska took a course at Cranbrook with Maija Grotell, and then found a job teaching design at Montana State University. Within a few years she was conducting ceramics classes and developing a ceramics department there.

Senska, like Andreson, studied with her students. She encouraged them to be experimental and, like African folk potters, to have a respect for clay. In an effort to mitigate Montana's remoteness from centers of ceramic activity, Senska brought the Natzlers, Edith Heath, and members of the Association of San Francisco Potters to the university for exhibits and workshops.

Two students in Senska's first classes were Montana residents taking advantage of the G.I. Bill—Peter Voulkos, a painting major, and Rudy Autio, whose interest was sculpture. Both men naturally took to ceramics. Each challenged the other, testing skills and exchanging ideas with Senska, who urged them to try new directions. Senska's linear surface decorations, abstractions of birds or animals, suggested to Voulkos a method of developing a raised line using wax and inlaid slip. A group of three bottles decorated using this technique earned Voulkos first prize at the fifteenth Ceramic National Exhibition of 1951.

Such an honor for a student from the artistically isolated state of Montana was a symbolic crack in the wall of regionalism. It was also a harbinger of an openness to new ideas by the postwar generation of teacher-potters. This group of artists now tempered Bauhaus precision with a more expressive style. In so doing, many of them, coming to pottery from other disciplines of art, further erased the mental boundary line between art and craft.

opposite:
174. PAUL SOLDNER
RAKU BOTTLE
*1964. Earthenware, height 9",
diameter 7". Everson Museum of
Art, Syracuse, N.Y.*

Part V

Abstract Expressionism:
Its Effects and Ramifications 1955–1965

Chapter 11
POSTWAR ARTISTIC FERMENT

The Growth of Ceramics Education

The G.I. Bill changed the nature of ceramics education. A government subsidy of the arts, the bill was different from, yet related to, the WPA/FAP programs of the thirties. The World War II veterans entering college (followed a few years later by Korean War veterans) shifted the emphasis from ceramics taught as art education for teachers to ceramics taught as an art form; because of government support, many postwar students felt encouraged to take courses not directly tied to a career, and which they previously might not have considered. The transformation of ceramics education from craft into art was abetted by the nation's rising affluence. There was money and time for things besides work, and adult education, community colleges, and university extension classes entered a period of expansion. The crush of students created a demand for potters to teach at the schools. As a result, the university became the teacher-potter's patron, providing employment, expensive studio equipment, and a new generation of ceramists. It was also the college teachers—and the generation they educated who became teacher-potters—who devised innovative solutions to the challenges of enrollment rising faster than funding.

During the mid-forties, Ted Randall (the son of Theodore Randall, one of the founders of the American Ceramic Society) designed a fly wheel more efficient and easier to build than the type used at Alfred during his college days. Randall's version, in bent steel with an orange tractor seat, was copied by many East Coast studio potters. There was also innovation in kiln construction. James McKinnell, who received his master's degree in ceramic engineering at the University of Washington in 1941, later used the G.I. Bill to learn the potter's wheel. He and his wife, Nan, spent most of the 1950s teaching ceramics, first in Colorado, then at the Archie Bray Foundation in Montana. It was in Montana that McKinnell experimented with a multi-chambered soft brick kiln capable of high temperatures.

opposite:
175. JAMES McKINNELL
COVERED JAR
*1958. Stoneware, height 17½",
diameter 9". Everson Museum of
Art, Syracuse, N.Y.*

above:
176. HENRY TAKEMOTO
VASE
*1962. Stoneware, height 4'½",
diameter 2' 9". Collection the
artist*

The artist was a student of Peter Voulkos's at the Los Angeles County Art Institute from 1957 to 1959. His work reflects the spirit of the Voulkos groups where the vessel served monumental, nonfunctional concepts.

177. ANTONIO PRIETO. TALL VASE.
1950. Stoneware, height 14", diameter 6". Everson Museum of Art, Syracuse, N.Y.

With the departure of Carlton Ball from Mills College in 1950, Antonio Prieto, a graduate of Alfred University, chaired the ceramics department. Prieto favored abstract surface designs on elegantly thrown forms. He was elected to the American Crafts Council Board in 1956, where he championed West Coast ceramics.

178. ANTONIO PRIETO
BOTTLE
1957. Stoneware, height 25", diameter 6½". Collection the Oakland Museum, Calif. Gift of Antonio Prieto

Uniquely portable because the bricks were not mortared and the structure was a system of lightweight supports, the kiln consumed less gas than traditional models. Kiln building became part of the curriculum in the classes the McKinnells taught in later years in Washington, the University of New Hampshire, and during the 1960s at Iowa State University.

This was also a time when the body of literature in ceramics education was growing. Glenn Nelson left his teaching job at Iowa State in 1955 with a fifty-page reference outline for his ceramics classes at the University of Minnesota in Duluth. Like Daniel Rhodes, he was tired of using makeshift material. As a result, he began writing an enlarged version of his outline. It was published in book form as *Ceramics: A Potter's Handbook* in 1960, a few years after Rhodes's book appeared.

Not everyone wanted to study pottery at a university. Harvey Littleton, a former student of Maija Grotell's, organized potters' guilds in Ann Arbor, Michigan, and Toledo, Ohio, where he taught at the city's museum. The guilds functioned as cooperatives, providing instruction, equipment, and a place to work without academic pressures. Besides guilds and museum classes, rural craft schools beckoned to teacher-potters. These schools, like the League of New Hampshire Craftsmen's classes, were an outgrowth of rural-based craft organizations. One of the earliest such centers was the Appalachian School in the mountains of North Carolina, which spawned the Penland School of Handicrafts in 1929. When Penland's enrollment swelled with returning World War II veterans, what had been a regional school soon acquired a national reputation for educating students in the art of fine handcrafts. The curriculum became a natural extension of the state's historical relationship to handcrafts, especially pottery and weaving. Another craft center that capitalized on this new interest in handcrafts was the Haystack Mountain School of Crafts in Maine which opened a summer school in 1950. Like the earlier handcraft leagues and guilds, the Penland and Haystack Mountain schools were concerned with preserving rural craft skills. However, their curriculum changed in the fifties as new faculty, with sophisticated training, taught classes, which in turn attracted a broader base of students. Each school's rural setting, one in the southern highlands, the other on a heavily wooded island off the Maine coast, appealed to both students and teachers; no place seemed more appropriate for the production of pottery than beautiful countryside.

The Organizational Network

As more trained ceramists graduated from universities, art schools, and other institutions, the pressure for additional exhibition opportunities increased. The Ceramic National exhibitions, discontinued during the war, resumed in 1946 with local juries in major cities. In response to the new uses of clay, the National added an addditional category. In 1952 Viktor Schreckengost received the National's First Architectural Ceramic Sculpture Citation for originality of design and for the best example of ceramic sculpture integrated with archi-

179. KARL MARTZ
FOOTED BOWL
1945. Earthenware, height 2¾", diameter 6⅜". Sheldon Memorial Art Gallery, University of Nebraska-Lincoln. F. M. Hall Collection.

After graduate work at Ohio State University with Arthur Baggs, Martz established the ceramics department at Indiana University in 1938. Like other newly initiated university programs in the 1940s, Indiana accommodated the flood of veterans taking advantage of the G. I. Bill.

tecture. The award was for a commission from the Cleveland Zoological Park in which Schreckengost portrayed the history of birds from prehistoric times to the present in a series of plaques.

During this period, a number of regional exhibits expanded their scope. The Wichita [Kansas] Decorative Arts and Ceramics exhibits, which began in 1945, quickly became national. In 1950, the Ceramic League of Miami initiated a national, juried exhibit which, after a few years, circulated work from the exhibit to museums and galleries around the South. Scripps College in California continued its annual shows under the direction of Richard Petterson. In 1950, Petterson included ceramics from Scandinavia, Germany, and Japan. Occasionally changing the format from the usual submissions, Petterson felt, allowed the annual to reflect shifts in aesthetic direction and new ideas.[1] The international exchange went both ways. When the International Academy of Ceramics organized its first exposition at Cannes in 1955, American entries were well endowed with awards: Peter Voulkos won a gold medal, and silver medals went to Mary Scheier, Robert Turner, and Antonio Prieto.

In the late 1940s, some teacher and studio potter members of the American Ceramic Society expressed unhappiness that their interests weren't being addressed in an organization more concerned with the problems of industry. A new column, "The Artist Designs," appeared in the July 1952 issue of the society's *Bulletin*, perhaps an attempt to mollify studio potters; the term "design" became the designation for several of the society's chapters whose members were not from industry. This concern with terminology was indicative of the increasing restlessness of the craftsman who saw this category as possibly ill-fitting. In 1953, the term "designer-craftsmen" was used as the title of an exhibit at the Brooklyn Museum sponsored by the American Craftsmen's Educational Council. The term "craftsman," however, was used as the title of an exhibition at the Brooklyn Museum sponsored by the American Craftsmen's Educational Council. The term "craftsman," however, was difficult to define to the satisfaction of all. The debate centered around the use of tools and apprentices (some considered the use of apprentices as another form of the factory system). An essay in the catalogue for the Brooklyn show observed that the modern craftsman, in order to survive, must have "aesthetic awareness as well as technical skill."[2] New conditions were influencing the crafts, the essay concluded, and therefore much depended on the purpose of the craftsman.

In another essay for the same catalogue, Anna Olmsted, the venerable director of the Ceramic National exhibitions, analyzed what she saw as new trends: the prevalence of earth tones rather than bright colors, the use of free-form, asymmetrical vessels (a prewar style influenced by Surrealism), a tendency toward sculpture, and a "garden-conscious era" that called for large, decorative pots relating to architecture.[3] Olmsted's observations proved highly prescient, and the Brooklyn exhibit turned out to be the seminal show of the decade.

The next big step for ceramics, as part of contemporary crafts, was a museum of its own. In 1956, with financial support from the business community and individuals, the American Craftsmen's Council converted an old brownstone building in New York City into exhibition space and offices, where it was named the Museum of Contemporary Crafts. The first exhibit, "Craftsmanship in a Changing World," acknowledged that while machines had raised the standard of living for a majority, crafts were needed to satisfy a hunger for creativity and personal expression.

In 1957, when all the barometers in the craft movement indicated rising growth, the ACC organized a conference of craftspersons. That summer a gathering of 450 artists from thirty states met at Asilomar outside of Carmel, California. Panel discussions by ceramists aired widely divergent views: the professional potter should produce only individual items; a professional's work should be adapted to mass-production needs; ceramists should have the same artistic freedom as the sculptor; aesthetic needs and impulses shouldn't be based on considerations of function; tradition should never bind the ceramist; he or she should be free to seek an original form.[4]

This debate regarding the role of the ceramist continued in letters and articles in *Craft Horizons*. Indeed, trade publications were the principal venues for discussions among ceramists. Published by the ACC, *Craft Horizons* had originally been a mimeographed sheet mailed to Handcraft Cooperative League of America members in November 1941 to a magazine format by its third issue. A year later, when the league was renamed the American Craftsmen's Cooperative Council, their publication was officially titled *Craft Horizons*. In two issues a year (until the end of the war), the magazine brought together craftspersons who shared similar concerns in such areas as clay, wood, glass, silver, and fiber. Other magazines such as *Ceramic Industry* and *Ceramic Age* were essentially industry-oriented, though they did publish articles by Carlton Ball and Herbert Sanders, which were of interest to the teacher and studio potter. *Ceramics Monthly*, beginning with its first issue in 1953, attempted to straddle the whole range of non-industrial ceramics—the hobbyist, teacher, student, and studio potter. Thomas Sellars and Spencer Davis, who began the publication, were graduates of Ohio State University and their orientation made the magazine in some ways the rightful descendant of *Keramic Studio*.

New Expressions in Clay

One of the outspoken critics of ceramics in the postwar period was Henry Varnum Poor. A painter as well as ceramist since the early 1920s, Poor questioned the value of technical perfection in American ceramic ware. Most Americans, he wrote in *Craft Horizons*, accept the sanitary, cold, machine-made objects conceived by efficient industrial designers. His point was whether people would want to spend their lives with these objects. Poor equated technology and mass production with conformity, which he felt would lead to an erosion of the creative life, contending that the antidote, good design, must come from a total familiarity with a material: "Clays are like wines—part of the flavor comes from knowing the hillsides and vineyards that grew the grapes."[5] He pursued this theme in later writings, championing the accidental as a necessary part of the process, "the material asserting itself; speaking to and informing the artist."[6]

180. HENRY VARNUM POOR
BOWL
1947. Red clay, white slip, sgraffito, height 4¾", diameter 6⅞".

181. PABLO PICASSO, IN COL-
LABORATION WITH POTTERS
GEORGES AND SUZANNE RAMIE
PLATE
*1957. Earthenware, diameter
13". Museum of Fine Arts,
Boston*

Poor was drawing attention to an expressive use of clay—an idea explored by Glen Lukens in the thirties and forties. Most potters in the 1950s concentrated on classical shapes and the perfection of form. A more personal expression was evident only in surface embellishment. However, a few artists were at work undermining traditional form. In 1947, Spanish artist Pablo Picasso formed an association with potters Georges and Suzanne Ramie in the small village of Vallauris in southern France. Wet or leather-hard bottles thrown by Ramie or one of his workers were refashioned by Picasso into the shapes of women, animals, or birds. Converting ready-made forms was an expression of Marcel Duchamp's philosophy of creating something new and different from a familiar material. Of greater significance was the artist's manipulation of clay in a spontaneous, intuitive manner. In addition, Picasso playfully emphasized or negated concave and convex areas by the way he painted the surface.

Equally innovative with clay, the Surrealist painter Joan Miró worked briefly during World War II with Spanish ceramist Josep Llorens Artigas, painting vases and plaques with the colors and symbols used in his canvases. In 1953 Miró returned to clay with Artigas. This time, objects of a pleasing texture and shape which he found near Artigas's Catalan farmhouse acted as inspiration for figurative clay sculptures. Miró's assembled forms were a synthesis of shapes from primitive cultures, rock formations, and images familiar to his paintings.

Both Miró and Picasso transferred concepts in their paintings to clay. Sculptor Isamu Noguchi also returned to clay in the fifties. In contrast to Picasso's flamboyant, whimsical birds and women, No-

guchi favored intimate structures with a personal iconography derived from dreams. One dollhouse structure, titled *The Apartment* (1952), is inhabited by a ladder and a figure with wings for arms. A series of similar structures along with plates, bowls, and vases exhibited in New York in 1954 were received with skepticism, considered too playful in the serious atmosphere surrounding Abstract Expressionist painting.[7]

Like Noguchi, American sculptor Reuben Nakian had worked in clay about twenty years earlier, for a short period. He adapted themes from classical mythology to an expressive ceramic style. In 1948, he began a series of plaques dealing with the Europa myth. Using an incised line, bold and calligraphic on a slab surface, Nakian interpreted Europa as a voluptuous, curvaceous woman languishing astride a bull whose form is merely suggested in a shorthand of linear configurations. The effect imparted a sensuousness inherent in clay that was infrequently expressed. Through their unorthodox use of clay that allowed for humor, chance, and spontaneity, this group of artists rejected boundary lines and traditional rules inhibiting expression in clay. The liaison between this group and potters still wedded to the wheel's precision was that figure of controversy, Bernard Leach. On his visit to Mills College in 1950, Leach demonstrated how work on the wheel could become more expressive. By slightly altering the wheel-thrown shape, the potter avoided imposing mechanical precision on a living form.[8] It was an oriental approach to clay, in keeping with the uninhibited ceramics of Picasso and Miró, and one which Leach had absorbed from many years of living in Japan.

182. BERNARD LEACH
JAR, VASE, PLATE
n.d. Stoneware. (left to right:) Jar, height 8¼"; Vase, height 14⅞", diameter 6⅞"; Plate, height 1⅝", diameter 12⅜". Everson Museum of Art, Syracuse, N.Y.

Missionaries of Personal Expression

When Bernard Leach returned for another tour of America in 1952, he was accompanied by potter Shoji Hamada, a lifelong friend with whom he had worked during his early years in Japan. The two were joined by Dr. Soetsu Yanagi, the founder and director of the Folk Craft Association of Japan. One of the trio's workshops was at Black Mountain College in North Carolina, where Karen Karnes and David Weinrib were the potters-in-residence. Hamada impressed the students with the Korean technique of brushing a white slip over a gray body using wayside grasses he had gathered and bound moments earlier. The wet surface of freshly made pots combed with grasses in such a nonchalant manner impressed his viewers.[9]

Another stop on the tour was the Archie Bray Foundation in Helena, Montana, where Frances Senska's former students Peter Voulkos and Rudy Autio ran the pottery. Here Hamada demonstrated throwing on a kick wheel while Voulkos provided the leg power. Yanagi lectured on Buddhism and Leach showed slides of his St. Ives pottery in England.

Before the group's arrival in Los Angeles, a committee organized by Richard Petterson of Scripps College brought together the now sizable ceramics community to plan a workshop-lecture schedule for the visiting trio—Leach, Hamada, and Yanagi. Working on the committee were Susan Peterson, a former student of Carlton Ball's who was teaching at Chouinard Art School, Harrison McIntosh, a studio potter in Claremont, and Vivika and Otto Heino, recent arrivals from New Hampshire. (Vivika handled Lukens's classes at USC

183. HARRISON McINTOSH
VASE
1960. Stoneware, height 13½", diameter 15½". Everson Museum of Art, Syracuse, N.Y.

While he was a teacher in the Los Angeles ceramic community, Harrison McIntosh was strongly influenced by Scandinavian design. His contribution to ceramics has been through teaching and studio production, and as a consultant in industrial design.

while he was in Haiti.) The Los Angeles visit was well publicized, and eleven hundred people crowded the demonstration at the Los Angeles County Museum, enthralled by the freshness of Hamada's brushwork and the freedom of his approach.

Assessing the impact of the trio's ideas on this and later visits was the topic of magazine articles, conferences, and seminars for several years to come. As a result of meeting Leach on his 1950 tour, many ceramists spent time as apprentices at his St. Ives pottery in England. Two of them, Warren and Alix MacKenzie, graduates of the School of the Art Institute of Chicago, began their apprenticeship with Leach there in 1950. After two years, they left for Minnesota to start their own pottery modeled on St. Ives in Stillwater, a small community near Minneapolis. The MacKenzies had learned from Leach that repetitive throwing gave the potter a sense of ease with the form and an intuitive feeling for the process; after that kind of concentrated effort the potter was free to approach form in an expressive manner. Still, the concept of making multiples of simple, utilitarian ware in a country workshop environment was somewhat antithetical to a period when most American potters believed their objective was to produce sophisticated, individual pieces. The MacKenzies decided that the Leach/oriental folk pottery style needed more exposure in America. It's not clear whether they proposed the 1952 tour to Leach, but Alix MacKenzie did assist with arrangements. The MacKenzies also offered workshops, but the opportunity to chair a ceramics department at the University of Minnesota in Minneapolis in 1954 gave Warren a more solid platform from which to spread the Leach concept of expression in clay.

After a number of years, the MacKenzies received a modicum of acceptance. By the late fifties, a kiln-opening in Stillwater brought

above left:
184. *Susan Peterson (left) working at the wheel with a student at the University of Southern California. (1960s)*

In the late 1960s, Susan Peterson developed an educational television program, "Wheels, Kilns, and Clay," which aired for two years. Peterson's discussions of good design, standards for evaluating ware, as well as providing technical information made the program a popular series.

above right:
185. SHOJI HAMADA
BOTTLE
c. 1950s. Stoneware, wax resist design, 9¼ x 7 x 5¾". Scripps College, Claremont, Calif. Collection Mr. and Mrs. Fred Marer

186. WARREN AND ALIX
MACKENZIE
SHALLOW BOWL
*c. 1958. Stoneware, wax resist
and inlay glaze decoration, oatmeal and saturated iron glaze,
height 2⅞", diameter 13³⁄₁₆".
Collection Warren MacKenzie*

customers to their door at 8 A.M., even in snowy weather. This kiln-
opening ritual, familiar to American folk potters in the Southeast,
was not yet part of the life of contemporary potters.

Voulkos: A New Concept in Ceramics

The approach to pottery taken by the MacKenzies was an obvious
reflection of Leach's influence. Less obvious—and more startling—
was Leach's effect on Peter Voulkos. In a way that Leach himself
probably could not have predicted, his philosophy helped guide
Voulkos into uncharted territory. The result was no less than an entirely new strain of American ceramics.

When Voulkos completed his graduate degree at the California
College of Arts and Crafts in 1952, he returned to Montana to join
Rudy Autio as a resident artist at the Archie Bray Foundation. In addition to organizing a production pottery (including garden planters
and ashtrays), the two taught evening classes and arranged workshops. James and Nan McKinnell, Marguerite Wildenhain, and Carlton Ball were some of the guests besides the Leach trio. Voulkos
picked up ideas from each workshop with these skilled ceramists,
producing large, footed covered vessels in Wildenhain's style, wax-
resist brush decorations like Hamada, and using white, brown, and
blue glazes and engobes (or slips) similar to the Leach/Hamada
palette.

In the summer of 1953, Voulkos went south to Black Mountain
College to teach a ceramics course. It was a heady atmosphere, and
Voulkos found himself in discussions with the likes of John Cage,

187. PETER VOULKOS
RICE BOTTLE
*c. 1951. Earthenware, height
13¾", diameter 10". Everson
Museum of Art, Syracuse, N.Y.*

188. *Peter Voulkos,
shown with slab-built
stoneware, late 1950s*

Merce Cunningham, and Robert Rauschenberg. Shortly afterward, he visited New York City where he was introduced to the Action painters of Abstract Expressionism—Jackson Pollock, Franz Kline, Willem de Kooning, and Mark Rothko—who challenged traditional pictorial space. Their spontaneous, intuitive, gestural approach to paint in a process that allowed factors beyond themselves to control the final results reminded Voulkos of the Leach workshop and Yanagi's lectures on Zen Buddhism. The common ground between the Action painters and Leach was a willingness to allow the material to express its inherent characteristics. Many years after the New York visit, Voulkos recalled, "I really got turned on to what the painters were doing. It was a special kind of time, a necessary kind of time...all the energies came together."[10]

VOULKOS: ASSEMBLED SCULPTURES

The effect on Voulkos of all this was a heightened desire for a new and different experience away from Montana. In 1954, he accepted a position at the Los Angeles County Art Institute (renamed the Otis Art Institute in 1960). Arriving in Los Angeles to find a classroom bare of everything except a table and sink, Voulkos and Paul Soldner, his only student for a short period, searched for equipment and supplies. Since neither liked the commercial wheels the school offered, they both built prototypes. Agreeing that Soldner produced the best model, Voulkos ordered the Soldner welded "x" frame kick wheel for the school. Over time, the Soldner wheel became the California classroom standard.

189. RUDY AUTIO
*Installation of terra-cotta panel
at Glacier County Library,
Cutbank, Montana, 1956. Made
at Archie Bray Foundation,
Helena, Montana*

Like Andreson, and because he didn't have a studio, Voulkos used the classroom as his workshop. As a result, his students became his colleagues in a community of mutual interest, diminishing the traditional academic distance between teacher and pupil. After Voulkos cajoled the institute's director, Millard Sheets, into keeping the classrooms open twenty-four hours a day, a macho camaraderie developed. (Few women joined the evening sessions.) Whether they were working together, or viewing the latest exhibit or architecture, the ceramists had formed their own closely knit group.

The pressures of an art school, Voulkos discovered, were quite different from those of a production pottery. No longer required to throw one hundred pots a day, Voulkos felt a restlessness with the restrictions of wheel-thrown forms. Picasso's method of stacking wheel-thrown forms and painting the surface to deceive the eye spurred his imagination. He particularly admired Picasso's ability to take risks, to detach himself from centuries of tradition.[11] Inspired, in 1955 Voulkos began a series of wheel-thrown, vertically and horizontally assembled forms, cylinders massed and banded together with strips of clay, playfully attached as though they'd been nailed together. Slabs, strips of clay, and coils combined in a seemingly haphazard manner expressly flaunted the Bauhaus concept of perfection and fine craftsmanship. Voulkos painted some of these multiforms with dark lines to emphasize or hide a protrusion, or to add gestural content.

At this point, there was no turning back. Voulkos's comrades at the institute—Paul Soldner, John Mason, Kenneth Price, and Jerry Rothman—understood the conflict that was engaging him since they were struggling with it themselves. Voulkos's statement as a juror for the Fifth Miami National Exhibition (1957) came to many people as something of a shock. What ceramics needed, Voulkos declared, was "a kick in the pants...to pull it out of the doldrums. ...Only when techniques and materials transcend themselves is there a chance for art."[12] Claiming that most of the entries lacked a sense of involvement, Voulkos revealed his personal concerns:

To make an idea good or bad, it takes not only craftsmanship but a sense of identity. [Most handcrafted objects] are made according to a narrow set of rules. There are too many rules and too little feeling. How is it possible to create without excitement?[13]

Creating with excitement ultimately negated the vessel's function, a point Voulkos demonstrated a year before the Miami show in *Rocking Pot* (1956) when he cut holes into the wall of a large bowl. Thrusting spears of clay through the holes, Voulkos positioned the vessel lip-side-down on blades of clay like runners on a sled. Literally overturning the container, he made it a sculptural element. When three large kilns were installed in the new building planned for the ceramics department, their size challenged Voulkos to build taller structures. It wasn't easy. At first, cylinders vertically stacked and assembled cracked, collapsed, or completely blew up in the kiln. Ultimately, Voulkos devised an exterior armature to support the weight. Building inside and outside together vertically, he adapted the appearance of the blocklike sculptures of Fritz Wotruba, an Aus-

190. PAUL SOLDNER
EXTENDED THROWING
PUSHED "TO THE LIMIT"
1955. Stoneware, unfired, height 8'.

Paul Soldner's master's thesis in art was an investigation of extended throwing. He was successful in pioneering a more effective method for adding height to a wheel-thrown object by the continual addition of thrown clay "doughnuts" to the rim of the piece. Whereas the more common technique was the attachment of thrown forms, Soldner's procedure allowed the ceramist both greater control and overall unification of the total column. (It also required that he throw while standing on a ladder.)

trian sculptor. Not since the monumental figures of Waylande Gregory, made almost sixteen years earlier, had anyone tried for such height in clay.

VOULKOS AND MASON,
TWO DIRECTIONS IN SCULPTURE

John Mason, working at the Los Angeles County Art Institute with Voulkos, went through a similar exploratory period. At first, Mason's large jars were decorated with strong, black lines in response to Franz Kline's harsh black and white paintings. Discontent with exterior decoration, Mason began altering wheel-thrown vessels by paddling the walls, distorting them into complex forms combined with hand-thrown additions. Less committed to the wheel than Voulkos, Mason expressed clay's plasticity by dropping a slab on an object to

191. PETER VOULKOS
MULTIFORM VASE
1956. Stoneware, wheel-thrown and paddled cylinders joined by slabs, with illusionistic "nail" holes, white and red iron slip, partially glazed, height 42".
American Craft Museum, New York

192. PETER VOULKOS
5000 FEET
*1958. Stoneware, height 41".
Collection the Los Angeles
County Museum of Art*

catch its impression. Slab and wheel-thrown combinations of the 1956–57 period have pronounced "x" and cross images, marks that reappeared frequently in Mason's later work. Large slab-plaques of 1957–58 were vigorously brushed with cobalt and iron, incised and gouged. These gestural strokes made plasticity the subject matter in objects that were both sculptures and paintings. Interwoven strips of clay became three-dimensional, gestural wall sculptures.

By 1957, Mason and Voulkos found working in the classroom too confining. They rented an old stable in Glendale and hired Mike Kalan, a ceramic engineer, to build one of the largest updraft reduction kilns in use at a private studio at that time—120 cubic feet of interior space. Voulkos worked simultaneously on as many as five or six assembled sculptures at a time. *5000 Feet* (1958) is unusual for its mass of wheel-thrown and paddled forms at the base, separated into columns at the top, its bulkiness offset by encompassing space. The overall color contributed to the effect of swelling organic growth. *Rondena* and *Little Big Horn* (both 1958) are more colorful, supporting large areas of dark blue and black lines over bulging, pregnant

opposite:
193. PETER VOULKOS
RONDENA
*1958. Stoneware, wheel-thrown
elements paddled and con-
structed; cobalt, iron, white
slips, and epoxy paint, height
66". Collection Mr. and Mrs.
Stanley K. Sheinbaum*

With this seminal sculpture, Peter Voulkos thrust wheel-thrown forms into a sculptural context, deliberately challenging traditional concepts of function. At the time, many colleagues and critics viewed this and similar work as an aberration, lacking precedent in ceramic tradition.

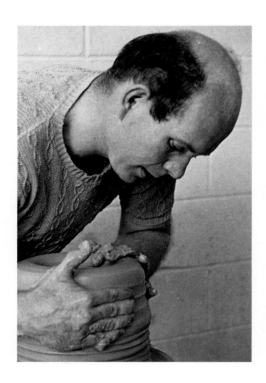

194. *John Mason, 1957*

195. JOHN MASON
GREY WALL
1960. Stoneware, 6' 7½" x 13' 9"
x 6". Collection the artist

forms. Two sculptures of 1959, *Camelback Mountain* and *Sevill-anos*, return to an overall brown surface of the previous year, but with important differences. Pierced, cut, or slashed areas relieved the heaviness while achieving a gestural quality through the clay rather than surface decoration.

As Voulkos, struggling against gravity, tried to keep stacked forms in a vertical plane, Mason covered a horizontal expanse with thick strips of clay. He rolled out clay on the floor of the studio, moving rapidly to incise, texture, cut, and impress the surface before the material became too dry. For sections too heavy to place in the kiln without support, he devised a rope armature and pulley system. The strips of clay in *Blue Wall Relief* (1959) cover a horizontal expanse of nine feet and echo the movement and gestural excitement of Jackson Pollock's paintings. Another wall relief of 1959 used altered vessels and handbuilt shapes, carved and incised. Low-fire, bright colored glazes accented some areas and contrasted with the natural, unglazed clay surface.

Mason's *Grey Wall* (1960) is traditional in the use of square

196. JOHN MASON
VERTICAL SCULPTURE
1961. Stoneware. 64 x 18 x 10".
Collection the artist

Mason built his sculpture
around a thick, interior wooden
pole. Confrontational because of
its human proportions, this assemblage of slabs also shows
Mason's feeling for the landscape of the Southwest.

units but not in its texture; the surface has the appearance of land
randomly roughened or smoothed by geological forces. This theme
dominated a 1960–63 series of vertical sculptures by Mason.

Few precedents in either sculpture or clay guided Voulkos and
Mason during this period of prodigious activity. They were not, however, the only ceramists working toward the liberation of form and
surface. Viktor Schreckengost's sculptures of the fifties show the influence of Brancusi. Toshiko Takaezu, a former student of Maija
Grotell's teaching at the Cranbrook Academy of Art, allowed glazes
to flow randomly, distorted wheel-thrown vessels, and obliterated
traditional function by completely closing the form. The Heinos
splashed and poured oxides over paddled vessels in a manner that
accented the form. But Voulkos's assemblages could no longer be
identified as vessels, and Mason's use of clay was architectural, more
closely related to landscape than traditional sculpture. By the 1960s,
Voulkos and Mason had moved clay into new places, difficult to
categorize except as three-dimensional Abstract Expressionist
sculptures.

197. BEATRICE WOOD. JAR WITH FISH. *1977. Stoneware, height 14", diameter 10¼". Everson Museum of Art, Syracuse, N.Y. Gift of the artist*

A member of the southern California ceramics community, Beatrice Wood studied with Glen Lukens, Vivika Heino, and Gertrud Natzler in the forties and fifties. In time she made luster glazes her special area of interest, developing exotic colors and surfaces (see fig. 269).

198. Toshiko Takaezu
PAINTED BOWL
*c. 1962. Stoneware, height 1⅞",
diameter 13½". Everson
Museum of Art, Syracuse, N.Y.*

199. Vivika and Otto Heino
BOWL
Early 1960s. Stoneware, diameter 9". Collection the artists

Beginning in the 1950s, Vivika Heino brought the technical expertise of an Alfred University master's degree to her teaching assignments in several southern California colleges. Otto Heino, Vivika's former student at the League of New Hampshire Craftsmen, maintained their Los Angeles workshop and gallery.

Chapter 12

TRANSFORMATIONS IN FORM AND SURFACE

The Vessel Redux

Voulkos's assembled sculptures and Mason's architectural walls substantially altered traditional concepts of form and surface for clay. Among the many factors fueling this change was the university and art school setting for ceramics education. Here the potter relinquished his previous isolation from mainstream art. Caught in the artistic momentum on the rise during the postwar period, not only Voulkos and Mason responded, but a number of Voulkos's students and fellow ceramists. For these ceramists—especially Rudolf Staffel, William Wyman, Ken Price, Ron Nagle, Paul Soldner, and Don Reitz—the 1960s became the period of experimentation for a new interpretation of the vessel. Although Mason and Price explored abstract sculpture in the context of Minimalism, the main thrust of the early sixties remained with the vessel.

The early 1960s also brought about a change in the orientation Peter Voulkos was taking. Between 1957 and 1960, Voulkos concentrated on his four- and five-foot-high sculptures. In 1959, when he accepted an assistant professorship at the University of California at Berkeley, he continued working on projects at the Glendale Studio, commuting from Berkeley until 1961. After that, Voulkos began constructing cast bronze sculptures at the university's new foundry, working on a scale not possible in clay. He did, however, also continue to work in clay. Though without a studio until 1963, Voulkos produced plates and vessels in the classroom and at workshops around the country. Between 1960 and 1964, for instance, he made several trips to New York City to conduct summer programs at the Greenwich House Pottery and run workshops at Teacher's College at Columbia University.

During the 1950s, the motifs on his plates either echoed paintings by Picasso and Matisse, or they reflected the gestural brushwork of his own paintings, which he continued to produce. Around 1959, this changed. Voulkos began testing the bright colors of low-fire

opposite:
200. PETER VOULKOS
USA 41
1960. Stoneware, epoxy paints, slips, light glaze, height 36". Corcoran Gallery of Art, Washington, D.C.

above:
201. RUDOLF STAFFEL
BOWL
c. 1950. Stoneware, glazed. 6 x 10". Courtesy Helen Drutt Gallery, Philadelphia

glazes on his plates, colors that had become unfashionable in the 1940s when the earth tones associated with stoneware were favored. Used sparingly, the reds and blues accented his stoneware plates. The plates themselves had become increasingly fragmented, scarred with ruptures, ripped edges, and surface bulges that strained the clay's malleability to its limit. With the overlays of slabs, brushed or splattered with oxides, and a dash of intense color these works were indeed Abstract Expressionist paintings in three dimensions.

A similar surface treatment appeared on Voulkos's containers. *USA 41* and *Red River* (both 1960) were wheel thrown, altered, and vertically stacked rather than assembled like the late fifties sculptures. This experimental series served as a study for the forms he created in the late sixties. Here the rips were more exaggerated than those on the plates and were filled with a darker clay body, a phenomenon Voulkos later referred to as a "pass through."[1] By the late sixties, the stacked, three-tiered vessel and the plate, thrown and altered, emerged as his primary forms. On both he made surface rips, some filled with wads of porcelain. Over the natural clay body or one darkened by slip, Voulkos sprayed a thin, clear, low-fire commercial glaze which he generally overfired—a deliberate rejection of a century of glaze research. What he was seeking through this process was the simulation of the slightly moist, leather-hard stage in the clay process, a skinlike appearance which conveyed the sensuousness of the material.[2] Less frenzied in surface and form than his earlier sixties vessels, work of this period reflects the impact of Minimalism, and its opposition to the emotionalism of Abstract Expressionism.

In 1954, Voulkos had his first one-person show in New York at America House and his first museum show in 1960 at the Museum of Modern Art. The work at the museum show was less than well received; in fact, it was largely ignored by an art world that persisted in thinking of clay as a decorative art. But a year earlier, the same body of work exhibited at the Pasadena Art Museum had garnered acclaim from the California art community. Voulkos's emergence as an artistic leader within the craft community was subsequently confirmed by an invitation to be the featured speaker at the first conference of the World Crafts Council held in 1964. This was followed by two exhibits that provided a context for his work of the late fifties. The first, "Abstract Expressionist Ceramics" (1966) at the University of California, Irvine, explained and documented the movement with examples of sculpture and vessels made by other ceramists who had worked with Voulkos at the County Art Institute.[3] The second, "American Sculpture of the Sixties" (1967) at the Los Angeles County Museum of Art, placed his work (and that of John Mason's) firmly in the category of sculpture, tacitly dismissing the tired prejudice against clay. Paradoxically, just as his position in sculpture was secured, Voulkos chose to continue working with the vessel. In so doing, he helped sustain the form's vitality and validity, particularly for those who'd begun their careers as vessel makers.

The sense of crisis that Voulkos felt when he first encountered Abstract Expressionist painting was similarly intense for Rudolf Staffel. But the conflict came earlier—in the late forties—and may have been deeper for Staffel, who was older than Voulkos and part of

202. Peter Voulkos
VASE
1962. Stoneware, height 28".
Collection Richard Swig

the Carlton Ball/Daniel Rhodes generation of ceramists. As Staffel described his dismay:

> *The Action school of painting destroyed my security. I was a craftsman and perfection was the standard that enabled an object to be a candidate for beauty. These new artists took our tools and said they are not worth anything. They overturned all past concepts of art.*[4]

Nevertheless, Staffel was challenged; he began translating the dynamics of the movement into abstract decorations on vessels, in particular gestural and calligraphic marks that recalled the automatic writing practiced by the Surrealists. The textural possibilities on stoneware intrigued him until the 1950s when he received a commission for a set of dishes that sent him in the direction of porcelain. As he searched for an appropriate clay body for wheel-thrown dinnerware, Staffel found a philosophical satisfaction with the translucent qualities of porcelain. Previously his studies of Buddhism had sensitized him to the harmony of opposites in light and shadow. And his postwar painting classes with Hans Hofmann had introduced him to the "push-pull" theory of color and made him aware of the value of contradictory elements in painting. In porcelain, Staffel found an embodiment of these ideas.

The dinnerware set never did materialize, but a highly translucent porcelain body did. Staffel's unglazed, thin-walled, wheel-thrown vessels of the sixties—altered by finger thrusts, bulging or depressed walls, and pinched particles of clay haphazardly applied to the exterior—conveyed the opposites of fragility/strength, thick/thin, and light/shadow. Staffel, along with Andreson, brought porcelain out of the exclusive domain of commercial dinnerware and into the studio where its expressive potential could be revealed.

Like Voulkos, William Wyman used the G.I. Bill for his college education, after which he began teaching. By 1958 he was an assistant professor of ceramics at the Massachusetts College of Art, his alma mater. Two years later, he opened the Herring Run Pottery in East Weymouth, producing individually crafted stoneware ranging from hanging planters to architectural murals. At the same time, Wyman constructed two-foot-high slab vessels whose surfaces he enriched with combinations of slips, glazes, sgraffito, and wax resist. To this brew he added words as a textural element. Soon the words began to take on a life of their own. Quotations, snatches of contemporary poetry, or random phrases that pleased him were scrawled in script or typeface-style letters. In the same way a phrase from the Bible or a saying from local folklore connected Pennsylvania German earthenware plates and salt-glazed jugs to the culture that produced them, Wyman used urban graffiti or an emotion-evoking phrase to link his work to the present.

In the hands of Voulkos, Staffel, and Wyman, the nonspecific container was less form and function than a receptacle for ideas. The cup and teapot, also basic to ceramic tradition, underwent a similar metamorphosis. The main instigators of the cup's transfiguration, Ken Price and Ron Nagle, were former Voulkos students—Price at the Los Angeles County Art Institute and Nagle at the University of

203. PETER VOULKOS
STEEL POT
1968. Stoneware, matt iron glaze, height 32½", diameter 11½". Arizona State University Art Museum, Tempe. American Art Heritage Fund

204. WILLIAM WYMAN
THE STRAINS OF JOY SLAB VASE
c. 1962. Stoneware, height 25". Private collection

California in Berkeley. Most of Price's early cups were delicate and tiny, hourglass in shape and glazed in luminous colors. After doing graduate work at Alfred University, Price returned to Los Angeles. Later, in the mid-sixties, Price produced a series of cups sporting small animals such as frogs and snails in place of handles, whimsical appendages reminiscent of the miniature dragon handles on Chinese Ming and Ch'ing dynasty vases. These small objects, whose poetic quality stood in dramatic contrast to the monumental statements of Voulkos and Mason, more than established Price's individuality— they transformed the cup into a vehicle for metaphor and humor.

For Ron Nagle, decorating teacups followed the direction of his mother, who was a china painter. Nagle started using china paints around 1962. It was in that year that he and Jim Melchert (another Voulkos alumnus and Nagle's colleague on the faculty at the San Francisco Art Institute) developed a low-fire, white talc body that could be thrown or slip cast. This clay body enhanced the delicate colors of china paints.

Nagle saw in Price's cups a directness and distance from big and bold forms associated with Abstract Expressionism, and which appealed to him. In the late sixties, Nagle began exploring lustrous glazes whose silky surfaces on small cups seemed to cry out for something to highlight their preciousness. For Nagle, the solution lay in encasing the cups in fitted, precisely crafted wood boxes. During a period when paper and plastic cups proliferated, Nagle basically

above left:
205. RUDOLF STAFFEL
LIGHT GATHERER VESSEL
*c. 1970. Porcelain, height 8¼",
diameter 6". Everson Museum of
Art, Syracuse, N.Y. Gift of
William H. Milliken*

above right:
206. KEN PRICE
SNAIL CUP
*1963. Earthenware, 2¾" x 6½".
Private collection*

207. RON NAGLE
CUP
1969. Earthenware, 3 x 4½ x
3½"; wood box 4½ x 4¾ x 6¼".
Collection R. Joseph Monsen

enshrined what seemed like a vanishing species: the ceramic cup. Framed and isolated, the Nagle cup extolled the cup's historical primacy in ceramic tradition.

In a sense, Abstract Expressionism gave ceramists permission to use traditional forms as a base for new ideas. One quasi-playful exercise at the Los Angeles County Art Institute during Voulkos's tenure was in producing a teapot—body, lid, spout, handle—in two minutes. The point of the exercise was a serious attempt to loosen old rules. Nor were those ceramists at the institute the only ones to challenge the teapot's classic form. Indeed, the freedom that many potters elsewhere displayed in altering the form was emblematic of changing times. The teapot in the mid-twentieth century became what variations of the pitcher stood for in the mid-nineteenth century: both moved a step beyond function. In the case of the decorative pitcher, the surface often reflected pride in the natural wonders of America, a narrative with figures interpreting romantic legends, or it took the form of a figure or face. During the 1960s, the range of interpretations for the teapot reflected a similar plurality of attitudes.

In 1965, the Museum of Contemporary Crafts (often a weather-vane for trends in the sixties) held an exhibition called "The Teapot," which demonstrated just how far, literally and figuratively, the form had been stretched. Karen Karnes's teapot in the exhibit represented a continuation of the Alfred/Harder/Bauhaus tradition, a form suitable for production ware with clean lines, a matt glaze, and within these limitations, personal expression. A combination of Japanese folk pottery and Scandinavian use of color inspired teapots by Ken Ferguson and Michael Cohen, while Peter Voulkos went to the extreme, emphasizing the plasticity of the material over considerations of function, thereby effectively obscuring the boundary between vessel and sculpture. Richard Shaw mounted the spout so low on his fragile assemblage of slabs that any possibility of function was immediately dismissed. Shaw's teapot was an act of ceramic satire, an execution of the form that suggested "a potter laughing at pots."[5]

The Encore of Traditional Techniques

Paul Soldner, Voulkos's first M.F.A. student at the art institute, graduated in 1957 and went to teach ceramics at Scripps College in Claremont when Richard Petterson took a leave of absence. It was in 1960, after he'd received a permanent appointment to Scripps, that Soldner first attempted raku, the low-fire process the Japanese developed in the sixteenth century for producing tea ceremony utensils. In preparation for the Scripps annual arts and crafts festival, Soldner decided to demonstrate raku firing, which he'd read about in Leach's *A Potter's Book*. Soldner expanded on Leach's minimal directions, and built a small portable kiln in the college courtyard. He placed a pot bearing a Leach lead glaze in the red-hot interior, and after about thirty minutes removed the blazing vessel, an act which impressed spectators. But after plunging the pot into the courtyard pond as a post-firing procedure, Soldner was disappointed with the results. On a hunch, he thrust another fired pot into a nearby pile of leaves. Encouraged by the more attractive surface decoration produced in the reducing atmosphere of leaves (rather than the oxidizing effect of water), Soldner spent the next several years experimenting with post-firing reducing agents and a heavily grogged clay body that would resist cracking under the extremes of hot and cold.[6]

THE AMERICANIZATION OF RAKU

Although Bernard Leach was the seminal influence on Soldner's exploration of raku, other Americans a decade earlier had experimented with the process. The fact that Soldner ultimately exerted enormous influence in the spread of the use of raku rather than these earlier ceramists should be explained. Carlton Ball attempted raku only briefly in 1947. Warren Gilbertson, a former student at the School of the Art Institute of Chicago, visited Japan in 1938–40 where he worked with Kanjirō Kawai and learned about raku. When he returned to America, he exhibited his tea caddies, covered boxes, vases, and teapots (some probably raku fired) at the Art Institute. Even though he wrote an article on raku for the American Ceramic Society *Bulletin* in the 1940s, Gilbertson remained ahead of his time in terms of wide public interest. Whatever opportunity to influence others he may have exerted was cut short by his unexpected death in 1954. Hal Riegger, a former Alfred student, worked in raku in the early 1950s and taught a class in raku at the Haystack Mountain School of Crafts. But it was the impact of Voulkos's transformation of form and surface in the late fifties and the artistic and cultural upheaval of the sixties that encouraged the rise of raku. With its often unpredictable results, raku fit the American Hippie/Zen attitude of "go with the flow." A new interest in low-fire ware and Soldner's post-firing use of different reducing agents contributed in large measure to its popularity.

One aspect of raku particularly appealing to Soldner was the relationship between planning and accident. The potter might plan the shape of the pot, but the firing and post-fire reduction ultimately de-

208. PAUL SOLDNER
VASE
1962. Stoneware, white engobe, cobalt and iron, greenish glaze, height 10", diameter 13". Collection S. M. Seganish, Falls Church, Va.

209. ROBERT WINOKUR
FIRST THEOREM: PLAIN GEOMETRY
1982. Salt-glazed stoneware, blue wood ash glaze, slips and engobes, height 9", width 9". Private collection

Winokur expanded salt firings, combining the texture derived from salt glazing with wood ash, glazes, slips, and engobes.

termined surface, texture, and color. Not bound by tradition (he knew little of the appearance of Japanese raku), Soldner was free to invent methods whose results pleased him.[7] His use of the process became an extension of the Abstract Expressionist mode. Uneven surfaces—like the flattened coil of clay defining the neck of his vessels—were heightened by the raku process. Incised lines, splashed or brushed with oxides and stains and combined with a minimal use of glazes, animated his vessels. For creating plaques, Soldner worked on the floor, like Mason, folding, creasing, and texturing slabs of clay with "available objects," including wood, burlap, or tennis shoes. Dissatisfied with his own drawings of figures, he made stencils from familiar figures pictured in magazines. Images of Twiggy, the Beatles, or the Marlboro Man linked Soldner's Abstract Expressionist plaques to Pop Art.

What Soldner developed was labeled raku—but as he discovered on a trip to Japan in 1971, his low-fire process had but a faint, technical relationship to sixteenth-century Japanese raku. While both procedures shared the philosophy of highlighting the character of clay, Soldner's raku displayed more kinship to the Action painters in its application of surface embellishment and in the potter's intimate involvement with every part of the process. Another factor separating the American variant from the Japanese original was that American raku had little or nothing to do with tea ceremony vessels. In fact, the Americanization of raku involved a firing process and techniques altered to the requirements of much larger objects. Steven Kemenyffy and David Middlebrook (both former Soldner students) developed larger tongs, but even tong size proved to be no limitation. Car and barrel kilns came into use so the kiln could be moved away from the pot instead of the reverse; clay bodies were altered to reduce thermal shock, and alternative post-firing methods involved digging holes in the ground and using large barrels, each filled with paper or sawdust as reducing agents. American raku didn't remain static; the repertoire of raku glazes, underglazes, overglazes, and reducing agents increased with each new potter who tackled the process.

SALT GLAZING FOR A GESTURAL SURFACE

In his 1960 edition of *Ceramics*, Glenn Nelson noted that salt glazing had become a forgotten technique, an obituary which turned out to be somewhat premature. There was Paul Soldner, for instance, who began experimenting with salt vapors around 1965. But he was not the leader of a movement back to salt firing. That role fell to Don Reitz. Working on his graduate degree at Alfred University in 1959, Reitz included salt glazing in his investigation of high-fire processes. Vapor glazing appealed to him because it doesn't obscure surface marks as do opaque glazes. Subtle textures and gestural, linear marks inspired by Japanese pottery (fourteenth and fifteenth century Shigaraki and Bizen, and 2000 B.C. Jomon) dominated Reitz's early ware. Searching for nuances of color beyond the gray and gray-brown of traditional ware, Reitz painted cobalt on a kiln brick to flash color on his pots, and threw wood ash or fruit into the kiln to produce dif-

210. *Don Reitz working on the wheel, 1975*

211. DON REITZ
9 TO 5
1971. Salt-glazed stoneware vessel, height 22".

ferent color blushes. Not since Arthur Baggs had an American ex- perimented so much with salt glazing.[8]

For over a decade, Reitz's salt-glazed forms remained functional. But by the late sixties they had transcended utility. Intertwined and baroque handles lengthened to become bas relief surface configura- tions, reminiscent of George Ohr's looped appendages. Besides the traditional pockmarked surface of salt glazing was a variety of tex- tures which Reitz had mastered. He had, in sum, done with salt glaz- ing what Soldner had achieved with raku—taken an aged technique and given it a contemporary identity.

Abstract Sculpture and Minimalism

For a small group of ceramists, certain aspects of Abstract Expres- sionism had, by the early sixties, lost their charm. Ken Price was an example of one who deliberately rejected the monumental for small-scale objects. In 1963, anxious to remove his work from the symmetry of wheel-thrown objects, Price began hand-building amorphous, humplike forms in beehive or bell shapes. These in- creasingly reductive objects ultimately became egg-shaped and cov- ered with glazes or acrylics. But, as Price explained: "I was striving for indistinguishable color and form...I wanted them to look like they were made out of color."[9] He experimented with lacquers bor- rowed from the world of Los Angeles hot-rod racing—hot pinks, ver- dant greens, and intense purples, reds, and blues. These glamorous, joyful colors were juxtaposed with ominous recesses sheltering mys- terious finger-like forms, emerging or retreating from suggestive, erotic cavities. The totality of the work recalls the organic sculpture of Constantin Brancusi and Hans Arp done in sophisticated colors complementary to color field paintings. Price constructed a pedes- tal for each form to emphasize its purpose as a sculpture for contemplation.

212. Ken Price
S. L. Green
1963. Painted clay, 9½ x 10½ x 10½". Whitney Museum of American Art, New York. Gift of the Howard and Jean Lipman Foundation

John Mason, one of the founders of Abstract Expressionism in clay, turned away from his totems of the early sixties and toward more geometric shapes. *Cross Form* (1964) and the circular *Dark Monolith* (1965), both with tiny openings to relieve massiveness, have surfaces smoothed by the artist's hand. By 1966, even these personal traces vanished in starkly geometric sculptures: *Red X, Cross, Oval Form,* and *Cube Form,* all almost five feet in height, and covered with a single brilliant or dark glaze. Like Price, Mason rejected gesture and spontaneity, the hallmarks of Abstract Expressionism's emotionalism. Mason's stark, symmetrical shapes, attractive for their rich, silky glazes, projected a geometric repetition with antecedents in Cubism. At the same time, they have much in common with the Minimalist sculpture of Tony Smith and John McCracken in which meaning is derived from the presence of the work.

The Studio Potter

Neither the sculptural movement in clay nor the reevaluation of function obliterated studio pottery. Encouraged by the life-styles of

213. JOHN MASON
RED X
1966. Stoneware, low-fire glaze, 58½ x 59½ x 17". Los Angeles County Museum of Art

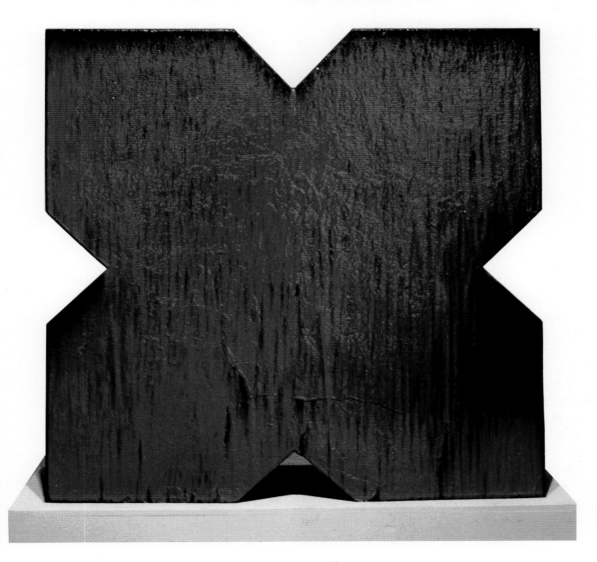

214. JOHN MASON
DARK MONOLITH WITH
OPENING
1965. Stoneware, 65 x 62 x 24".
Private collection

Marguerite Wildenhain and the Natzlers who depended solely on pottery production for their livelihood, and inspired by teachers such as the Heinos, Andreson, and Harder, countless graduates of university classes turned to studio production pottery. Many ceramists seeking a profession in the postwar era saw pottery as a path to independence, a way of having control over one's destiny. This independence also allowed the studio potter to respond to the ferment occurring around the vessel and clay sculpture.

Ken Ferguson exemplifies the kind of potter who incorporated experimentation into studio pottery. An Alfred student during Charles Harder's tenure, in 1958 Ferguson became the director of the Archie Bray Foundation. Six years later, he moved to the Kansas City Art Institute as chairman of the ceramics department. The work he first produced in Kansas displayed the influence of early American ware—well-proportioned covered jars with sturdy lids, ear-shaped

215. KAREN KARNES
COVERED CASSEROLES
*1957. Stoneware, diameter 10".
Private collection*

body handles, and attractive orange iron spots. However, by the late sixties, Ferguson had branched out into wood firings, salt, and low-fire ware. His admiration for Japanese Bizen pottery led him to wrap his pots in straw, disperse salt and organic materials around the kiln, and wood-fire the ware for a rich and varied surface.[10]

Some potters abandoned a college connection altogether. For example, Robert Turner's successors at Black Mountain College, Karen Karnes and her husband, David Weinrib, decided that the future of the school was uncertain. They left in 1954, joining other artist friends in developing the Gate Hill Cooperative at Stony Point, Long Island. Here Weinrib constructed small, slab-built sculptures combining geometric and biomorphic forms. Karnes produced sturdy casseroles thrown with pronounced finger ridges which played against the thickness of a glaze for a two-toned color. Her pulled lid handles, looped forward and back and attached at angles, captured the pliability of wet clay. Birdhouses, weed pots, and fountains made of vessels became identified with her production. Ultimately, Karnes added salt glazing to her repertoire of techniques.

In 1964, the Museum of Contemporary Crafts sponsored "Designed for Production," an exhibit that surveyed the diversity of studio potters, from designers-in-residence for large companies to those like Karnes who maintained individual potteries as their sole source of income. Heath Ceramics of Sausalito, California, founded by Edith Heath, represented that end of the spectrum linked to its industrial legacy. Also in that category was David Gil, an Alfred University graduate, who updated the past by reorganizing Bennington Potters in Vermont for contemporary dinnerware production. The newest production pottery represented in the exhibit was one just founded by Byron Temple, who had trained for studio pottery as a thrower at St. Ives. In 1963, Temple opened a studio in New Jersey, where he produced the tableware shown in the exhibit. His work could be characterized as a form of new classicism—Leach's Japanese aesthetic combined with a Bauhaus austerity.

Another studio potter entering the movement in the sixties was John Glick. A former student of Maija Grotell's at Cranbrook, Glick initiated a number of procedures at his Plum Tree Pottery in Michigan that became the model for many studio potters. His use of assistants, considered more European than American, was one way of placing studio pottery on a business basis without sacrificing its purpose of handcrafted ware. Glick's first assistant threw the forms, allowing him to concentrate on decoration and finishing. When Glick added handbuilt forms to his production, assistants assembled the slabs from his patterns. Glick's ware was primarily functional, with iron spots bleeding through the glaze as the only decoration. Later, stains, oxides, and glazes, dripped, dipped, and brushed on, produced expressive abstract designs. Forms changed when they no longer interested him. Borrowing from tradition, Glick reintroduced the extruder, a tool used by the Moravians in North Carolina and others around the late eighteenth century. Glick widened the tool's possibilities beyond handles by using it to construct sections of his slab-built ware.

216. JOHN GLICK
PITCHER
1980. Stoneware, altered form, height 10". Collection the artist

MERCHANDISING PRODUCTION POTTERY

The mid-century generation of studio potters sold ware through a few department stores, some gift shop galleries, regional summer fairs, or, like the MacKenzies and the Heinos, at their studios. As the number of professional potters increased, the pressure for wider public access grew.

Like Richard Bach decades earlier, Eudorah Moore, president of the Board of the Pasadena Museum of Art, proposed a department within the museum structure to bring together good design in a wide range of manufactured and handcrafted products for a juried exhibition. The art and industry exhibits of the twenties and thirties were the precedent for "California Design," originally an annual exhibit which first opened at the Pasadena Museum in 1956. By 1962, "California Design" ran the gamut from the state's leading craftspersons and designers to young artists seeking recognition. That year entries numbered an overwhelming eight hundred objects, an abundance that not only made an aesthetic evaluation close to impossible, but forced the show to become a triennial event. Ceramics were a significant part of each display, ranging from functional, production pottery to one-of-a-kind objects and architectural sculpture. "California Design" attempted to balance a commercial context with aesthetic principles, just as its predecessors thirty years earlier had done.

The American Craftsmen's Council offered its own solution to merchandising by adapting the League of New Hampshire Craftsmen's successful fairs to a national format. The ACC initiated its first annual fair in Bennington, Vermont, in 1964.[11] More a marketplace than an exhibition, the fair provided a convenient meeting ground for craftsmen, wholesale buyers, and the public. The site changed three times in the next seven years as the number of exhibitors and viewers rapidly increased. Settling in Rhinebeck, New York (the site from 1973–84), the fair developed a jury system and became the model for the mass marketing of quality crafts at fairs around the country. When it outgrew Rhinebeck in 1984, the fair's sponsor, American Craft Enterprises, moved the show to Springfield, Massachusetts. The popularity of these fairs was a sign of prosperous times. The affluent economic climate of the sixties and seventies made it possible for a wide audience to acquire studio pottery; it was no longer solely the purchasing province of an elite few.

The American Potter in the Mid-sixties

Clearly, the potter in the mid-sixties didn't fit into a single neat category. Teaching had become a primary part of the potter's life, whether full or part-time, at a university, art school, or community college. Some ceramists, like Robert Turner, maintained a production pottery for a short time, then began teaching and producing more individual ware. Turner and others who viewed their careers as twofold—pottery and teaching—often confronted conflict in both areas. Supported by teaching, potters such as Voulkos and Soldner felt they could afford to take risks, to experiment, to make mistakes. But their public, and in many instances their college students,

weren't prepared for the unfamiliar. And that included nonfunctional vessels and abstract clay sculpture.

There were more than a few who believed that the issues facing the potter in academia weren't being addressed by the main organization representing potters, the American Ceramic Society. Dissatisfaction with the society (whose primary concern remained the problems of industry) led to the founding in 1959 of the Ceramic Education Council within the ACS; the council, in turn, formed a Design Section in 1961 to stimulate, promote, and improve teaching. Functioning as a forum for ideas and technical information, the group changed its name in 1965 to the unwieldy National Council on Education for the Ceramic Arts (shortened to NCECA and pronounced "N-seek-ah").[12] Then in May 1966, a disagreement with the ACS board resulted in a close vote by NCECA members to become an independent organization. Some of the teachers who led this move for independence included Ted Randall (teaching at Alfred), Vivika Heino, Robert Turner, and Don Reitz (teaching at the University of Wisconsin). The first official meeting of NCECA occurred in 1967 at the invitation of Louis Raynor, who hosted the event at Michigan State University in East Lansing.[13]

The new organization encompassed the range of work in clay produced by the teacher-potter—from functional ware to vessels beyond function, from small, pedestal sculpture to lifesize and architectural sculpture. NCECA arrived at a propitious moment, a time when college ceramics departments were expanding and the complexity of issues facing the ceramics community was further complicated by the aesthetics of Realism and Pop Art.

217. ROBERT TURNER
ASHANTI FORM
1980. Stoneware, applied, stamped, incised decoration, height 13¼". The St. Louis Art Museum. Decorative Arts Society Fund

opposite:
218. TONY COSTANZO
PEACH SQUARE BAFFLED
1982. Cast low-fire slip and wood, 44½ x 41". Collection the artist

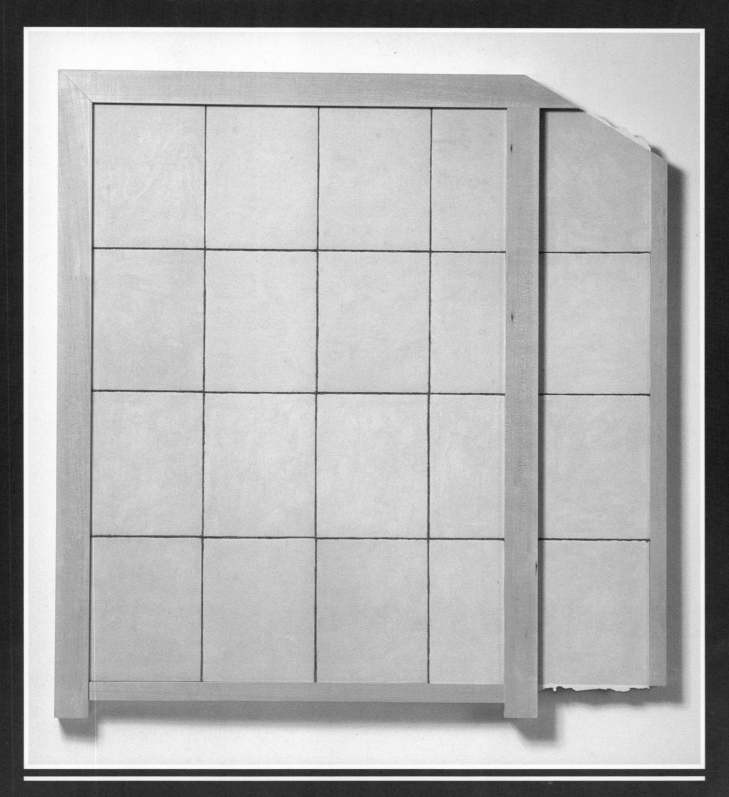

Chapter 13
REALISM AND THE COMMON OBJECT

The Rise of the Common Object

Experimentation and instinct characterized the work of Voulkos, Mason, and Soldner. In the mid-sixties another group of artists emerged whose use of clay was equally expressive, but whose subject matter was entirely different. For these artists, clay was a tool, a method of statement and a way to take aim. The target was nothing less than popular culture.

The first "clay arrow" to strike out at popular culture was probably fired by Robert Arneson. It occurred at the 1961 California State Fair where Arneson, then a teacher at Mills College in Oakland, was demonstrating on the wheel. Instead of producing the usual bowls and vases, Arneson made a series of bottles; he crowned one with a real pop bottle cap and labeled it "no deposit, no return." This act, predating as it did Andy Warhol's painting *Green Coca Cola Bottles* (1962), was indeed prophetic. But it was not until 1963, after he began teaching at the University of California at Davis, that Arneson's choice of everyday objects as subjects for clay began dominating his work. That year he was invited to participate in "California Sculpture," an exhibition at the Oakland Museum including the work of Voulkos and Mason, his idols. Arneson recalled his exhilaration: "[The invitation] put my mind in gear...and I cut myself loose and let every scatological kind of notation from my mind flow freely."[1] The result was a rush of clay images of toilets, bathroom scales, and sinks just as a cartoonist—which Arneson had been in college—might imagine them. They seemed like menacing, devouring, anthropomorphic machines, in some ways aesthetically akin to Marcel Duchamp's ready-made *The Fountain* (1917) and Jim Dine's *Black Bathroom* (1962), the latter a painting supporting a real sink. The difference was that Arneson depicted his objects with surrealistic overtones and Miró-like symbols. Even with all its humor and surrealism, for its time the work was strong stuff: Arneson's *John Figure* was not accepted for the 1963 Oakland exhibition because it was

opposite:
219. ROBERT ARNESON
SMORGI-BOB, THE CHEF
1971. Earthenware with vinyl tablecloth and wood table, 73 x 66 x 53". San Francisco Museum of Modern Art

above:
220. ROBERT ARNESON
6 PACK
1965. Stoneware, 10 x 12 x 18". Collection René and Veronica DiRosa, Napa, Calif.

considered an attack on American capitalism. Undaunted, Arneson produced six more toilets, a bathroom sink with a smear on the basin reading "hard to get out stain," and a bathroom scale that, like his toilets, looked as if it might devour the user.

Arneson's ironical, satirical works in the sixties retained the gestural mode of his pre–Pop Art vessels and sculptures; he continued to adhere to an expressionistic style in contrast to the cool, distant approach of Pop Art painters such as Andy Warhol. Returning to the pop bottle in 1965, Arneson toyed with commercial slogans in *Things Go Better With Coke* by adding a real Seven-Up bottle to the six-pack, and surrealistically portraying *Diet Coke* as six skinny bottles. Besides representing an actual object and giving it human qualities, Arneson's pop bottle was both a symbol of American culture and a three-dimensional pun linking the visual image to the verbal in his titles or words on the object itself.

The idea of machines as devouring creatures reappeared in another series based on familiar objects: *Toaster* (1965) is a nightmarish depiction of slightly burnt fingers emerging from one of the slots; in *Typewriter* (1966), fingertips with painted nails stand in place of keys. Aggressive and macabre, both machines provoke uncomfortable, nervous laughter from the viewer.

A technical achievement allowed Arneson to shift from stoneware to a low-fire clay body. Stoneware clays tended to dull the

221. ROBERT ARNESON
THE PALACE AT 9 A.M.
1974. Terra-cotta and glazed ceramic, 24 x 118 x 84". Courtesy Frumkin/Adams Gallery, New York

The original *Alice House* made in 1966 was unavailable for Robert Arneson's retrospective exhibition at the San Francisco Museum of Modern Art in 1974. As a result, he produced this version which, compared to the earlier work, shows the house aging under hard use and landscape growth. The title pays homage to a 1932–33 sculpture of the same title by Alberto Giacometti.

222. ED FORDE
UNTITLED [Carrots Doing
Pushups]
*1974. Stoneware, length 5–15".
Individual pieces variously
owned*

Robert Arneson was among the
first to use multiple images and
to alter perspective by their size
and placement, as in his *Smorgi-
Bob, The Chef* (fig. 219). Forde is
working with similar ideas, and
in this instance playing up the
decade's concern for health food
and exercise.

bright color accents that Arneson preferred for his handbuilt sculptures. When Ron Nagle and Jim Melchert formulated their white
earthenware (or whiteware) clay in 1962, which enhanced bright colors, it likewise seemed tailor-made for his purposes. In a 1966–67
series, Arneson utilized whiteware to its advantage. The series was
produced shortly after he moved his family to a suburban tract
home. In the series, cups, plates, small murals, and boxes carried an
image of the new Arneson home, so named "Alice House" after the
street. The pièce de résistance was an eight-foot-long floor sculpture
of the house and its surrounding landscape. The sixty assembled
parts included lush shrubbery, the garage with its basketball hoop,
and the family's Volkswagen bus in the driveway. Images of Alice
House obsessed Arneson, in part because he'd always thought that
being an artist meant living in a cold garret in Greenwich Village,
rather than in a tract house in comfortable and conventional
suburbia.

Arneson's embracing of banal objects was part of a unique expression which critic Peter Selz defined as "funk." Borrowing a term
from jazz for a word referring to "the blues that gives you a happy/
sad feeling," Selz regarded Bay Area Funk as owing a debt to Dadaism for its irreverent, sensuous, and scatological qualities.[2] At
University Art Museum, University of California, Berkeley, the
1967 exhibition of "Funk" that Selz curated included, among others,

Arneson, David Gilhooly (one of Arneson's students), Voulkos, and former Voulkos students Melchert, Price, and Manuel Neri. Like "Abstract Expressionist Ceramics" a year earlier, "Funk" provided a context for work in which ideas were foremost, and which took shape quickly and freely, without regard for material or form. Unlike Dadaism, which aspired to change the world, Funk's intentions were to change perception of the world: by putting familiar objects in an unfamiliar context the world could be seen afresh.

For those ceramists whose careers began in the mid-sixties, Arneson, like Voulkos, opened a new arena for work in clay; he legitimized the common object as acceptable subject matter. The object of choice for Fred Bauer in the mid-sixties was the nonfunctional machine. A Tiffany Foundation Grant in 1966 allowed Bauer, who was teaching at the University of Michigan, the opportunity to construct bizarre, fantasy machines supporting an assortment of steering wheels, fire truck hoses, and protruding fins. *Steam Drill—Slot Pump* (1967), a five-foot-high gadget tower having windmill-like arms, wings, and shooting flames suggested movement although that would in fact never occur. Appropriately labeled Funk for its seductive colors and sexually suggestive hose, Bauer's pump and similar works that followed were, like Arneson's *Toaster*, surrealistic and disquieting. Bauer's machines enticed the viewer with lively colors until the sight of human entrails and slightly disguised genitals shifted delight to feelings of dread or shock.

Arneson's fascination with domestic suburban life directed his energies away from appliances to habitat. In 1971, he went "inside" to examine Alice House's contents. Working from slides he took of the aftermath of family dinners with their partly empty platters and plates, Arneson produced a clay compendium of domestic detritus. In the *Dirty Dishes* series (1971), he approached the half-eaten doughnut, the knife and fork askew on a plate, and *The Last Slice of Apple Pie* somewhat like an archeologist who can reconstruct the history of a culture from tiny shards. The culmination of this food fixation was a self-portrait of sorts with Arneson in the guise of a lip-licking chef (*Smorgi-Bob, the Chef*, 1971) supervising a table laden with platters of turkey, ham, cheeses, wine, tossed salad, etc. Arneson heightened the perspective by creating an exaggerated, trapezoid-shaped table. The color, or rather, the lack of it, makes the construction remarkable. Chef, table, and its contents are glazed a glossy white. By eliminating color with one stroke Arneson defied centuries of luridly colored food pictured in paintings as well as food's contemporary depiction on television, in magazine ads, and on billboards.

The ubiquitous representations of food in the media made cuisine prime subject material for some Pop artists. Claes Oldenburg's giant hamburgers with cheese and tomato, and his slices of pie, cake, and popsicles which appeared in the early sixties made of plaster, vinyl, and kapok served as monuments to the food preferences of American consumers. Mineo Mizuno's 1975 trompe l'oeil hamburgers and slices of apple pie on paper plates with paper cups were ceramic counterparts of Oldenburg's work. The health food culture of the seventies inspired Ed Forde's field of forty-nine ceramic *Carrots Doing Pushups* (1974). Lined up like an Army drill team, the carrots

223. FRED BAUER
STEAM DRILL-SLOT PUMP
1967. Painted earthenware, height 65". American Craft Museum, New York

224. ROBERT ARNESON
JOHN FIGURE
*1965. Earthenware, 11 parts,
37 x 27". Collection the artist*

incorporated Funk humor and serial imagery. But amusement regarding food consumption eventually evolved into indictment of
gluttony. Victor Spinski's late-seventies ceramic series focused on
overconsumption and waste—garbage cans filled with half-eaten
meals, bones, and empty bottles. Arneson's six-pack had become
trash.

Traditional Forms Meet Pop Art

Characteristic of early Pop Art was the use of a single image repeated
in different versions. In clay, that image often took traditional functional forms. Arneson captured a mood of the late sixties in a series
of thirty-five teapots, some thrown and constructed with a casual-
ness reminiscent of Voulkos's "two minute teapot." *A Social Gathering in the Late Afternoon* (1969) speaks of the social ritual of tea
and its connection to a specific form, but here Arneson moved beyond the familiar. If "teapots and cups are [to the potter] as the human figure is to the sculptor" as one critic suggested, then Arneson's
substitution of human genitalia for teapot spouts and lids, as in *A
Tremendous Teapot* and *Spiked Tea* (with its reference to the drug
culture), had an inherent, if not surrealistic, logic.[3]

Another artist who transformed traditional forms into Pop Art
was Roy Lichtenstein. An established painter, Lichtenstein was
known for his use of comic strip characters delineated in a manner

225. ROBERT ARNESON
A SOCIAL GATHERING IN
THE LATE AFTERNOON
*1969. Earthenware, 11 x 9 x 5".
Private collection, Boston*

that flattened both figure and ground as in reductive industrial repro-
ductions. For a year's time beginning in 1965, Lichtenstein collaborated with ceramist Ka Kwong Hui at Rutgers University, where both
men were teaching; together they produced a series of mold-made,
thick, hotel china cups. Influenced by Picasso's *Glass of Absinthe*
and Leger's use of primary colors on his ceramic sculptures, Lichtenstein, with Kwong's technical assistance, decorated the cups with
the benday dots, solid color areas, heavy outlines, and shadows characteristic of the artist's paintings.[4] Four, five, or six cups, painted in
black and white or in intense colors, were then precariously stacked
on a saucer as though they were waiting to be washed. Thus arranged, the cups metamorphosed into sculpture. Their purposeful
lack of content or gesture and their seeming abandon by human care
turn the cups into a metaphor for people in a mechanized culture.

Arneson returned to the cup form in 1971–72. His *Coffee Cup
with Round Holes and Porcelain Balls* was an exercise in appearing
to destroy volume while flaunting function; holes punched through
a cup and saucer didn't prevent the set from being filled with small
porcelain balls. *Taste Test* and a series of *Mountain* cups spoof commercial market research and advertising (the latter poking fun at
Folger Coffee ads about "mountain grown" coffee). Arneson, like
Lichtenstein, Price, and Nagle, moved the cup beyond function,
thereby turning tradition into sculpture capable of conveying a diversity of ideas.

Michael Frimkess saw this same possibility in the vase form.
After he left the hermetic confines of Voulkos's Los Angeles and
Berkeley classrooms, Frimkess studied classical pottery, especially
Greek and oriental, through regular visits to museums in New York
and Boston. He applied his new knowledge to the production of exaggerated Chinese ginger jars. After Price and Nagle shared their technology for low-fire ware, Frimkess covered the jars with a white slip
and decorated them with contemporary scenes, using china paints
and low-fire glazes. Instead of oriental women in kimonos serving

226. MICHAEL FRIMKESS
THE MARRIAGE OF AUNTIE
SUSANNA
*in the form of lotrophoros hydra.
1977. Stoneware, china paint,
height 34", rim diameter 11½".
Private collection*

tea in tree-covered arbors, Frimkess depicted his environment—such as a college ceramics class in *Things Ain't What They Used to Be* (1965). (Like scenes from a comic strip, his figures make typical classroom comments while they throw and fire pots, their conversation inscribed in clay.) *Jumpin' at the Moon Lodge*, a similarly shaped vessel, is an explosion of figures in bright china paint colors; Uncle Sam, Superman, Hare Krishna, and Santa Claus, who is wearing a Hitler mask, symbolize the artist's social and political concerns. The destruction of indigenous cultures is the theme of a jar titled *Homenaje a la Maquina* ("Homage to the Machine," 1973). In a more hopeful mood Frimkess produced a series in the mid-seventies of four-foot-high columns of stacked vessels, which he named hookahs or melting pots. A rhythmic combination typical of Greek, Zuni, Chinese, and Peruvian pottery, the melting pots physically embody Frimkess's desire for harmony between cultures. Other ves-

227. MICHAEL FRIMKESS
JUMPIN' AT THE MOON
LODGE
1968. Low-fire clay, 27½ x 14¾ x 14¾". Scripps College, Claremont, Calif. Collection Mr. and Mrs. Fred Marer

228. HOWARD KOTTLER
PEACE MARCH PLATE
*1967. Porcelain blank plate with
ceramic decals and luster,
diameter 10¼". Collection the
artist*

229. MARILYN LEVINE
TENNIS SHOES
*1969. Stoneware, slab construc-
tion, lifesize. Collection Sue and
Richard Bender, Berkeley, Calif.*

sels from this period pay homage to his favorite jazz musicians and singers.

Art of the sixties and seventies abounded in social commentary, and this was certainly the hallmark of the ceramic Pop artist. Indeed, for some ceramists, this emphasis on social commentary nearly obliterated the more conventional concepts of crafts. Such was the case with Howard Kottler, whose fascination with the ceramic decal and its ease of application led him to a series featuring repeated images. More concerned with idea than with form, Kottler worked with porcelain blanks, commercial plates used by china painters whose industrial finish enhanced decal colors. American history, art history, and conflicts of the 1960s were Kottler's themes: a plate made in 1968 featured a multiple portrait of Lincoln, the dome of the Capitol, a pistol, and the Lincoln Memorial stretched across its diameter— poignant reminders of past and present political assassinations. Another series of plates with decals of the American flag's stripes in disarray symbolized for Kottler the national disarray of the sixties. Like Lichtenstein with his mass-produced hotel cups, Kottler regarded industrial blanks and repetitive images as epitomizing the mechanization of American culture.[5] However, many of Kottler's colleagues didn't sense his intentions, and were profoundly dismayed by his use of materials so blatantly removed from the craftsman's tradition.

Super Realism and the Common Object

Kottler's combinations of industrial ceramics for their shock value was characteristic of art in the 1960s. The social and political earthquakes of the sixties and early seventies produced their share of aftershocks in the arts, and ceramics was no exception. One consequence was the increasing appearance of objects in clay not previously considered appropriate subject matter. Consistent with Arneson's use of one object to encompass many levels of meaning and experience, Marilyn Levine chose apparel and leather accessories as her clay images. A Canadian with a master's degree in chemistry, Levine arrived at the University of California in Berkeley in the late 1960s to pursue an advanced degree in clay sculpture. In her first attempt to simulate clothing in clay she produced a series of tennis shoes and socks. Then a friend presented her with a worn pair of leather boots. Examining the scuffed and scratched gift, Levine realized leather was a material so much more capable than others of recording and preserving a personal history of its use or abuse. Well-worn leather bespoke living and life.

In her early work of handbuilt slab boxes, shoes, hats, and socks, Levine reinforced the clay slabs with fiberglass, at the time a new industrial material. (The use of fiberglass with clay had been pioneered a few years earlier by Daniel Rhodes.) When she began fashioning the clay to imitate leather, Levine shifted to nylon fibers for greater strength.[6] *Knapsack* (1970), a mass of pocket straps, buckles, and eyelets, is characteristic of the trompe l'oeil nature of her objects. Instead of adopting Arneson's expressive use of clay, Levine

230. MARILYN LEVINE
H.R.H. BRIEFCASE
*1985. Clay and mixed media
hand-built (slab construction),
16 x 17½ x 6¾". Collection
Marilynn and Ivan Karp*

231. RICHARD SHAW
PLATE
1976. Porcelain, diameter 15".
Collection the artist

232. RICHARD SHAW
OPEN BOOK II
1978. Porcelain, 3¼ x 12⅞ x
11⅛". Everson Museum of Art,
Syracuse, N.Y.

moved toward realistic representation. *Knapsack* and other objects of the early seventies—a man's leather jacket worn at the elbows and hanging on a hook, a doctor's old black bag with its well-worn handle—implied use in the real world. The one instance when this wasn't true of Levine's work occurred when she was invited in 1971 to send cups to a Los Angeles exhibition, "The Cup Show" (one of many shows in the 1970s featuring cups). A series resulted—cups with zippers, eyelets, fringes, buckles, straps, handles. To confuse reality further, Levine laced some of the cups with real leather.

In time, Levine's suitcases, briefcases, and golf bags became increasingly realistic in detail. She began using nonceramic materials such as oil paint, shoe polish, and hardening oils, which gave her surfaces an exceptionally leather-like appearance, further eroding the viewer's ability to distinguish between representation and reality. Into the 1980s, Levine continued to operate within the Super Realist realm of sculptors like John De Andrea and Duane Hanson, who undermine the viewer's sense of reality with lifesize, lifelike figures in fiberglass and vinyl.

Levine's work is a reversal of Claes Oldenburg's aesthetics. Oldenburg's use of soft materials to represent hard objects (for example, his *Soft Toilet* of 1966), was turned on its head by Levine's use of clay, which was fired to hardness, to represent leather, a soft material. In contrast to industrial, ubiquitous plastic, leather has the ability to assume a personality, to inject narrative content and mood which Levine projects through creases, worn and frayed edges, broken straps, missing buckles, and overall composition.

THE SLIP-CAST, MOLD-MADE OBJECT

Trompe l'oeil expression also became part of Richard Shaw's objects during the early 1970s. Shaw had harbored an affinity for eighteenth-century English Staffordshire, but that interest had gone unreflected in his work until Ron Nagle introduced him to the use of china paints. Then, in 1971, Shaw spent a year collaborating with sculptor Robert Hudson at Shaw's studio in Marin County near San Francisco. An inveterate junk collector, Shaw had selected a variety of store-bought small objects, along with rocks, pieces of logs, and twigs for slip casting. Wheel-thrown and handbuilt forms completed the inventory of component parts which both men proceeded to assemble into teapots, jars, and cups. Underglazes, china paints, air brushing, and fabrics pressed on the surface added texture and decoration. The majority of pieces from their joint casting—each made his own objects from the collection of parts—were surrealistic assemblages of unrelated forms. Like their eighteenth-century Chinese and European counterparts, these assemblages imitated familiar materials in the form of containers. Exhibited at the San Francisco Museum of Art in 1973, the Shaw/Hudson slip-cast porcelain objects overturned the Arts and Crafts prohibition against this industrial technique by suggesting a wide range of contemporary possibilities.

Whereas Howard Kottler purchased ready-made molds and decals, Shaw made his own molds and decals or employed a professional mold maker for certain objects. A grant in 1973 from the National Endowment for the Arts to explore a photo-silkscreen method of reproducing decals allowed Shaw to work with a professional silkscreen artist, perfecting ceramic inks that burn into the clay surface when fired at a low temperature. This technological advance appeared shortly thereafter in Shaw's work in representations of fragments of postcards, stamped envelopes, newspaper clippings, labels from canned goods, and playing cards. Historically, similar subject matter had been part of the still-life paintings of nineteenth-century American trompe l'oeil artists John Peto and William Harnett and the early Cubist collages of Picasso and Braque. At first, the flat surfaces of plates, wooden boards, or corrugated cardboard simulated in clay served as bases for these collages. Around 1977, Shaw shifted to a series of book jars—actually containers whose lids were disguised by objects strewn over the top book—stacked in twos, threes, and fours. With meticulous attention to detail, Shaw used decals to recreate book pages, marbleized covers, and spine patterns. Odd tidbits on the top book such as playing cards, a matchbook, or pipe conveyed the notion that someone had carelessly assembled, then abandoned the objects.

Along with the ceramic books, Shaw began another assortment of trompe l'oeil, this time slip-cast objects in the shape of peculiar walking figures: paint cans became heads, odd pieces of lumber and twigs assumed the position of legs, tubes of paint served as fingers, and a plunger substituted as a foot. Shaw's choices for body parts and their stance, sitting or striding forward, gave each figure a distinct personality. Humorous and strangely appealing, these assembled objects call to mind the detritus of affluence, the constant proliferation of used and abandoned products in a throwaway, consumer society.

233. LUKMAN GLASGOW
HANDPAINTED SKYSCAPE
1975. Whiteware, china paints,
lusters, height 20", diameter 14".
Collection Mr. and Mrs. Anson
Moore

Super Realism was given a surrealistic twist by David Furman in 1976 with a series of sculptures representing ceramic studio tools. Furman assembled slip-cast sponges, syringes, and wood-trimming tools, balanced precariously on cloth-covered boards. In an amusing interpretation of the essential rolling pin (used to form large slabs), *The Irresistible Force vs. The Immovable Object* shows a relaxation of the laws of nature as one rolling pin flattens another. In a collaboration similar to that of Shaw's and Hudson's, in 1979 Furman and Ed Forde produced a series of wall drawings that combined graphic lines with assortments of pencils, erasers, and paintbrushes normally found on an artist's drawing board. Like a magician willing to reveal his trickery, in *Wall Drawing #2* Furman included the molds he used to create his pencils.

This trend toward trompe l'oeil objects led to an exhibition at the Laguna Beach Museum of Art in southern California in 1977, "Illusionistic Realism in Contemporary Ceramic Sculpture," which presented the works of Furman, Forde, Arneson, and others. In *Handpainted Skyscape* (1975), ceramist Lukman Glasgow's slip-cast disembodied hand held a paint brush as it swept down a wall trailing a swatch of luminous sky and puffy, iridescent clouds. Like other works in the exhibit, Glasgow's hand, brush, and sky were objects culled from their usual context, employing trompe l'oeil details and surrealistically flaunting the physical laws of balance and spatial tension. Like the paintings of René Magritte, Salvador Dalí, and Giorgio De Chirico, the variations on Super Realism displayed in the

234. DAVID FURMAN
THE IRRESISTIBLE FORCE vs.
THE IMMOVABLE OBJECT
1976–77. Slip-cast earthenware, press-molded, underglazes, 4 x 18 x 19". Private collection

exhibit conveyed more than just a sense of mystery and ambiguity through surreal exaggeration.

THE ARTIST IN THE FACTORY

In spite of the fact that technological improvements were deemed essential for the advancement of ceramics by such paragons as Charles Binns, Arthur Baggs, Charles Harder, and others influential in earlier years, the closer the ceramic artist came to the use of tools intimately associated with industry, the more such practices alarmed segments of the ceramic community. Even though the results of the Shaw/Hudson collaboration served to break down some objections to slip casting, resistance remained.

One effort to diminish this division between industrial methods and craft came from industry itself. In 1974, the Kohler Company of Sheboygan, Wisconsin (in association with the John Michael Kohler Arts Center), invited ceramists Jack Earl and Tom LaDousa into its

235. HOWARD KOTTLER
DREAM STREET OR THE OLD BAG NEXT DOOR IS NUTS
1976. Earthenware, unglazed, height 13". Collection Joan Mannheimer

factory as temporary artists-in-residence. Funded in part by a grant from the National Endowment for the Arts, Kohler's offer of access to its technology was innovative and also appropriate given the company's primary working material—slip-cast vitreous china used to produce bathtubs, urinals, toilets, and sinks (though not, of course, of the Robert Arneson variety). The four weeks that Earl and La-Dousa spent assembling sculptures by carving, modeling, dissecting, and joining Kohler's precast forms introduced the artists to power tools and to working with clay in a dried condition.[7] The Kohler Company was so pleased with the interaction between artist and factory that it initiated year-round programs offering individual fellowships, group workshops, and conferences. A conference on industry and the artist-craftsman held at the Kohler Company plant in 1975 moved beyond the usual discussions of the artist-designer and industry to that of artists working alongside plant production. In the years that followed, participants in the Kohler program found aspects of industrial technology—larger kilns, electric clay mixers, a variety of extruders—enormously useful for work on a grand scale. Karen Massaro used ceramic slabs as surfaces for glaze paintings; George Mason turned flat slabs into large modular wall and floor pieces. Liberated from using the wheel in the Kohler program in 1979, Coille Hooven temporarily abandoned functional ware for a combination of cast and handbuilt figures and animals in elaborate tableaux. Instead of changing her direction, a few years later Deborah Horrell enlarged the scale; she built a five-foot slab figure for *Flesh and Bones* (1983), balanced against a six-foot-high nest of bones.

However, until the end of the 1970s, incorporating industrial methods and products into the work of individual ceramists remained problematical. Howard Kottler in particular was singled out. The ire of traditionalists toward Kottler's combinations of commercial molds and factory-made decals was focused on his *Dream Street or the Old Bag Next Door is Nuts* (1976). This pedestal sculpture, featured in an article on "Illusionistic Realism" for *Ceramics Monthly*, showed a commercial mold of a Victorian house next to an overscale grocery bag filled with walnuts. The unglazed white color of the nuts and the house evoke a dreamlike fantasy in trompe l'oeil detail in contrast to the realistic wood grain pattern on the out-of-scale paper bag. The visual/verbal pun almost distracts from Kottler's intentions, namely a juxtaposition of old-fashioned values represented by the Victorian house with the falsification of materials in the form of the wood-grained bag. Kottler's statement about the demise of ethical standards in the post-Watergate, post-Vietnam era escaped the readers of *Ceramics Monthly*. Instead they condemned the technique in letters to the editor, fueling a controversy that raged for months over the ethics of Kottler's use of commercial molds and decals.

The irate letter-writers were jousting with windmills. In the exhibition "Clay from Molds" (1978) at the John Michael Kohler Arts Center, eighty artists explored subjects ranging from political statements to psychological portraits. Whether the molds were purchased from a company or made from objects selected by the artist, the aesthetic potential was apparent and would soon overcome the label of a disreputable technique.

Chapter 14

THE RESILIENT VESSEL

By the late 1960s, American ceramics had changed to such an extent that it was hardly the same medium it had been only twenty years previous. Though there had always been American potters who leaned toward sculpture, the Voulkos/Mason revolution had, in the simplest sense, dramatically divided ceramic activity into two major branches: one composed of those who used clay for sculptural purposes and the other for whom function remained paramount. Shooting off the sculptural branch were many other extensions, each with its own outgrowths—from the large forms of Voulkos and Mason to Soldner's plaques to Arneson's last slice of apple pie. The complexity of the ceramic art scene was such that even these two seemingly different approaches intertwined. And surviving—indeed, flourishing—in the midst of all this new and strange growth was that most enduring of clay forms, the vessel.

Nor, however, had the vessel remained static among so much revision and upheaval. There continued to be those potters who upheld the importance of function, whereas others weren't prepared to abandon the vessel as a form, yet regarded function as too restricting. In spite of the polarity of these views, each group influenced the other.

Functional Pottery and the Consumer Society

The first half of the twentieth century had witnessed the birth of the studio potter in America. By the late 1960s this way of working, fostered in part by the émigrés of the thirties and forties, and the impact of Bernard Leach's visits, had become as much an American tradition as a European one. The strength of this new tradition was also responsible for helping to sustain the vitality of functional pottery. At the same time, the far older tradition of American folk pottery, revitalized in the 1930s in Jugtown, North Carolina, and by the Meaders family in Georgia, blossomed during the sixties. Circumstances peculiar to this period and the following decade contributed to the flourishing of both the studio and folk pottery movements.

opposite:
236. LUCY LEWIS
BIRD VASE
c. 1983. Earthenware, with designs on polished white slip, height 10", diameter 14". Private collection

The matriarch of a family of women potters at the Acoma Pueblo in New Mexico, Lucy Lewis and her daughters adapted designs based on pottery of the Mimbres, a prehistoric Southwestern culture. The younger generations in the Lucy Lewis and Maria Martinez families, taught by the older women, are continuing the tradition.

above:
237. MICHAEL CARDEW
PITCHER
1972. Glazed earthenware, height 8¼", diameter 6½". Collection Albert A. Struckus

THE FOLK TRADITION

The affluence of the 1960s was one reason for the renewed interest in collecting and preserving traditional American crafts. Another was the threatened loss of folk arts in the face of increasing technology. The view that folk pottery was a tradition to be cherished—and one that had been gaining momentum since the thirties—helped to instigate several Smithsonian Institution projects involving folk potters of the southeastern states. Folk ware was featured in Smithsonian museum shops, and in 1967 the Smithsonian sponsored a documentary on the prominent pottery families in the South, including the Meaders of Georgia. Lanier Meaders continued the family pottery after the death of his father, Cheever, in 1967. Along with other north Georgia pottery families, the Meaders were yielding to the pressures for increased production. Documentation by the Smithsonian was important because there were few records of how folk pottery was made and present-day technology was now altering these traditional methods. The use of electric pug mills, commercial glazes, and modern gas kilns inevitably changed the shape, feel, and surface decoration of folk pottery.

Although many family potteries of the Southeast were benefiting from modern equipment, financial problems were forcing Vernon Owens of Jugtown Pottery to close shop. This was prevented unexpectedly when in 1968 a Massachusetts pottery teacher, Nancy Sweezy, helped out. To save Jugtown, Sweezy enlisted the help of several folklife foundations, as well as the Smithsonian Office of Folklife Programs and Country Roads, a nonprofit corporation dedicated to preserving American folk arts. Once in charge, Sweezy retained some of the oriental shapes and glazes introduced by Jacques Busbee in the thirties, and returned to more traditional forms and glazes. With the addition of a new kiln, electric wheels, a large sales room, and an apprentice program, Jugtown gradually returned to solvency.

Jugtown's revival came at a period when other area potteries also were experiencing a renewal of interest from the community and the tourist trade. Both Zedith Teague Gardner of Teague Pottery and the Cole family, which operated several potteries, welcomed new customers but resisted sweeping technological changes. They continued working in sheds built over earthen floors, digging their own clay, and using wood-burning kilns. Piedmont tradition, as Nancy Sweezy observed, is "being raised from childhood in sureness that this is the right way to do it, then doing it for a lifetime."[1]

The same regard for tradition could be applied to native American potters. Responding to the pressure of merchandising, in 1973 the Eight Northern Pueblos Indian Council of New Mexico initiated the first juried crafts show in order to attract collectors. Educational programs on Pueblo tradition at the Indian Pueblo Cultural Center (incorporated in 1975) in Albuquerque, New Mexico, increased public awareness of Indian crafts and provided an additional marketing outlet.

Of equal consequence was the recent interaction between native American potters and the community at large. In the late sixties, Maria Martinez (now over eighty years old and the grande dame

238. VERNON OWENS,
JUGTOWN POTTERY
CHURN WITH LID, TWO EAR
HANDLES
*1982. Salt glaze, fired in oil-
burning kiln to 2300°F, height
18", width 9". Private collection*

of Pueblo potters) visited Colorado State University where she and her son Popovi Da demonstrated coil building, decorating, and the firing of a dung kiln. (Popovi Da was an accomplished potter in his own right and in the sixties had developed new ware, sienna in color.) With this workshop, colleges became the meeting ground for a cultural exchange between students and Indian potters. In 1974, Martinez and several members of her family spent four weeks at a summer workshop directed by Susan Peterson and sponsored by the University of Southern California. The students' enthusiastic response made the program an annual event, with different Pueblo potters participating over the years. Peterson's ongoing friendship with Martinez resulted in a book, *The Living Tradition of Maria Martinez* (1977), which added substantially to the literature on native American potters.

Peterson's book focused on one of the families introduced earlier in a landmark exhibit, "Seven Families in Pueblo Pottery" (1974). At the Maxwell Museum of Anthropology in Albuquerque, New Mexico, the show authoritatively identified the most prominent Indian potters in the state. Curated by Rick Dillingham, the exhibit and catalogue illustrated the development of Indian style and tech-

239. KAREN KARNES
COVERED JAR
*1981. Wood-fired stoneware,
height 18". Private collection*

240. CHARLES COUNTS
PLATE
*1981. Stoneware, diameter
10½". Collection the artist*

nique at a time when most native pottery was submitting to subtle modifications. Aesthetic considerations rather than traditional symbols established designs. Watertight utility was no longer possible for the production of highly popular black ware, which required a very low firing temperature. Tradition also accommodated practicality. Santana, Maria Martinez's daughter-in-law, smoothed her pots with an old Calumet baking powder lid (instead of a river-washed stone used by many native American potters), after which her husband, Adam, sanded her ware with paper imported from England, a nod to technological improvements.[2]

THE MELDING OF STUDIO AND FOLK POTTER

Although no present research has documented the parallels between the increasing prominence of the folk and studio potter during the 1960s and 1970s, certain events point to interaction in this development. In the 1940s and 1950s, rural studio potters Wildenhain, Karnes, and Turner had inspired many to join their ranks. The increasing visibility of folk potters in the following decade more than reinforced the virtues of this life-style. Then too, the conditions of life in the late sixties—crowded cities, the civil rights upheavals, and the counterculture's emphasis on reconnecting with nature, on finding a meaningful activity and purpose in life—likewise affected many potters of the period who began to question their goals and direction. As a result, one group of potters who opted for a rural life specifically chose areas known for their regional crafts. Kentucky-born Charles Counts with his wife, Rubynelle, also a potter, built Rising Fawn in 1963, a studio-workshop in northwestern Georgia, which also served as a marketing outlet for local craftspersons. Updating regional craft skills and a belief in honest workmanship inspired similar efforts in Massachusetts by Richard Bennett, who opened the Great Barrington Pottery in the late sixties as a center for folk pottery. Sid Oakley and his wife, Pat, opened the Cedar Creek Pottery in Creedmoor, North Carolina, in 1969. The Oakleys, natives of North Carolina, had studied ceramics at schools in the South. In the next decade, Cedar Creek added a gallery for contemporary regional crafts and for the Oakleys' collection of North Carolina folk pottery.

African Folk Pottery in America

Up until this time little attention had been given to African pottery, but that began to change when Charles Counts invited Michael Cardew to address the Southwest Region of the American Crafts Council in June 1972. Cardew, an Englishman and former student of Bernard Leach's, had spent many years in Ghana and Nigeria where he developed pottery training centers. His book, *Pioneer Pottery* (1969), distilled his experiences in Africa, and was as significant for many potters as Leach's book had been thirty years earlier. In his lecture, Cardew suggested an exchange between Nigerian and American potters. Counts raised money in 1972 for a six-week tour of the Southeast by Cardew and two of his students—Kofi Athey and

Ladi Kwali, who became the star performer. Counts described the reaction to her coil-building demonstration before NCECA members at the Arrowmount School of Crafts in Tennessee: "Ladi Kwali was a sensation. She kept 1,500 pottery teachers literally spellbound while she did the ritual dance that is the only way she works at home in her village."[3]

Cardew had hoped black Americans would respond to their African heritage through his students' pottery demonstration, but instead the unexpected occurred. Though there were American-Nigerian exchanges during the years 1972–76, *white* Americans rather than black Americans were most receptive to Kwali's pottery and Cardew's philosophy. Although Cardew failed to attract southern blacks to pottery production, the Englishman charmed Counts and his colleagues. As Counts explained:

> *Cardew gave voice to those of us who want to be pottery makers—no more, no less. He was a living example of Yanagi's unknown craftsman and of course, Leach's great call on the universal spirit deep inside each of us. Yes, a new generation of mug makers and bowl and pitcher potters took strength from Cardew's message.[4]*

241. WARREN MACKENZIE
LIDDED JAR
1973–74. Fluted stoneware, temmoku exterior, oatmeal interior, height 8⅝", width 7³⁄₁₆". Collection the artist

Like the Leach tour, the Cardew road show touched a sensitive chord, and changes were moving swiftly in the art world of ceramics. Voulkos used the vessel to respond to Abstract Expressionism and Minimalism; Soldner returned respectability to earthenware (or low-fire ware) and his post-firing procedures offered increased opportunity for interaction between potter and pot. And Arneson had made of clay an instrument for social commentary. In this "new world" of ceramic endeavor, many production potters wondered what place was left for them. What the production potter needed Cardew's visit reinforced—the confirmation that functional pottery could be a legitimate, artistic, and noble pursuit.

Studio Pottery in the Seventies

By the 1970s, Warren MacKenzie's conviction that the sensuous, tactile aspects of clay should enhance function led him to the formulation of a soft, more responsive clay body and new designs—his drinking bowls (cups without handles) brought the user into more intimate contact with the vessel. MacKenzie's aesthetic regarding function became the rallying point for a group of Minnesota studio potters. Labeled the "Minnesota Syndrome," these potters—among them, Jeff Oestreich, Shirley Johnson, Randy McKeachie-Johnston, and Mark Pharis—were united by a concern for the quality of the material, the process, and the subtle relationship of surface to form and to their environment. As such, MacKenzie sought to define the group: "The pots are like the people of this area, who, less aggressive and fashionable than their counterparts on the East or West Coast, reveal their strengths and qualities only to close friends."[5]

MacKenzie and the Minnesota Syndrome were part of a burgeoning group of production potters. Ken Ferguson, whose production pottery experience at the Archie Bray Foundation deepened his admiration for those like Wildenhain and Karnes who worked outside the academic system, organized an exhibition in 1976, "Eight Independent Production Potters," drawn from around the country. Ferguson called the group's self-sufficiency "an embodiment of the American experience."[6] The studio pottery movement's new strength was evident in the annual exhibits of "Functional Ceramics," begun in 1974 by the College of Wooster in Ohio and by "Craft Multiples," an exhibit in 1975 at the Renwick Gallery in Washington, D.C. After some thirty years during which the definition of a craftsperson had been hotly debated, Lloyd Herman, the curator of the Renwick show, supplied an answer in the catalogue. Of less importance was whether or not the craftsperson used machine tools, Herman wrote; the quality of work was what counted, and craftsmanship should be defined not by its tools but by a life-style and the retention of a personal touch in the object produced.[7]

The seventies was indeed a decade of increased regard for American crafts. Recognition of the high quality of American production crafts even extended to the White House. In May 1977, First Lady Rosalyn Carter honored the achievements of American craftspersons by using handcrafted place settings at a luncheon for senators' wives (the luncheon's settings were subsequently displayed in museums around the country). It was also in the seventies that a new magazine for ceramics was launched. First published in 1972 and based fittingly in New Hampshire, *Studio Potter* addressed the practical and aesthetic aspects of production ware. At a 1979 symposium, the magazine's co-editor Gerry Williams noted that about twelve thousand Americans were engaged in studio pottery; they were part, he said, of a "cultural continuity" that could be traced back to Indian potters of 2,000 B.C., whose work had been discovered in Georgia and Florida.[8] The recent rise of the professional crafts and its continuing identification with the principle of function was, according to Williams, an affirmation of an American cultural heritage.

The Vessel: Yielding to Modernism and Metaphor

While Gerry Williams spoke for those committed to function, there were other potters equally devoted to the vessel who, following Peter Voulkos and Paul Soldner's explorations of the vessel in the six-

243. *Warren MacKenzie conducting a workshop at Clayhouse, a potter's center, in Santa Monica, California, 1983*

ties, sought a broader vocabulary. These potters believed it necessary to remove the vessel from its functional context and give it fresh, contemporary meaning. Once again contemporary potters found themselves reevaluating the past by employing the most ancient of firing techniques—raku—and broadening the spectrum within raku to primitive processes.

THE LOW-FIRE SPECTRUM

The initial appeal of raku—an instant firing technique yielding unusual surfaces—broadened the many possibilities within low-fire. Evidence of both the growth of interest in raku and the expansion of the process since Soldner's explorations of the early sixties was the publication ten years later of two books on raku, *Raku: Art and Technique* (1970) by Hal Riegger, and *Raku Pottery* (1972) by Robert Piepenburg. Riegger's affinity for low fire, plus an early sixties visit to Santa Fe, New Mexico, had led him to explore primitive firings, which like raku demand a close relationship between potter and process. In his book *Primitive Pottery* (1972), Riegger defined "primitive" as neither crude nor unsophisticated, but rather as an approach that required careful observation and a sensitivity toward the environment in which the pottery is created.[9] In expressing the need for such sensitivity, Riegger was also reflecting the environmentalism of the times.

The low-fire spectrum—raku, primitive firings, and the variations practiced by native American, Mexican, and African potters—appealed to potters rejecting some of the encumbrances of a technological society. For potters more concerned with appearance than function, the low-fire spectrum was intriguing for its capacity to produce striking surface effects. For Rick Hirsch, lusters and iridescent glazes opposing smoked areas initially attracted him to raku and away from high-fired stoneware. While teaching in Ontario, Canada, Hirsch was approached to write a book on raku with his colleague Christopher Tyler. In *Raku* (1975), Hirsch and Tyler provided historical background information with their discussion of contemporary practices, and it wasn't long before historical forms began showing in Hirsch's work. In the same year the book was published, Hirsch added legs to his globular vessels using a tripodal design similar to traditional Japanese iron teapots and Chinese bronzes, which he admired and collected. As the vessel's legs became more pronounced and the container more diminutive, Hirsch labeled the transformation "space vessel" or "ceremonial cup," a juxtaposition of the ancient with the futuristic. He exploited the seeming fragility of these three-legged forms by balancing them as gracefully as a ballet dancer on point; music—especially jazz—influenced Hirsch's improvisations with the tripodal cup. Some pieces appear to hover in space while others recall human skeleton bones.

Another potter whose knowledge of the past blended into his work was Rick Dillingham. As a young man, Dillingham had collected Indian pottery, and his continuing interest in the indigenous culture of the American Southwest led him to attend college in New Mexico. Besides curating the seminal exhibit of seven Pueblo fam-

opposite:
244. RICHARD HIRSH
SPACE VESSEL #29
*1983. Red, green, orange terra
sigilattas, cupric sulfate, raku
fired, height 32", Museum of
Fine Arts, Boston*

245. RICK DILLINGHAM
LARGE BROKEN GLOBE
*1981. Earthenware, fired in an
electric kiln, gold leaf, height
13", diameter 16". Courtesy the
artist. Private collection*

246. BENNETT BEAN
VESSEL
*1982. Pit-fired and painted,
glazed, height 6". Private
collection*

247. RICK DILLINGHAM
VASE
1981. Earthenware, height 8½",
diameter 9". Everson Museum of
Art, Syracuse, N.Y. Gift of
Everson Museum Members'
Council

ilies in 1974, Dillingham worked as a volunteer restoring ancient Pueblo pottery for the University of New Mexico Maxwell Museum of Anthropology in Albuquerque. There he noticed the fluid, linear marks made by the repairing process. Using one of his own broken vessels, Dillingham accented these lines with glue which had been dyed black. Experiments with shards refired and restored developed into a study of random surface patterns. The subtle interaction of clay shards and fire-flashed marks on Dillingham's early work changed in the late seventies when he added glittering enamels, gold leaf, and lusters, a sophisticated contrast to the primitive quality of a smoke-blackened surface.

The elements of native American pottery and raku found in Dillingham's vessels are also essential to the work of Bennett Bean. His vessels of the late seventies use surface for the interaction of controlled geometric patterns with the chance effects of random smoke and fire flashes. Bean pit-fired his vessels, then overlaid confetti-like dots, flecks, diamonds, and rectangles for atmospheric spatial depth, not unlike the random dots in Larry Poons's paintings of the mid-sixties. For Bean, the significance of the vessel lies in the evidence on its surface of a dialogue between the controlled designs and the accidental actions of the kiln. That multi-leveled dialogue incorporates the smoke patterns of primitive firings, the burnished surface of native American pottery, and the geometric configurations and fragments found in contemporary art.

248. BENNETT BEAN
BOWL
c. 1984. Earthenware, height 9".
Collection David R. and Jean C.
Guthery

249. KEN PRICE
PLATE FROM TOWN
UNIT #2
1972–77. Earthenware, length
11¾". Private collection

250. ROBERT TURNER
RED IFE
*1980. Stoneware, sandblasted,
height 10¼ x 6⅜". Collection
the artist*

For Californian Ken Price, not archeology but the folk traditions of Mexico, Peru, and Central America were, for a time, his point of reference. Living in New Mexico in 1971, Price embarked on a period of prodigious creation, in which as a folk potter he produced innumerable sets of cups, plates, and vases. Using earthenware clay and a vocabulary of scenic and geometric designs true to the spirit of the Mexican village potter, Price regarded his five-year output as "potters talking to potters through vessels."[10] Like Lichtenstein, Price was interested in transforming production pottery into a sculptural environment. In 1978, Price's project culminated in "Happy's Curios," an exhibition at the Los Angeles County Museum of Art. The show conveyed a vast curio shop's ambience while the ware itself, with its brilliant colors and myriad shapes, transcended the ordinary vessels it emulated. As an intricate and enormous mosaic, the individual pieces formed a single cohesive and stunning work. Price had turned low art into fine art.

ORGANIC, ARCHEOLOGICAL APPROACHES TO THE VESSEL

Michael Cardew wrote that primitive pottery should be seen as expressive form rather than the product of a technique or evidence of the archeological and historical past.[11] For those potters uninterest-

above left:
251. KEN FERGUSON
T-POT
*n.d. Stoneware, height 13".
Donation by Peter Voulkos to
Nelson Atkins Gallery, Kansas
City*

above right:
252. KENNETH FERGUSON
STORAGE JAR
*c. 1963. Stoneware, height 15",
diameter 8". Everson Museum of
Art, Syracuse, N.Y.*

ed in primitive firings, yet concerned with making archaic connections, organic expression so dramatically exploited previously by Peter Voulkos offered a viable direction. Initially attracted to the dark, two-tiered vessels Voulkos made in the early seventies, Robert Turner shortly turned to one of the ceramist's sources—Japanese Bizen ware, which not only caused him to reject the Bauhaus austerity previously dominating his studio pottery, but to revise his thinking about the vessel. For Turner, "Form became an inside sense, not outside (perfect and boring)."[12] Other influences followed from the Bizen pottery. Aware of Cardew's experience in Africa, Turner visited Charles Counts when the latter was teaching at the University of Nigeria (1972–76). This experience in Africa introduced Turner to an animistic culture imbued with a spiritual basis for even the most mundane activity. The impact on his pottery gradually took shape. During the seventies, returning to the cylinder as his primary form, Turner rounded the shoulder into a dome with phallic attachments. Late in the decade, the cylinder itself became a phallic shape touched by a single, spontaneously incised line. These ideas coalesced into a series in 1980 he titled *Ife*, in which he incorporated oblique references to African shrine images and tribal dances.

Though not as minimalistic in his expression of the organic character of clay, Ken Ferguson also found inspiration from a culture not his own. One of many American potters who visited Japan during the seventies, Ferguson's trip in 1973 reinforced his orientation

toward a repetition of forms. There he learned that the Japanese potter and calligrapher (like the jazz musician) believe that through repetition an artist becomes comfortable with a form so that he can improvise with feeling.[13] Ferguson's slightly distorted, faceted teapots with paunchy spouts, and his large baskets with tall twisted handles emphasized the improvisational and gestural potential in clay.

Human anatomy and the celebration of symbol and ritual is alluded to in Richard DeVore's vessels. His wide bowls and deep cylinders, in the form of seductive openings, subtle folds, and creases, suggest body cavities—mouths and vaginas. DeVore, a former student of Maija Grotell's, incorporated into his vessels delicately cracked, skinlike surfaces, uneven rims, and random markings that recall stone age vessels and the historical pottery of the Anasazi and Mimbres indians. Ambiguous notches imply compass points similar to those prehistoric monuments meant to mark the movements of the sun. To the symbolic-ritualistic connotations of the vessel, DeVore added a contemporary slant with references to the new science of archeoastronomy, which combines a study of ancient civilizations with the study of the heavens.[14]

CONTEMPORARY HISTORICISM

With its lengthy tradition, the vessel form had been appropriate for references to archaic pottery bearing archeological and anthropological information. As it moved further from traditional function, this harkening to ancient beginnings eased the transition for the vessel as a carrier of ideas. The transformation for clay vessel and object as social commentary had occurred earlier in a Pop Art context through the works of Robert Arneson, Michael Frimkess, and Roy Lichtenstein, but many ceramists rejected the limitations of its commercial subject matter. Instead, this group expressed a greater affinity for aspects of Art Deco and eighteenth-century European ware.

Adrian Saxe combined diverse historical styles into his vessels, whereas Ann Currier and Elsa Rady revived the spirit of Art Deco. Saxe's tripartite covered jars rest on a rough earthenware base suggesting stone or wood ravaged by nature; the body of the jar provides a surface for a variety of patterns—brushwork, incised lines heightened by a celadon glaze or biomorphic relief fragments. An antelope (an animal associated with Art Deco sculpture) gracefully balanced on the lid completes the contrasting aesthetics of earthy, primal clay with refined eighteenth-century French porcelain. Hedonistic in their luxurious surface, Saxe's jars appear to taunt the decorative arts period while at the same time reflecting the eclectic climate of the late seventies, evident in the mix of historicism in the architecture of the period.

The black-and-white color schemes of Ann Currier's teapots of the mid-seventies are geometric puzzles that usually merge two cups, a sugar jar, and creamer into a horizontal or vertical structure. Unusual in the sense that when unassembled the parts are functional, the assembled pieces had another objective. They resembled variously thirties architecture with their rounded corners or the multi-

opposite:
253. ADRIAN SAXE
UNTITLED ANTELOPE JAR
1986. Porcelain and stoneware,
height 24½". Private collection

above:
254. ADRIAN SAXE
UNTITLED ANTELOPE VASE
1976. Porcelain and stoneware,
height 18", diameter 13".
Collection Jeffrey Clawans,
Los Angeles

above:
255. ELSA RADY
STILL LIFE #1
1987. Porcelain, from left to
right: 13½ x 6"; 13¼ x 5½"; 4¾ x
10½". Private collection

left:
256. ELSA RADY
CLIPPED WINGS
1984. Porcelain, 5½ x 14⅞ x
11½". Everson Museum of Art,
Syracuse, N.Y. Gift of Jill and
Marvin Cole

257. JERRY ROTHMAN
RITUAL VESSEL
1976. Whiteware, height 23" (approx.). Private collection

decks of a modernist, sleek luxury liner. Elsa Rady's porcelain vases also appear equally svelte and trim, although they share a sense of balance, purity, and classical shape with the sophisticated pottery of the Sung and Ming dynasties of China. Working on a functional scale with the bowl and cylinder, Rady tempered the Bauhaus austerity of form with elegant, sensuous, monochromatic glazes. These early 1980s vessels, often presented in groups of twos and threes, were cut or notched diagonally along the rim. The eggshell-thin walls and the swirling upward thrust produced a sense of graceful, circular movement. Along with references to Color Field painting in the unblemished surfaces, the Art Deco spirit dominates, echoed in Rady's use of curves and straight lines fulfilling her purpose, the investigation of relationships in the placement and presentation of objects in space.

In contrast to the severity of Currier and Rady's ware, Jerry Rothman's voluptuous *Ritual Vessels* and Elena Karina's *Tidepool Vessels* bulged with baroque attachments. Rothman embellished tureens, teapots, and covered jars with winged fish, spirited birds, phallic protrusions, and vegetal references, recalling to a degree eighteenth-century European Rococo tureens. Like Ferguson, Rothman did not overtly portray human anatomy, yet the forms suggest his models were buxom women. Appropriately baroque for an age of excess, the glossy, all-black or all-white covered containers would serve an extravagant, indulgent life-style. Equally lavish, the interior of Karina's vessels glistened with opalescent glazes on thin, pleated, and pierced layers of porcelain, undulating upward like huge, convoluted seashells. The contrasting encrusted exterior supported barnacle bumps, mother-of-pearl bulges, and dark algae gardens. During the mid-seventies, Karina expanded the handbuilt, cast, and sculptured forms from a vertical to a horizontal direction, creating branched sections exposing interior cavelike entrances and tunnels. A reflection of the rocky ledges, crevices, and coves within walking distance of her California studio, these theatrical, sensuous forms suggested seascapes, eccentrically carved snuff bottles, and the ubiquitous scallop shell, whose image can be traced back to classical sculpture and forward to eighteenth-century English ceramics.[15]

Support and Conflict

References to ceramic tradition through contemporary historicism occurred in the seventies in part because the impact of shifting val-

below:
258. PHILIP CORNELIUS
FT. WORTH
1982. Porcelain thinware, charcoal fired, 8 x 7 x 2". Collection the artist

Thin slabs of porcelain molded like an airplane wing form the body of "thinware," as the artist calls it. Though delicate in appearance, the vessel has sustained the harshness of a charcoal firing.

opposite left:
259. VAL CUSHING
UNTITLED
1982. Stoneware, height 24". Collection Daniel Jacobs

The artist has taken the covered jar, a form derived from folk pottery, and introduced new elements. Form and surface contain allusions to fruits and vegetables, whereas the lid is based on Islamic architecture.

ues brought on by Abstract Expressionist and Pop Art aesthetics had altered the way ceramists viewed the potential within their material. On the one hand, diversity and the freedom to pursue any one of a multitude of directions threatened the stability of the medium; as a counterbalance, the use of stylistic approaches from the past provided an anchor in tradition for ceramists like Rothman, Karina, Saxe, and Currier. This backward glance offered some reassurance after a period of so many changes and styles; the concern these changes produced was evident in the number of exhibits exploring the past. Like the 1940s, when national pride took the form of a rash of exhibitions displaying early American ware, many museum shows of the late seventies once again verified the strength of American accomplishments by tracing prominent developments.

CLAY ROOTS

One of the first exhibitions of this nature, "Foundations in Clay" (1977), at the Los Angeles Institute of Contemporary Art, celebrated the work of Michael Frimkess, John Mason, Ron Nagle, Kenneth Price, Paul Soldner, and Peter Voulkos. In essence an update of "Abstract Expressionist Ceramics" (1966), the show compared earlier work with the present. A small catalogue offered a chronology of im-

below:
260. ROSELINE DELISLE (left to right:) FUSIFORME. *1986. 13 x 5". TRIPTYQUE 6. 1986. 21 x 6½". JARRE SIMPLE 6. 1986. 6½ x 4½". Porcelain. Collection Mr. and Mrs. Charles Diamond, Newport Beach, Calif.*

These meticulous, pristine, porcelains based on triangular elements recall spinning tops or a rocket whirling into orbit. The concept of opposites is prevalent here, with regard to color (black and white), medium (porcelain as fragile but strong), and appearance (the piece is stationary but its depiction conveys movement).

portant dates for the decade and reprinted John Coplans's essay from the mid-sixties catalogue. Ceramic historian Hazel Bray curated "The Potter's Art in California 1885–1955" (1978) for the Oakland Museum, tracing the contributions of those potters who had established a clay tradition in the state. For "Ceram-a-rama" (1977) in San Francisco, curator Jim Stevenson printed a genealogical chart of student-teacher relationships for the two dozen northern California ceramists in the show. Another show, "Northern California Clay Routes: Sculpture Now" (1979), paralleled the 1977 Los Angeles "Foundations" show, exhibiting the work of seminal Bay Area ceramic sculptors.

The accomplishments of ceramists in the Northwest were underscored by a 1979 exhibition and book, *Ceramics in the Pacific Northwest*. Formidable research by author and curator Le Mar Harrington was acclaimed as the first overview of that area's prodigious activity since World War I. But it remained for the Everson Museum in Syracuse to sponsor a national, definitive historical exhibit. When the venerable Ceramic National exhibitions ceased in 1972 (controversy and massive numbers of entries had plagued the forum since the sixties), the museum saw the void as a unique opportunity to explore a new approach.

The approaching Bicentennial prompted serious consideration of the country's artistic past, so the proposal by critic Garth Clark and ceramist Margie Hughto for an extensive survey of ceramics at the Everson Museum of Art appeared most timely. "A Century of Ceramics in the United States 1878–1978" (1979) displayed four hundred objects chronologically, decade by decade. For the first time, the visualization of historical progression (tantalizingly hinted at in earlier shows) substantiated the achievements of one hundred years of American ceramics. The show traveled the country, making inroads into the established aesthetic prejudices on the status of work in clay. The accompanying catalogue became a reference guide; art critics who knew little about clay, past or present, and rarely discussed ceramics, expressed surprise at the extent and vitality of the work in the show. Art historian Donald Kuspit wrote that the exhibit demonstrated "the artistic importance and esthetic independence of American ceramics."[16]

The affirmation of contemporary clay's vitality and significant history through such shows was underscored further by a support system of new annual exhibits, galleries, collectors, and federal funding. The affluence of the period enabled the National Endowment for the Arts to initiate a crafts program in 1972. Newly appointed Crafts Coordinator Elena Karina, along with a panel of artists, made available grants to institutions and individuals specifically for crafts exhibitions and projects. Municipal and college galleries, which in the past had rarely exhibited crafts, yielded to the pressure from enlarged ceramics departments, and with federal money produced special ceramics shows; symposia, and workshops which brought together ceramists, students, and collectors were also among the grant recipients. Annual exhibits such as the Marietta College Crafts National (of Ohio, functioning from 1971 to 1983) and Clay Conjunctions (beginning in southern California in 1970), found needed financial aid from the NEA.

261. TOSHIKO TAKAEZU
PORCELAIN FORM
*1982. Porcelain and glazes,
10 x 7 x 7". Private collection*

Both Toshiko Takaezu and Catharine Hiersoux treat glazes much like a painter approaching a canvas. For Takaezu, the porcelain clay body sustains the quality of the color through layers of glaze applied in a spontaneous, intuitive manner.

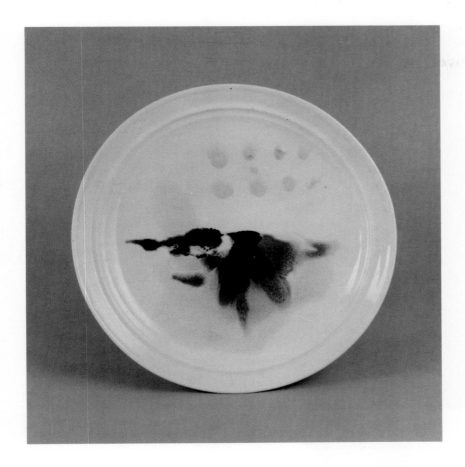

262. CATHARINE HIERSOUX
PLATE
*1986. Porcelain, diameter 16".
Collection the artist*

Invited to produce twelve place
settings for an anonymous cli-
ent, Catharine Hiersoux only
learned the destination after she
had packed the ware—no less
than the White House. The
publicity brought welcome attention (as it had for Lenox, Inc.
some sixty years earlier) to
American ceramics.

Simultaneously, the audience for contemporary ceramics broadened to include serious collectors, among them Fred and Mary
Marer, who discovered Peter Voulkos and his fellow ceramists at the
Los Angeles County Art Institute, purchased their work, and encouraged their then-undiscovered talent. Seattle residents Joseph and
Elaine Monsen began collecting in 1965, and became early support-
ers of the University of Washington ceramic community. A crafts exhibit attracted Pennsylvania attorney Robert Pfannebecker, whose
extensive collection ultimately required housing in special facilities
at his home. Iowan Joan Mannheimer conceived the idea of sharing
her growing number of ceramic objects with the University of Iowa.
During the 1970s, other collectors were motivated to open craft or
ceramics galleries: in New York, Kay Eddy established The Elements Gallery for Contemporary Crafts; in Philadelphia, Helen
Drutt's gallery opened in 1974; a year later, Ruth Braunstein, with
partners Rena Bransten and Sylvia Brown, founded the Quay Gallery
for ceramics in San Francisco; Alice Westphall's Exhibit A moved
after nine years in Evanston, Illinois, to Chicago in 1979. Among
these pioneer craft galleries was The Egg and The Eye (later becoming the Craft and Folk Art Museum) offering omelets along with fine
crafts to Los Angelenos.

The effect of all this activity sharply accented what had become
the dual character of the vessel, widening the breach between function and nonfunction. In spite of Cardew's assurances about the aesthetic position of functional pottery, the work of most production

263. ELENA KARINA
SIREN'S TRUMPET
1980. Porcelain. height 11",
diameter 18". The Kessel
Collection

264. SALLY BOWEN PRANGE
EDGE-SCAPE VESSEL
n.d. Porcelain, with grog clus-
ters, matt crystal glaze, 8 x 5 x
5". Collection Gwen Laurie and
Howard Smits

The sandy beaches, seashells,
and ocean sunsets near the
artist's North Carolina home
inspired a series of cylinders
suggesting nature's construc-
tive/destructive powers in
ripped, slashed, and folded walls
and edges. This eggshell-thin
vessel takes its color from that
marine environment.

265. DANIEL RHODES. SCULPTURE. *1980. Stoneware, 36½ x 20 x 11". Collection the artist*

On this torso-like form, patterns found in nature mix with the layering associated with Buddhist ceremonial robes. In his sculptures of the 1980s, Rhodes concentrates on two forms, the torso and the head.

266. WAYNE HIGBY
"CANYON LAKE"
LANDSCAPE CONTAINER
1976. *Four boxes with lids,
earthenware, raku technique,
hand-built with inlaid clay,
12 x 30 x 12". Private collection*

potters went not to galleries but to exhibits specifically for functional ware or to the Rhinebeck, New York Fair (then the largest of the craft fairs), and similar operations around the country. Fewer national shows of vessel and sculpture included functional pottery, a fact noted by potters, critics, and gallery directors. Warren MacKenzie, who spoke for many production potters, saw function becoming an odious boundary line between art and craft. The concern over the negative attitude developing toward function erupted in debates at symposia, workshops, and the annual NCECA meetings, recorded later in the pages of the NCECA *Journal* and other magazines. Mac-Kenzie, who viewed function as a vital part of the potter's language, said that tactile communication was essential in linking the user to the potter and to the multi-sensory experience of a vessel.[17] On the other side of the debate, vessel maker Wayne Higby, of Alfred University, regarded function as inhibiting, stating emphatically, "Functional pottery is not and cannot be a part of contemporary art as it is now constituted."[18] In a panel discussion on "Function-Nonfunction," Garth Clark commented on the high regard the Japanese aesthetic accords functional ceramics, a concept still alien to westerners.[19] Critic Judith Bettelheim addressed the prejudice of institutions like the Museum of Modern Art in New York, which accepted well-designed machinemade objects but rejected handmade, craft-oriented objects.[20] The art issues that Arneson and others approached in their sculpture of the sixties (specifically the nonfunctional vessel) further confused the issue. The concern was twofold: the position of the functional vessel in the ceramic spectrum and whether the vessel's utilitarian tradition (regardless of its rejection of function) would permit an association with clay sculpture of the seventies as it moved toward acceptance in the mainstream of American art.

267. LYDIA BUZIO
UNTITLED VESSEL
*1982. Burnished earthenware,
diameter 9½". Private collection*

268. Brother Thomas (Bezanson). Mei P'ing. *n.d. Porcelain, chrysanthemum glaze. Height 12¾", diameter 9". Private collection*

Mei p'ing, a vase shape dating from the Sung dynasty (960–1279), was the particular influence for this object's shape. Characteristic of Brother Thomas's work was the organic use of glazes, which continue the classical tradition based on oriental porcelains initiated in 1888 by Hugh Robertson.

269. BEATRICE WOOD
BLUE AND GOLD CHALICE
*1987. Earthenware with lusters,
height 11", diameter 7".
Collection Mr. and Mrs. Charles
Diamond, Newport Beach, Calif.*

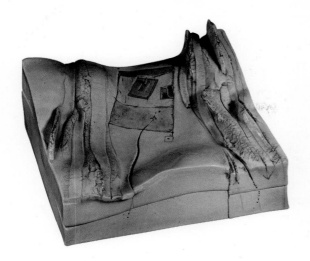

Chapter 15

ABSTRACT AND ARCHITECTONIC IMAGERY

A Dialogue with the Architectonic

Paralleling the bifurcation of the vessel into function and non-function were the divisions within sculpture. During the sixties, the object derived from Pop Art—in an expressive or super-realistic mode—dominated sculpture, with evidence of abstract, organic, and geometric directions also present. A dominant theme appearing in a wide variety of forms was a sensuous expression of the earth's terrain and the forces of nature. Some artists explored a relationship with landscape as a site for ritual monuments interacting with the environment. Others dealt with the concept of dwellings in a range of expressions, from romantic to sociological, inspired by primitive structures to the contemporary urban house. Ceramic sculptors also delved into architecture, following the momentum of John Mason's expressive, monumental walls of the sixties. Mason's use of strips of clay, coils, and textured slabs questioned the traditional meshing of clay and architecture in the form of tiled walls, floors, and bas-relief decorations. By the seventies, ceramists had not only disputed the role of function for the vessel, but had also viewed mere decorative embellishment in architecture as inadequate to the demands of diversity. A more formidable challenge—that of orchestrating mass, space, plane, and image—appealed to the ceramists seeking a broader, more sculptural interpretation of clay's relationship to architecture.

CLAY ON THE WALL

Among the first clay objects to tackle this new role was the nonfunctional plate.[1] No longer confined to a table or pedestal, the plate moved to the wall, competing for the vertical plane traditionally reserved for paintings. Soldner's plaques and Voulkos's plates of the sixties and early seventies, mounted at eye level, were intended to

opposite:
270. ROBERT SPERRY
MURAL
1985. Glaze and porcelain slip on tiles, 96 x 96". Private collection

above:
271. PAULA WINOKUR
"AERIAL VIEW, WINTER PLOWING" LANDSCAPE BOX
1980. Porcelain, sulfates, stains, lusters, 14 x 12 x 8". Private collection

evoke a different emotional response than conventional tiles. They were works unto themselves, demanding an attention greater than that afforded to simple decoration. And like Mason's walls, they expressed a sensuous, textural richness differently conveyed than in paintings. The tensions of weight and mass added new elements to the painterly concerns of line, color, and texture.

Ceramists Frans Wildenhain and Ruth Duckworth, along with Mason, were among the first to explore the possibilities for a large expanse of clay on the wall. Both favored abstractions of imagery derived from nature, first tried on plaques, then on murals. Teaching at the School for American Craftsmen, Rochester Institute of Technology in New York, Wildenhain produced a series of plaques in the late 1950s whose semi-abstract shapes recall Paul Klee's linear patterns. A sense of whimsy enlivened not only these plaques but the murals Wildenhain was later commissioned to do. His 1960 frieze for the National Library of Medicine in Bethesda, Maryland, sweeps across four walls in textures and abstract shapes reminiscent of seed pods, leaves, and the crackle pattern of ice melting on a pond. *Allegory of a Landscape*, a 1972 mural for the auditorium of the Student Union at the Rochester Institute, records Wildenhain's impressions of the Finger Lakes region of New York State as seen from the air. Cut like the pieces of a puzzle in high and low relief, the sections project a sense of brown plowed fields, the soft contours of hills, and the unusual formation of the lakes. The mural's position on an inner hall and its shades of brown suggests the archaic ambience of a cave.

Like Wildenhain, Ruth Duckworth translated her keenly felt emotions about her surroundings into romantic expressions of nature and landscape. Duckworth's three wall murals for the Hinds Laboratory for the Geophysical Sciences in Chicago also enclosed space, but for an atmospheric effect. She blended the three themes of *Earth, Water and Sky* (1968) in a four-hundred-foot expanse of stoneware with abstract elements resembling sunbeams and rippling water. These motifs were further developed in Duckworth's subsequent series of stoneware panels—the movement of water, clouds, and the earth within the earth's solar system. The flat landscape around Chicago (Duckworth's home since leaving England in 1964), and the meteorological environment created by Lake Michigan inspired *Clouds Over Lake Michigan* (1976), a twenty-four-foot mural for the Dresner Bank in the Chicago Board of Trade building.[2] Celebrating the air flow that typifies the Windy City, Duckworth's abstract forms can be read as the wind-rippled lake or as complex cloud formations. The atmospheric quality of Chicago's winter sky and Lake Michigan's shades of gray are conveyed in a number of Duckworth's porcelain raku wall sculptures of the late seventies. Smoked edges and subtle color variances on undulating surfaces create a rhythmic sense of movement between the sectioned plaques.

Understandably, not all ceramists attracted to using vertical space worked on such a massive scale. Nor were they as effusive in their approach. In contrast to Duckworth's use of high relief and abstractions of natural phenomena, Tony Costanzo's slip-cast eggshell-thin sheets of porcelain rejected emotion and gesture for a reductive, smooth, almost unrippled surface. In the mid-seventies, Costanzo, a Californian, incorporated concepts from Color Field

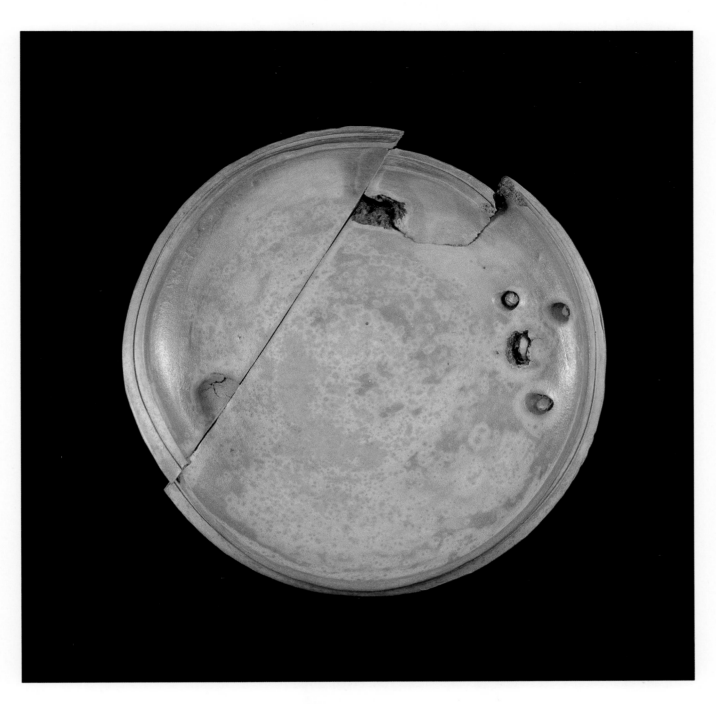

272. PETER VOULKOS
PLATE
*1978. Stoneware, height 4¾",
diameter 23". Everson Museum
of Art, Syracuse, N.Y.*

painting into the fragile-appearing, pale-colored clay. Rips interrupted the surface to form linear grids; lightly drawn lines mimicked the
pattern of a tile wall. Interior tears and fragmented edges revealed
supporting struts evoking a larger structure or the wall of a building
in disrepair. The elegant, refined, uncluttered porcelain combined
with the elements of decay and decomposition connected Costanzo's work to the past and the present—to the precision and classicism of ancient Greek architecture, and to contemporary
Minimalism.[3]

Grids and panels were also integrated into Marylyn Dintenfass's
sensuously folded and draped porcelain in *Autumn Palette* (1978).
Closer to Duckworth in her use of organic, curvilinear shapes, Dintenfass continued this stylistic treatment on a larger scale for the
sixteen square units forming *Quadrille* (1979), installed at the advertising agency Benton & Bowles in New York. Handling porcelain
like cloth or paper, during the 1980s Dintenfass moved beyond
panels to a complex system of parallel and diagonal elements,
engineering increasingly larger walls. Like the large canvases of contemporary paintings, Dintenfass's monumental structures were con-

273. *Ruth Duckworth, who
works on several projects simultaneously, is surrounded in her
Chicago studio by examples of
the many directions her work
has taken. (1986)*

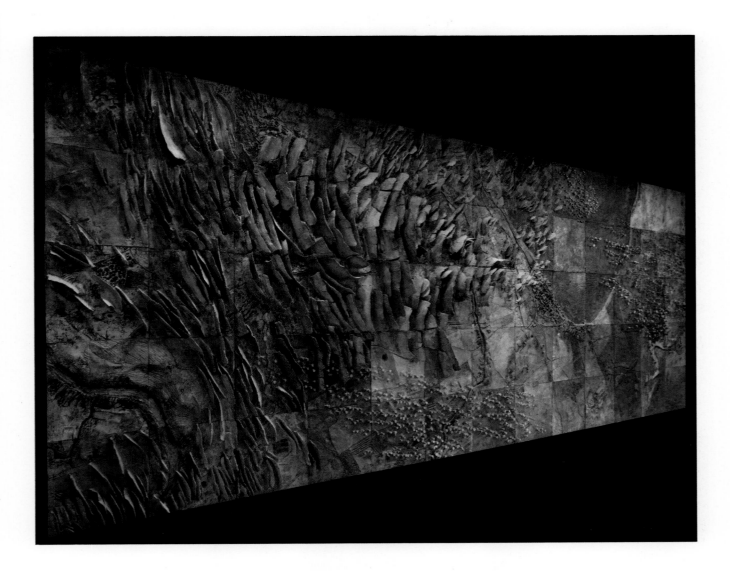

274. RUTH DUCKWORTH
CLOUDS OVER LAKE
MICHIGAN
*1976. Stoneware mural, 24'
x 9'7". Collection Dresner Bank,
Chicago*

frontational. However, despite this increase in scale, her work continued to employ an aesthetic similar to Costanzo's of encompassing space through a geometric, minimalistic expression.

In the striving for innovation, tradition wasn't completely abandoned. While others searched for new approaches to the expanse of a wall, the conventional form of the tile intrigued Robert Sperry. As the successor to the position Paul Bonifas held at the University of Washington, Sperry was initially involved with functional pottery. Then his large stoneware platters of the mid-seventies grew into sixteen-inch thrown, footed, and altered square slab plaques which seemed to require mounting on the wall. For the glazes, Sperry capitalized on earlier experiments that dramatized the incompatibility of shrinkage rates between porcelain slip and stoneware. Like the Natzlers years earlier, Sperry took what once was considered a glaze defect and manipulated it into a varied crackled pattern by altering the thickness of the white slip. *Triptych* (1979), three sixteen-inch squares, demonstrated his ability to shape the crackle glaze in the form of large and small circular mazes. By 1981, he had devised Velcro fasteners to secure black mullite kiln shelves on an easel structure, permitting him to coat large groups of tiles either by pouring or painting, using a long-handled mop dipped in slip. Like a Paul Bunyan with a giant-sized armstroke, Sperry, using his calligraphic brush-mop, produced loops and sprays of white crackled and crater-like slip. Once fired, these gliding, splashing sprays of slip became cosmic images resembling sun spots and volcanic eruptions against a stark, black background.

More than decorative architectural embellishment, clay on the wall addressed the transformation of space. Combining dimension with texture, weight, mass, and plasticity, and as part of a structure in a vertical position, clay acquired a range of expressions—abstract to geological, highly decorative to environmental. Painting, relief sculpture, and a historical eclecticism toward architectural ceramics became more important.

STRUCTURES FOR THE LANDSCAPE

As part of a reaction against the preciousness of sculpture in bronze or marble, sculpture in the mid-sixties frequently made use of industrial materials—bland, ready-made, bricks, lead plates, and steel

275. JOHN MASON
HUDSON RIVER SERIES VIII.
SCALE: 7
1978. Firebrick, each square 63".
San Francisco Museum of Modern Art Installation, 1978.
Collection the artist

beams, often identical units—whose component parts were interchangeable. In conjunction with this use of industrial material was a broadening of the plane upon which work was constructed. Carl Andre's railroad ties and Anthony Caro's aluminum panels and steel rods (among other works) moved sculpture from a vertical stance to a horizontal position.

After John Mason completed his series of monumental geometric forms toward the end of the sixties he turned to firebricks, an industrial material, as formal units for sculpture. And he moved to horizontal construction. While the use of firebricks separated Mason from a hands-on approach to ceramics, the firebrick as a basic unit in kiln building kept him connected to clay, though that wasn't Mason's concern. His first consideration was the material's industrial nature, uniformity, and efficiency. The horizontal construction of work was less a departure for him. Indeed, making the floor a space for sculpture was quite in keeping with his past work. Mason's *White Horizontal Relief* predated by six years sculptor Carl Andre's 1966 horizontal path of bricks titled *Lever*, which was considered startlingly innovative at the time.

Instead of the intuitive approach essential to his Abstract Expressionist sculptures, Mason relied on geometric logic for the spatial relationships in his firebrick sculptures. His first sculptures in 1972 and 1973 were narrow, diagonal backbones or wide platforms, through stepped-up segments, rising from a flat surface. In *Hudson River Series* (1978), Mason designed twelve installations for six museums located across the country, each installation planned for a specific space. Mathematical sequence and unit progression governed the un-mortared arrangements. Architectonic platforms, patios, plazas, meandering paths, building foundations, and arches formed by the alignment of firebricks imparted a feeling of movement and grandeur associated with massive historical monuments. A direct connection to landscape lay in the wandering quality of some of the squares, connoting nature's random arrangement of rocks in a streambed. Subtle color variations in the brick suggested light filtering through trees.

Mason's sensitivity to landscape took an archaic direction in the works of Paula Winokur and Tony Hepburn. Foregoing the monumental, Winokur's landscape boxes were small and intimate. Derived from porcelain slab-built ware whose lids were female faces in repose, these Art Noveau images gave way in the late seventies to more extroverted expression. Partly as a result of a plane trip taken to the West Coast, Winokur's perspective, like Frans Wildenhain's a decade earlier, shifted to an aerial view and with it came a heightened attachment to the land. The sensuously curved boxes easily adapted to a terrain shaped by gentle rather than aggressive forces. The hills, meadows, and valleys were marked with tiny sticks, colored rectangles, and arrows whose purposes remained unknown and ambiguous. The placement of poles suggests directional clues within a primitive ritual, if such a thing were possible.

Similar mystical implications were present in Tony Hepburn's mid-seventies assemblages of earthenware rods. Hepburn, an Englishman who has lived in the United States for many years, has acknowledged his affinity for prehistoric sites such as Stonehenge. His primitive ritualistic configurations—tepee-like burial mounds and crude kiva-related ladders—attained monumental height. By 1980, however, Hepburn had altered his clay vocabulary and scale, but not the motif. Closer to Winokur's boxes in size, Hepburn's circles within square slabs of clay were irregularly marked with stones or pieces of graphite. The size and shape suggested an aboriginal compass or a plan made by primitive man for marking an area of land with boulders or other natural forms.

Dennis Gallagher's stacked, nine-foot-high blocks of clay bear similar references. Although less expressionistic in form than Mason's totems of the sixties, Gallagher's column blocks, if placed in a circle, would stand in as ancient ritual monuments. Scarred, gesturally incised and pitted, they appear to carry the final record of a vanished civilization. Also looking to the past, Luis Bermudez took inspiration from pre-Columbian architecture and vessels in the use of stepped pyramids, vessels with a tripod base, or in bowls for grinding corn. With these forms as his base, Bermudez mimicked nature seen at its most dynamic moments. In a seven-foot-high orange arch, *Synapse* (1981–83), jagged lightning is momentarily suspended in time, or a three-legged vessel with an inward spiral captures the action of water swirling in a whirlpool. Like the rain gods depicted in human form by the Mayans and Aztecs, Bermudez's sculptures represented those same powers. Yet the imagery symbolic of natural phenomena incorporated architectural elements appropriate to a pre-Columbian civilization.

The layers of references in Hepburn, Gallagher, and Bermudez's minimalistic forms also incorporated gestural elements, evidence of Abstract Expressionism's persistent, if subtle, presence past the height of its influence. Combined with the rejection of permanence in art, the Abstract Expressionist concept that the making of art was as important as the object itself influenced California ceramists George Geyer and Tom McMillin. Both had produced functional ceramics before they met in 1973. They soon discovered their mutual interest in incorporating scientific and ecological information into their projects. McMillin's *Rammed Earth* in 1975—a wall of earth firmly compressed revealing layers of strata extremely sensitive to the touch of a finger—and Geyer's *Tidal Erosion and Pollution* three years later (the latter a group of earth-compressed panels randomly altered by water pollution and the motion of the tide), demonstrated the beauty in metamorphosis and the fragility of earth materials. In 1981, Geyer and McMillin collaborated on *Surf-line Erosion* for an exhibition at the Newport Harbor Art Museum, "California: State of the Landscape." Each five-foot-square panel of earth, sand, and an organic hardener was compacted into a wooden mold, which was then placed in the sand during the ocean's low tide. The dark geometric shapes complemented the eroded, sienna-color bluffs above the beach cove, changing with each day's onslaught of waves and wind from an off-shore storm. Geyer and McMillin's emphasis on allowing natural phenomena to alter form and surface has its roots in the rituals of pre-technological societies as well as in the Earthworks of Robert Smithson, whose *Spiral Jetty* of 1970 extended into a salt lake and linked art and nature.[4] Inherent in a process where variables of natural forces—wind, rain, tides—determine the final structure is

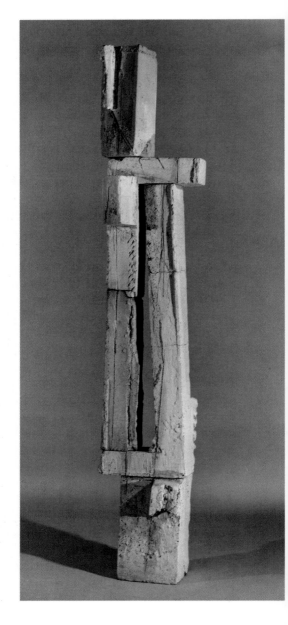

276. DENNIS GALLAGHER
UNTITLED (6.83.VI)
1983. Ceramic, 86 x 16 x 15".
Private collection

the metaphorical association with the temporal aspect of all life on earth.

Ephemeral material and Process Art were also part of John Roloff's landscape sculptures. Using a kiln to visualize the transformations occurring in nature and art, Roloff, in a 1979 on-site sculpture workshop, experimented with inserting a propane burner into a structure of bricks covered by a ceramic fiber blanket. Perfecting the technique by 1980, Roloff suspended the blanket on steel frames of various shapes—a starfish, a ship, and the head of a fish. During firings held outdoors at night, propane burners inserted in the blanket

illuminated the form while also containing the heat. Photographic documentation, essential to Process Art, accompanied the action of these "land kilns," as Roloff named them. One such land kiln in the shape of that most transitory of images, the curl of an ocean wave (*Wave Kiln*, 1980), symbolically reenacted during the firing the impermanence of its form in nature. The action of the kiln on the glaze materials placed on the ground beneath it transformed the earth, leaving a mark bearing the shape of the kiln. As Roloff himself put it, his intent was to develop "a poetic relationship between the kiln, its contents, and the firing. These are interlocked and inseparable elements of the process."[5]

The American landscape tradition in painting which developed during the mid-nineteenth century, the complexities of a techno-

277. TOM MCMILLIN
RAMMED EARTH SCULPTURE, CONTINENTAL SHELF
1975. 30 tons of earth compressed with pneumatic tamper (destroyed after exhibition), 8 x 6 x 14'.

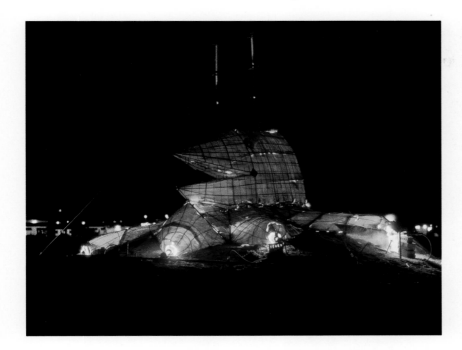

logical culture, and the extravagance and waste in an era of diminishing natural resources—all contributed to artistic expressions of concern for nature and the environment in the mid-1960s and 1970s. Stirred by a recognition of the earth's preciousness, ceramists searched for ways of making more basic connections to the planet, and articulating fundamentals about human existence. The result took a variety of forms, but one recurring theme, particularly in the mid-seventies, was that of shelter.

Images of Shelter

Nothing is more indicative of a society and its aspirations and values than the buildings it constructs and inhabits. This was especially true of Robert Arneson's autobiographical *Alice House* (1967). The shrub-lined tract house, the Volkswagen bus in the driveway, and the garage door basketball hoop reflected the suburban experience of millions of Americans. In a later piece, Arneson altered his focus from what we build to what we build with. In *Fragments of Western Civilization* (1972), the subject matter was the building material itself, brick—some of it was ready-made, some handbuilt with Arneson's name or bearing his astrological sign or a fragment of a self-portrait in an arrangement alluding to a ruin. For Arneson, the brick represented the fundamental unit associated with the development of Western culture.

One of the first to follow the autobiographical vein of *Alice House* was David Furman, who created small-scale sculptures of rooms in his home. Furman's clay rooms, produced between 1973 and 1974, were constructed with four walls, forcing the viewer to become a voyeur looking down into the work. Furman's presence is represented in each room by Molly, his personable dog, who lounges

opposite above:
278. GEORGE GEYER AND TOM McMILLIN
SURF-LINE EROSION
Laguna Beach, Calif. 1981. Earth, wood, steel, water, sand, 75 x 13 x 7'.

opposite below:
279. ROBERT ARNESON
FRAGMENTS OF WESTERN CIVILIZATION
1972. Terra-cotta, handcrafted and commercial bricks, 41 x 120 x 120". Collection Australian National Gallery, Canberra

above:
280. JOHN ROLOFF
ANCIENT SHORELINE/ ISLAND FOR LAKE LANONTAN (FIRING OF BLACK CORAL STARFISH ELEMENT)
University of Nevada, Reno. 1985. Steel, ceramic fiber blanket, ceramic and natural materials, propane, height 14", diameter 20'. Collection Sheppard Gallery, University of Nevada, Reno

Roloff researched the geological history of this site in Nevada near Reno. Some of his information, such as the presence of fish fossils, shows up in the piece and in the title.

on a bed or chair, on a rug in the hall, or near the fireplace (as *In the Living Room with Molly*). These precisely detailed miniature room tableaux defined Furman's intimate space in a narrative of tranquillity that suspends time. Shelter in these sculptures is a place of refuge, a retreat to a world of calm, neatness, and order.

The notion of archeology central to Arneson's *Fragments* was expressed in an entirely different form in the work of Charles Simonds. Simonds created groups of tiny dwellings, circular, spiral, and cliff-clinging structures in which a miniature brick was the basic element, a unit so small he used a pair of tweezers to move each piece into place. Between 1973 and 1977, Simonds's dwellings, built on the streets of New York in vacant lots or building ledges and crevices, emphasized roundness, a form alluding to regeneration. By interacting with a specific site, Simonds designed his projects to suggest the erosion of time or destruction by physical forces. Inspired by Robert Smithson's spiral, *Entropic Landscape* (1970), Southwest Indian kivas and pueblos, and unspecific primitive shelters, Simonds's work contains the themes of settlement, destruction, abandonment, and disappearance. An earlier affinity for the relationship between body, landscape, and habitation reappeared in Simonds's work of the seventies in the sensual manipulation of clay to incorporate pudendal or labial orifices, suggesting sexual energy and procreation.[6] By the late 1970s, Simonds was making connections between his forms and biological functions: the labyrinth inferred seduction, the incinerator digestion, and the mastaba, death.

281. DAVID FURMAN
IN THE LIVING ROOM
WITH MOLLY
1974. Ceramic, 11 x 13 x 7". Collection Marietta College, Ohio

opposite above:
282. CHARLES SIMONDS
RITUAL GARDEN
1980. Clay, sticks, blood, sand over styrofoam, masonite armature, 9 x 29⅞ x 29⅞". Collection the Museum of Contemporary Art, Chicago. Gift of The National Endowment for the Arts Museum Purchase Grant, Gift of the Men's Council, the Women's Board, and the Collector's Group

opposite below:
283. CHARLES SIMONDS
"DWELLING," DUBLIN
1980. Unfired earthenware; destroyed

Haunting, ephemeral, and poetic, Simonds's archeological edifices served as a visual history of an imaginary society responsible for its construction—the civilization of the Little People. This fantasy of myths, rituals, and cultural behavior could be derived by the viewer from the configuration of the ruins. The structures also served as a metaphor for the cyclical and temporal quality of human existence. Like Geyer and McMillin's transitory works, Simonds's site projects continue to exist only in photographs. The temporary nature of his work stood in defiance of the gallery system. In 1978, Simonds made a concession to more conventional exhibition with *Circles and Towers Growing*. This series of twelve kiln-fired and transportable landscape environments traced the evolution of the Little People from life on a bare, parched plain through the construction and destruction of complexes of towers, gardens, and observatories. During the 1980s, Simonds was invited to build his structures on the streets of Europe and China. In 1982–83, he built *Age*, a whorl structure and his largest work, as an installation piece for the Guggenheim Museum. The sculpture encompassed organic and inorganic forms which suggested the transformation of land into body or the reverse, a cosmos touching on man's origin and that of all creativity.

The sense of mystery and the unknown in Simonds's projects also pervaded the work of William Wyman. In 1965, Wyman spent three months in Honduras working on an international development project. While there, he had the chance to visit nearby ancient Mayan ceremonial centers which left a profound impression on him.[7] Nearly a decade later, Wyman, by then an accomplished ceramist, began creating a series of temple-like objects in clay. These thirty-inch-high unadorned shelters conveyed a spiritual presence inspired by the Mayan sanctuaries he had seen. Most of Wyman's temples

284. WILLIAM WYMAN
TEMPLE 7
1977. Ceramic, 19 x 29 x 9½".
The Metropolitan Museum of
Art, New York. Gift of Helen
Palmer Andrus, in memory of
Vincent Dyckman Andrus, 1980

285. JENS MORRISON
CASA DE LOS SIERRA
*1984. Earthenware, 18 x 12 x
15". Private collection*

had a sparse appearance emphasized by unglazed and unmarked surfaces; others pulsated with color shaded into the clay by conte crayon or pastels. Entry openings varied from narrow slits to wide
apertures, allowing glimpses of enigmatic interior stairways with
unknown destinations. Broad exterior steps, severe geometric lines,
and projecting windows demonstrated Wyman's high regard not
only for Mayan structures but for Egyptian pyramids and North African architecture as well. Viewed as metaphors for a tomb, retreat, or
the womb, these temples serve as symbolic dwellings for the human
spirit.

Another artist who took inspiration from a different culture was
Jens Morrison. Instead of monumental structures, however, Morri-

son's series of slab-built objects focused on the exterior of the house. The series evolved from his interest in cultural anthropology, specifically the Tarascan Indians of Mexico and the Somba and Dogan cultures of West Africa. The adobe with a pitched roof served as a model for a group of *Tea Temples* (1980–82), whose pastel-colored walls were ornamented with winglike shards, delicate teacups, fragments of incised drawings, and cacti sprouting from the roof. Another series, *Casas* (1983–86), inspired by the small rural roadside shrines of Mexico, added such unpretentious offerings as pesos, flowers, and seashells to the space around the shelter/shrine. A small, central niche often held a heart-shaped object, a cactus ear, or a miniature cup. Rural architecture's close ties to nature are embodied in the cactus; the precariously balanced teacups on the rooftop or in the niche symbolized simple household rituals, and along with the shards added humor to Morrison's references to ceramic tradition. The naive quality of children's drawings of houses and folk art is conveyed by *Casas'* boxy construction and high pitched roof. This paradoxical incorporation of folk art elements into the work of urban artists such as Morrison and Ken Price, whose training and sophistication are antithetical to that of folk artists, spawned the term "academic folk art."[8] The *Casas* and their predecessors communicate with studied intention the values of a simple life-style which have been forsaken by technological cultures.

286. MEL RUBIN
FOSTER FREEZE II
*1982–83. Low-fire clay, acrylic paint, wood, 30 x 37 x 3¾".
Collection Norman and Lyn Lear*

URBAN REALISM

Gritty reality remained a compelling tableau for many ceramic artists creating architectonic work. For ceramists such as Raymon Elozua, Gifford Myers, and Mel Rubin, the urbanized industrial American city, with all its decay and redevelopment, was the thrust of their work.

Like Simonds's primitive structures, Raymon Elozua's industrial buildings appear abandoned, some even in a state of ruin. Elozua's decaying railroad trestles, wharves, coal sheds, and oil derricks document a fading American industrial heritage, a familiar sight in the South side of Chicago where Elozua was raised. Building these structures with the skill of a carpenter, Elozua then allowed the clay to warp as it dried, damaging and repairing the parts until the edifice appeared properly worn. (As in Marilyn Levine's work, clay's ability to imitate many different materials is underscored.) In an odd way, the skeletal appearance of Elozua's small-scale warehouses and billboards resembles Giacometti's thin, lonely figures, also seemingly abandoned in a landscape.

Gifford Myers and Mel Rubin's wall plaques recorded ordinary city architecture in realistic detail. Closer to Simonds in scale, Myers's homes, apartments, and office buildings appear newly painted and ready to display a "for sale" sign. His *Real Estart Series* (1981–83) is a group of tiny wall plaques, two to four inches long, involving perspective, two and three dimensions, and the illusion of depth. Myers's minute embellishments—corbels on bay windows, slightly fading brick surfaces, hood moldings, pediments over doors, and reflections of neighboring buildings in some of the minuscule windows—demonstrate a high level of technical achievement. But

287. GIFFORD MYERS
RANCHITA BONITA
1982. Glaze and acrylic on ceramic, 4 x 5 x 2⅜". Ann and Tully Friedman Collection

the real significance of the plaques lies in Myers's emphasis on the house's economic importance, social status, and use as a commodity for speculation. Titles for many plaques read like newspaper real estate advertisements—"Xlnt. Loc./Upper Brackets," "Cozy Bungalow/Terrific Terms." Architecture associated with geographic areas of the country, apartment houses whose architecture and landscaping struggle for an exotic atmosphere, inflated property values, and modern redevelopment are the issues in objects whose small size belies their capacity for tackling such complex, contemporary socioeconomic problems.

The red brick buildings of Philadelphia where he grew up, inspired Mel Rubin's late-seventies relief plaque series of graffiti-decorated building walls. Like Elozua's objects and Arneson's *Fragments*, Rubin's large plaques of abandoned buildings had the appearance of contemporary ruins. Moving to Los Angeles's central district altered his perspective; his 1980s depictions of fast food establishments, Mom and Pop markets, abandoned theaters, diners, and seedy motels recall Edward Hopper's paintings of lower-class urban neighborhoods. Connections to the past—the Ash Can School of painting—and the present—the Photo-Realists—linger in the details of ordinary architecture. The wall-plaque format required that Rubin unobtrusively "lie, cheat, and exaggerate perspective" by utilizing relief elements such as telephone poles, palm trees, and mail boxes.[9] His storefronts appear the victims of time and use, an urban landscape devoid of people. The richness of the details which contribute to an overload of daily information in billboards, signs, posters, and advertisements contradicts that quality of big city loneliness suggested by deserted streets.

A number of exhibitions opening in the mid-eighties focused on the variations within the theme of house/shelter. "On the House" (1984) at the John Michael Kohler Arts Center in Sheboygan, Wisconsin, explored the house image in clay in terms of personal narratives and political or social themes. Multi-media exhibits such as "Artists Look at Architecture" (1985 at the Transamerica Pyramid in San Francisco) and "Shelter" (1986 in Richmond, California, at the Art Center) concentrated on the widespread and universal use of the shelter image. A smaller show of eleven ceramists held at the Esther Saks Gallery in Chicago in 1985 interpreted most effectively the psychological and sociological possibilities for this image. Curated by Susan Wechsler, "Is Anybody Home" revealed ambivalent, nontraditional conceptions of the home as seen in the figure in Christine Federighi's *Side Rider* (1984), which, too large for the windowless, doorless house, rides astride the roof. Michael Lucero's small gray house is equally inaccessible, overwhelmed by its landscape, while Patrick Siler's figures continually run around a closed building. The harboring of anxieties, dreams, fears, and hopes transforms these images into metaphors for personal narratives and perceptions of space altered by these emotions. The self-involvement characteristic of the 1970s made references to the human figure an important part of these structures. The emphasis on a human/personal connection was also responsible for figurative imagery, another dominant feature of this period.

opposite:
288. DOROTHY HAFNER
MARDI GRAS RIBBONS
1983. Porcelain serving tray, 17".
Private collection

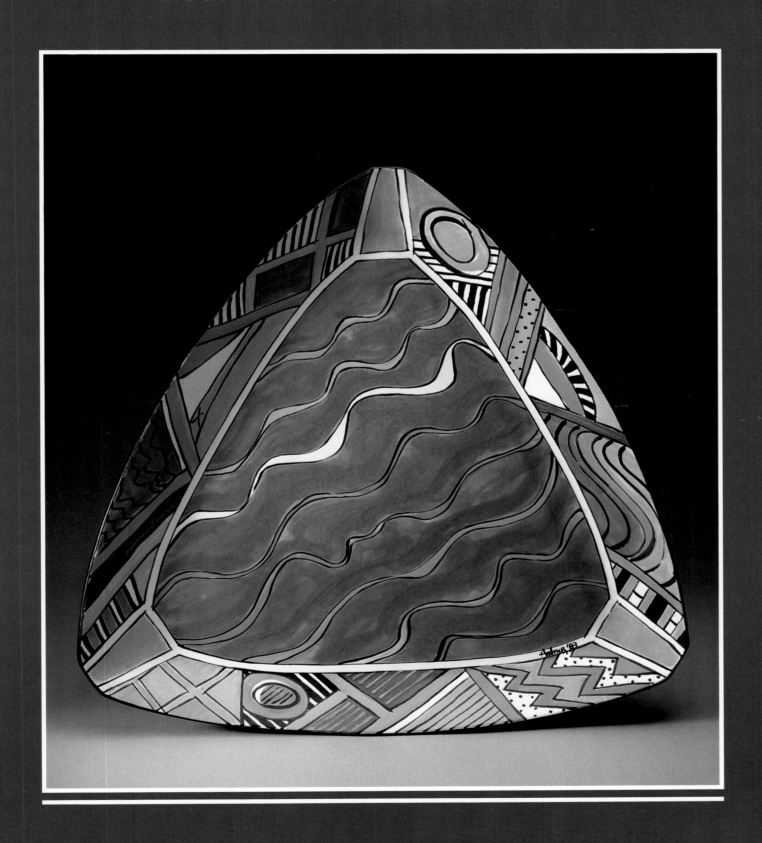

Chapter 16
FIGURATIVE IMAGERY AND THE HUMAN CONDITION

The Human Connection in Animal Sculpture

Animal sculpture in American ceramics has ranged from the whimsical lions of nineteenth-century Shenandoah Valley potters John and Solomon Bell and the stiff poodles of Bennington, Vermont, potters to the Depression-era decorative and personable horses, hippos, and cats of Carl Walters, and the lanky giraffes and camels of Viktor Schreckengost. Humor was part of the equation then and was essential in the return to animal imagery in the seventies.

But the amusing, decorative animals of the thirties could not satisfy ceramists whose thinking had been transformed by a decade of civil unrest; in the seventies, the role of animals in clay was as commentary—on the culture and narcissism of the times. As surrogates for the human experience, animals were exempt from the social taboos imposed on men and women. David Gilhooly's frogs, Jens Morrison's pigs, and Douglas Baldwin's ducks lived out their creator's fantasies about how each wanted the world to function.

In 1970, Gilhooly's nearly human-size Frog Fred became his dominant image, often appearing in the form of a revered historical or biblical figure or a god from an ancient culture. For example, in his work satirizing the ecological concerns of the period, *The Honey Sisters Do a Garden Blessing* (1973), Gilhooly portrayed Fred Frog as the Egyptian god of resurrection, Osiris, presiding over fertility and regeneration. This fecundity for Gilhooly also signified abundance (including consumer consumption), and Frog Osiris took on a variety of roles including an inaugurator of supermarkets, a blesser of vegetable gardens, and the singular begetter of look-alike-Osirises in *Cloning* (1973). In a piece attacking overconsumption, Fred Frog is nearly buried under an avalanche of canned food.

The 1970s were defined as the "me" decade by critic-writer Tom Wolfe; Gilhooly translated the hedonistic possibilities inherent in this label into visual tableaux. Frog Fred could be seen swim-

opposite:
289. DAVID GILHOOLY
TANTRIC FROG BUDDHA
CAMPING OUT
1975. Glazed earthenware, 26½ x 16 x 15". Collection Mr. and Mrs. Robert H. Shoenberg

290. DAVID GILHOOLY
OSIRIS CANNING FACTORY
*c. 1972. Earthenware, 28 x 15 x
14". Everson Museum of Art,
Syracuse, N.Y.*

ming delightedly in chocolate vegetables, or as a self-indulgent Buddha in *Tantric Frog Buddha Camping Out* (1976). In the latter, the two-foot-high, plump, blissful frog wrapped in strips that resemble lustered lasagna rests ecstatically above a frieze of animals copulating. Where Carl Walters's animals were polite but cheerful, Gilhooly's frogs were openly raucous, pampered spirits, disrespectful equally of institutions like the stock market to female movie idols. In short, Frog Fred was just as sybaritic and sensuous as was American society of the seventies.

In contrast to Gilhooly's three-dimensional figures, Jens Morrison's archeological chronology of the imaginary Farmounians was recorded on flat, circular, or square glyphs in bas-relief. Between 1973 and 1977, while teaching at Coe College in Iowa, Morrison transformed his fascination for ancient history, cultural rituals, and his first experience of the agricultural Midwest into a fanciful record of an ancient and imaginary corn-belt society. The anthropomorphic porcine Farmounians were depicted as industrious and devoted, planting crops, building a "hoguaduct," or succumbing to the influence of mind-expanding "pigote." Magicians ("cornjurors"), gods, legend recorders, and the corn farmer shaped the graphic representation of an agrarian culture viewed by a foreigner (Morrison) from a technological society. The saga of the Farmounians, explained in elaborate texts shamelessly distorting farm terminology into relentless puns, accompanied each display of their relics, mollifying Morrison's personal angst at living in an alien world.[1] Captivated by the anthropological investigations this project required, Morrison immersed himself in the details of early civilizations such as Meso-

291. JENS MORRISON
THE GREAT CORNWALL
STONE
1978–79. Earthenware, 40 x 24 x
28". The Denver Art Museum

292. DOUGLAS BALDWIN
BEGINNING THROWING 101
from the "GREAT DUCK
CERAMIC SCHOOL"
*1976. Brick, clay, porcelain,
length 7". Private collection*

potamia. Contemporary parallels and ironic commentary are part of the narrative. His creation of an energetic, hard-working utopian society confronted a period when American workers were being described as indifferent to the work ethic and accused of contributing to the declining quality of American products.

The world as it should be in academic ceramic departments inspired Douglas Baldwin's alter ego—a small, anthropomorphic duck. In the early seventies, while he was teaching at the Maryland Institute College of Art, Baldwin placed his duck-teachers in a series of tableaux demonstrating the correct stages in throwing a cylinder. (Back in 1967, Robert Arneson had illustrated throwing a cylinder by painting the hand positions on a thrown cylinder.) The culmination of Baldwin's aquatic academia was the *Great Duck Ceramic School* (1976), which besides normal facilities featured a massage parlor, a school psychologist, and a vault for secret glaze formulas. Separate models of particular activities allowed Baldwin, like Morrison, to elaborate on his utopian vision. The pressure of large classes, academic responsibilities, and time for his own creativity led Baldwin to fantasize a perfect world of energetic, dedicated students who were neat, efficient, orderly, and extraordinarily creative.

Not all ceramists working with animal figures felt confined to the societal context. Two ceramists, Frank Fleming and Joe Bova, working in the Southeast, brought imagery from that region into animal sculpture. The symbolism in Frank Fleming's tableaux of animals is rooted in personal experiences. *Savior Penguin* (1977), standing before a two-headed dog and flanked by a staff and holding a book, recorded Fleming's encounter with a devoted disciple of the Southern Baptist church. Fleming's anguish over the tragic death of a friend was vividly expressed in *The Soul Screamer*. His unglazed, porcelain creatures—penguins, rabbits, monkeys, goats—are precisely detailed. The illogical assignment of parts of one animal to another, combined with human actions and gestures, mocks southern social customs and imparts a surreal quality reminiscent of animal/human figures in native American art.

Fleming's identification with the rural South (he was born in Bear Creek, Alabama) is evident in an ironically humorous series of wall plates. In *Southern Triptych* (1984), the main character is a saucy catfish who foolishly leaves his Alabama ("the heart of Dixie") home, has a few adventures, and then wisely returns home. Commenting on the interior world his sculptures expose, Fleming observed: "We're in an age where we are bombarded by all kinds of external media. It's most important for each of us to be able to turn inward—to listen, hear, and respond to the personal myths that might, but not necessarily do, dwell inside us."[2]

Like Fleming, Joe Bova juxtaposed human and animal. In Bova's work the creatures were modeled after animals and fowl indigenous to the landscape most familiar to Bova—the lakes and bayous of southern Louisiana, his home since 1969. A startling, powerful set of images came from a series produced in the late seventies of animals and birds springing out of heavy-jawed male heads. In *Michocán Memories* (1979), the pale, unglazed head whose eyes are closed as if dreaming or in reverie recalls the dynamic, realistic pre-Columbian portrait stirrup jars. The tropical species of a bird emerging from the bald skull bears references to the ceremonial headdresses used in primitive rituals and to the magical powers early cultures attributed to nonhuman species. In individual heads and figures of pigs, dogs, and rabbits, Bova fused the attributes of animals to human moods. The pottery traditions of Mexico and Peru, ones he most admires, have captured this integration of man and nature; Bova's intent was "to address the same essential human concerns these works convey to us today."[3]

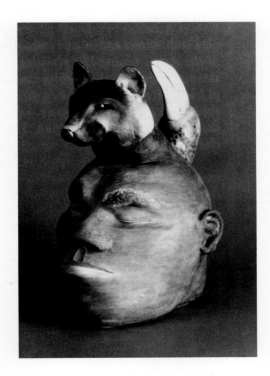

293. JOE BOVA
CLUES
1979. Ceramic, height 14½".
Collection Mary and Alfred R.
Shands, III

The Portrait and the Figure

Frank Fleming's admonition to turn inward and Joe Bova's self-involved dreamers exemplified a preoccupation with the self characteristic of the seventies. World and national events appeared beyond individual control, and the intellectualism of previous art modes—Color Field painting, Minimalism, and Conceptual Art—played a part in turning artists once again toward recognizable images, especially the human figure, and, in some cases, more emotional expression. The figurative paintings of Philip Pearlstein and Alex Katz, and the Photo-Realism of Chuck Close's portraits and self-portraits all explored, with diversity, the figurative modes. As early as the mid-sixties, that same diversity began to reveal itself in clay.

PSYCHOLOGICAL PORTRAITS

The psychological turmoil inherent in daily life and human relationships, portrayed in animal sculpture in the 1970s, was also among the first issues addressed by a group of ceramists who preferred depicting the human figure. Confronting his own complex anxieties,

Robert Arneson began self-portraiture both for the challenge within clay technology and as a personal emotional release.[4] In *Self-Portrait of the Artist Losing His Marbles*, (1965), Arneson expressed his distress quite literally—marbles cascade out from a large crack in a bust of himself. A few years later, Arneson, perhaps feeling the strain of running a populous ceramics department, portrayed himself in the guise of a tall kiln (*Kiln Man*, 1971), his features in brick—with a characteristic cigar in his mouth—still recognizable.

That same year Arneson produced a series of self-portraits of exceptional emotional power and strength. In *Hollow Gesture* and other busts that followed, Arneson's personal anxieties, as a consequence of his divorce in 1972, were frozen, as in a photograph, in

mid-action. The nervousness of a compulsive eater driven by unbearable pressures was evident in *Snac*. The open-mouthed scream in *Crazed* (1972) echoes Edvard Munch's woodcut of *The Scream*. However, Arneson lightened the mood of *Crazed* with a pun of his own on the crackled (or crazed) glaze covering the head—a portrait not so much of terror as of frustration. In discussing these portrayals of emotion, Arneson compared his work to the psychotic self-portraits of the eighteenth-century European sculptor Franz Xavier Messerschmidt, describing his own busts by observing, "that's where my obsessiveness really came through...."[5]

Arneson's self-portraits of the next several years were by contrast quietly humorous, larger-than-lifesize, and often concerned with the subject matter of Pop Art—mundane or trivial human experiences. Around 1977, he expanded his portrait subjects to include friends, colleagues, and historical artists to whom he felt he owed a debt. *Vince* (1978) was modeled after Van Gogh's thickly painted self-portrait of 1887. Other artists likewise received the Arneson treatment. Marcel Duchamp, costumed as Rrose Selavy (1978), and Pablo Picasso, in a pose similar to the women in his painting *Les Demoiselles d'Avignon*, were individuals who "by what they did,"

294. ROBERT ARNESON with bust,
WHISTLING IN THE DARK
1976. Terra-cotta and glazed earthenware, 35½ x 20 x 20".
Whitney Museum of American Art, New York. Gift of Frances and Sydney Lewis

295. ROBERT ARNESON
ELVIS
*1978. Glazed ceramic, 47 x 30 x
19". Hirshhorn Museum and
Sculpture Garden, Smithsonian
Institution, Washington, D.C.
Gift of the Frances and Sydney
Lewis Foundation, 1985*

296. ROBERT ARNESON
VINCE
*1978. Stoneware, 40 x 19 x 19".
Private collection*

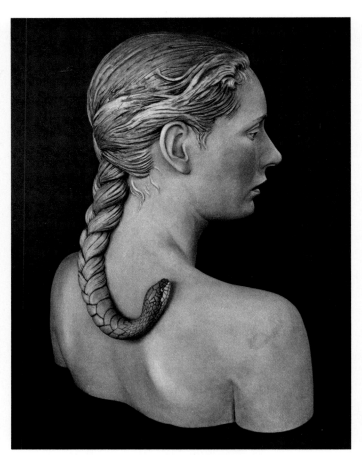

Arneson remarked, ''allowed me to do whatever little thing I do as an artist.'' [6]

As should be obvious by now, Arneson typically undercut the emotion in his work with wit. Other artists, however, chose to express emotions in the raw. Judy Moonelis's subjects exposed their deepest feelings of fear, anger, loneliness. Unconventionally structured, Moonelis's large stylized heads of 1983 were thin, flat slabs placed together for two profiles in low relief, incised, vibrantly colored. Some were as large as three feet tall, expressed as double portraits of conflicting moods. Neo-expressionist in the sensuously and spontaneously textured surfaces, the portraits recall Greek masks or African and archaic sculptures. A year later, using two partial figures in *Embrace II* (1984), Moonelis eloquently confronted the range of feelings possible within human relationships.

Duality and aggressive images were also characteristic of Ken Little's figures and portrait busts of the late seventies and eighties. In a series of busts and figures, Little appropriated the cowboy apparel of his native Texas along with a blending of human and animal imagery. The seemingly friendly western, cowboy ambience is contradicted by the gun-bearing figure in *Fit to Kill* (1983), whose smile appears to be changing from human to animal; a covering of spiked shards reiterates an underlying hostility. Another merging of contradictory ideas lies in the shard-covered figure of *Deluge Ken*.[7] The

above left:
297. JUDY MOONELIS
''EMBRACE II''
1984–85. Ceramic, 42 x 36 x 21"
(view 1). Collection the artist

above right:
298. BEVERLY MAYERI
THE BRAID
1980. Clay, acrylics, 18 x 16 x
9". Collection Jay Cooper

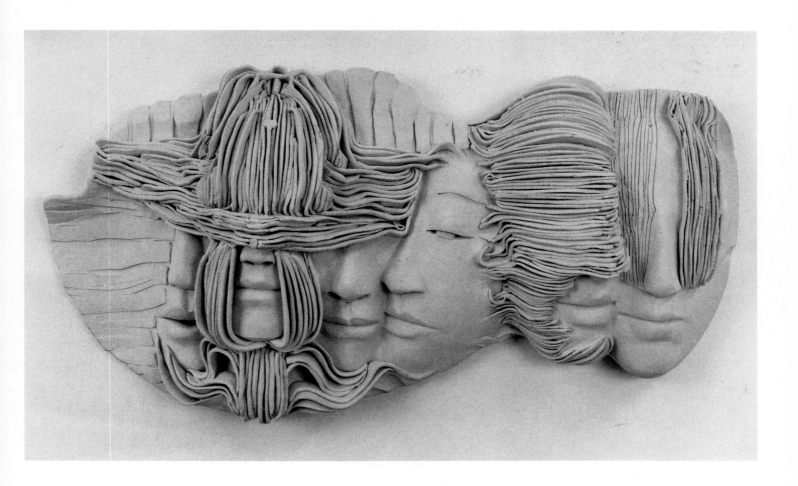

299. Dora De Larios
INNER EYE
*1982. Stoneware, cone 10, un-
glazed, hand-built sculpture, 12
x 24". Collection the artist*

suffering, distorted features of the figure are launched like a space-
ship through the roof of a small house to show emotional strain. Little juxtaposed earthbound, painful domestic conflicts with the
scientific and technological advances that can place a man on the
moon.

INTERIOR IMAGES

Where Arneson and Moonelis's portraits externalized a roller-coast-
er ride through human emotions, for many figurative sculptors their
work reflected a desire both to retreat from an open expression of
life's anxieties and to reconnect with the atavistic. Beverly Mayeri's
busts of women in 1980 combined the Surrealism of Arneson with
the inwardness of Bova to project a Magic Realism. Mounted on
small pedestals like their eighteenth-century classical counterparts,
the women in *Renaissance Woman*, *The Braid*, and *The Daughter*
have heavy lidded eyes and averted gazes, a dreamlike state suggesting an altered consciousness. Clothing clasps made of tiny lizards
and a hair braid that becomes a snake recall the prehistoric and
mythological roles these animals had as symbols of fertility and wis-
dom. Mayeri's busts and masks of 1985 were stretched into long narrow faces similar to Modigliani's portraits. A rough surface covering

all but the subject's eyes and mouth appeared to offer some protection against unknown dangers.

A similar elongation of facial features was characteristic of Peter Vandenberge's portraits of the 1980s, although the rough texture of their coil construction is reminiscent of folk art, further underscoring their unpretentious nature. Larger-than-lifesize, solemn and tight-lipped, Vandenberge's men in their derby hats and bow ties are enigmatic, in control of their emotions, and self-involved. *Hooded Woman* (1984), her head and face covered down to the tip of her nose, conveys a feeling of inward isolation. Instead of a hood, ribbon-like layers of clay strips partially obscured Dora De Larios's groups of three or four wall-mounted faces. Long narrow noses and full lips connect these masks of the early 1980s to the distinctive features of Mayan Indians, historical references to De Larios's cultural heritage.

The sublimation of feelings indicated by face coverings played a part in Arthur Gonzalez's figure fragments. A minimal disguise of white slip exposed only eyes and mouth on the faces of his early 1980s wall-mounted torsos. Adorned with ambiguous objects symbolic of diverse cultures, art movements, or magical powers, Gonzalez's women seek the unattainable from men (or women) who attempt to pull away from their possessive grasp. Similarly, the par-

300. ARTHUR GONZALEZ
NEW BEST FRIEND
1985. Clay with mixed media, 31 x 30 x 15". Collection the artist

tial figure is a vehicle for communicating Gonzalez's ideas about human longings, fears of commitment, and the exercise of power by one individual over another.

Equally enigmatic in dress and activities, but rooted in a medieval ambience, were Elaine Carhartt's figures. About four feet tall with chunky bodies and hands, Carhartt's men and women have faces resembling dwarfs and wear clothing similar to the people in a Breugel painting, which, strangely enough, bear allusions to contemporary astronauts. Interaction for Carhartt has become more positive. Whereas the interior visions of Mayeri and Vandenberge's people were solitary, Carhartt's figures share and relate to one another. Though their world remains private, strange, and unexplained to the outsider, it is mysteriously captivating for its alluring combination of rich colors, fantasy, and physical accuracy.

A FEMINIST PERSPECTIVE

The concerns of women ceramists in the late twentieth century were so vastly different from the women who gathered to produce china-painted teacups a century earlier that comparisons are almost

above left:
301. PATTI WARASHINA
WASH & WEAR
c. 1976. Low-fire clay, under-glaze, approximate height 27", width 16", diameter 16". Memphis Brooks Museum of Art, Tenn. Gift of Audrey Taylor Gonzalez

above right:
302. ELAINE CARHARTT
THE GOSSIP from THE
MEETING (detail, 1 of 3)
1982. Low-fire clay, acrylic, 30 x 28 x 27". Private collection

303. Patti Warashina
CAR KILN
1972. Low-fire whiteware, hand-built, glazes, lusters, 15 x 14⅜ x 35¼". Collection John Michael Kohler Arts Center, Sheboygan, Wis.

meaningless. What is comparable is that women, both in their numbers and in the quality of their work, had remained integral members of the craft. By the 1950s and 1960s, male domination in ceramics was especially pervasive, notwithstanding some notable contributions by women in the field. But women ceramists in the seventies re-emerged to challenge their male colleagues. Indeed, the strength of the women's movement encouraged a feminist reevaluation of women in American culture and of men.

Patti Warashina had not consciously decided to attack the prevailing machismo head-on, but, as she remarked recalling that period, "When Voulkos came along, no one had to deal with the past anymore."[8] She applied herself to the present, combining the Pop Art mass culture image of the automobile with the kiln as a symbol of male domination. In *Car Kiln*, part of a 1970–74 series, she contrasted a car destroyed by fire with the creativity of fire in a kiln. Other car/kilns parodied kiln terminology (the fact that the equipment is pronounced "kill") with the car's life-threatening capacity. Humorous and surrealistic, the car/kiln imagery deftly undercut male pretensions.

Karen Breschi, reacting more overtly to the feminist movement, created figures that matched the movement's early literature castigating men. She applied animal heads on the busts and torsos of men. *Man Disguised as a Dog* is a barrel-chested, arrogant canine/man wearing a leather vest and a leer on his lips. The counterculture terminology of the sixties was part of *Pig Boss* (1973). Unlike Frank Fleming's use of animal heads on human bodies, Breschi's figures combined raucous humor with raw anger. That anger likewise infected her images of women; in a series of sculptures produced between 1973–78, female figures occupied shrine/altars. Although the relationship to nature myths, madonnas, or romantic love goddesses was implied, those figures projected the power of an enraged Earth Mother, with glowering facial expressions and violent gestures.

In the mid-seventies, Patti Warashina's imagery for a feminine iconography shifted from the car/kiln to pyramids and tetrahedrons, the latter stacked like Japanese food containers. Related in form to

Buddhist household shrines, the pyramid series signaled a change from icons of male domination to images describing a woman's servile position in American culture. Painted on the surfaces of this series of twelve altarpieces (1976–77) were women as housewives and mistresses, presented in the media as the core of happiness and contentment. Three-dimensional forms playing against a two-dimensional background depicted smiling, open-mouthed women exuding a kind of television-commercial cheerfulness as they washed clothes and attended to chores. But an electric cord extends from the back of one figure (*Love it or Leave it*), implying that she functions just like an ordinary kitchen appliance; another woman, clothed in the apparel of a geisha, cheerfully holds a heart punctured by arrows.

By 1977, Warashina had freed her women from servitude and the flat surface; cast porcelain, unglazed nude figures created on a scale to fit her cars became her principal image. Unlike the stilted poses and faceless anonymity of Guy Cowan's dancing figurines, these women had vibrant personalities and were bursting with the purposeful energy of the reborn. The myth of Europa, a popular subject in the 1930s, was refashioned by Warashina into a woman riding a household iron. Now in control, the figure commands the iron, fearlessly swinging the electric cord like a lasso. The Chevrolet coupe returned, this time commandeered by women who rode on the roof, or in other ways were figuratively in the driver's seat, freed from conventional social roles. Warashina's personal experiences and her view of herself as an artist contribute to energetic images of transformation—from cocoon-like restraints to the freedom of flight.

Like Warashina, Nancy Carman used dreams and fantasies as the basis of figurative narrative scenes; her sketches, drawings, or doodlings, similar to the automatic writings of the Surrealists, often shaped the tableaux.[9] But unlike Warashina's vibrant women, Carman's figures frequently lacked gender definition or distinct facial features. Carman's themes—complex male/female relationships, romantic tragedies, and women confronting a personal struggle—were characteristic of a feminist approach in the late seventies and eighties. The fairy tale of the frog prince was modernized in *Desperate* (1983). The disappointments, failures, and confusions over social interaction were expressed through figures out of scale with their surroundings or in ambiguous and mysterious associations with animals and other figures.

In contrast to Carman and Warashina's sophisticated, cast, and china-painted sculptures, Mary Frank's recumbent women, assembled from unglazed slab fragments, evoke an archaic landscape. The sectional figures capture the fluidity and sense of movement Frank admired in sculptor Reuben Nakian's clay plaques of the early sixties. That influence led her in the early seventies to a series of incised and cut plaques depicting women and horses in dreamlike fantasy voyages. A later series of figures associated women with the mythology of sea nymphs, who gradually metamorphosed into land creatures. Like Warashina's transformations, Frank's figures are shown in the act of becoming; for example, a woman's hair flows down her body like a waterfall down a mountain, while she balances on tree-trunk-thick limbs. These transitions connect Frank's women to nature in a serene, ingenuous context, not with the aggressive

304. NANCY CARMAN
DESPERATE
1983. Low-fired white clay, underglaze glaze, and china paint, height 18". Private collection

305. REUBEN NAKIAN
UNTITLED
1959–60. Terra-cotta, 13⅜ x 11½ x 5¼". National Museum of American Art, Smithsonian Institution, Washington, D.C. Gift of Mr. Philip Stern

306. MARY FRANK
PERSEPHONE
*1985. Terra-cotta, 28 x 73 x 40".
Collection the artist and Zabriskie Gallery, New York*

307. MARY FRANK
SWIMMER
*1978. Ceramic. 17 x 94 x 32".
Whitney Museum of American
Art, New York*

anger associated with nature in Breschi's sculptures. The bent knees, raised arm, and rise of a stomach in *Woman with Outstretched Arms* (1975) mimic mountains, valleys, and tall trees. The subtle imprint of ferns, leaves, and grasses transformed body fragments into fossil-bearing, earth-connected natural objects.

The sensuous assemblages of flowing body forms lend themselves to themes of idyllic or erotic love (as in *Lover*, 1977) and present undisguised sexuality. Frank's spontaneity, intuition, and exploitation of the immediacy of the material suited a hedonistic expressionism. Like her contemporaries, Frank incorporated mythology to suit inner visions, fantasies, and dreams. But where Breschi and Warashina expressed resentment and frustration with the restraints imposed on women, Frank's context was altogether a different one; her work connected womanhood to the primary elements of water and earth. Unlike exhibits on trends in contemporary ceramics, feminist perspectives in this field were never made the subject of a prominent show. Instead, the work of these artists was sometimes shown with that of other women artists, but more often as part of shows on figurative sculpture.

THE ARCHAIC LANDSCAPE AND THE FIGURE

Mary Frank's association of unglazed clay fragments with a natural environment paralleled the work of Hepburn, Simonds, and the ves-

308. MARY FRANK
FEMALE FIGURES
1976. Ceramic, 13½ x 9". Collection Selma and Alfred Knobler

right:
309. STEPHEN DESTAEBLER
*Fired clay. (left:) Seated Woman
with Mimbres Womb 1978. 71 x
16 x 29". Private collection.
(right:) Standing Figure With
Ribs. 1978. 79 x 17 x 28". Private
collection*

below:
310. MICHAEL LUCERO
*Ceramic and metal (left to
right:) Untitled (fish). 1981. 94 x
36 x 15". Untitled (cucarachas).
1981. 102 x 67 x 24".
Untitled (turtle). 1981. 92 x 36 x
32". Collection the artist*

sel-makers involved in raku and primitive firings. The emphasis on clay's origins in the earth and lengthy primitive tradition exerted a strong appeal for other figurative sculptors interested in expressing clay's roots.

The meshing of landscape and figure in Stephen DeStaebler's columnar forms is more closely related to geology and archeology than are Frank's fragmented forms. Coming West in the late sixties from Missouri to attend the University of California in Berkeley, DeStaebler was impressed by the rugged mountains and geological formations, images of which eventually entered his work. Like Mary Frank, DeStaebler initially began with sculptures in a horizontal axis, but by 1971 he was searching for a way to sustain a vertical axis in spite of the material's resistance to such efforts. He resolved this problem by rearranging wet assembled segments and allowing the clay to crack, shrink, and warp—factors prior to Abstract Expressionism considered "taboos" of clay technology.[10] By 1975, DeStaebler's fragmented figures had attained a pyramidal form with sheer cut sides. Appearing to emerge from the earth while simultaneously retreating into a final resting place, the forms expressed a dynamic tension. Horizontal cuts, a result of DeStaebler's rearrangement of segments, suggest geological stratification and the wearing effect of erosion; both give his work the timeless quality inherent in Mason's totems of the sixties. More monumental, slender, and upright by the 1980s, DeStaebler's enigmatic fragments can be read as abstraction or figuration, as bones, fossils, or fleshy human anatomy. The sculptures sustain intrinsic connections to primitive ritual, to a poetic expression of the archaic, and to DeStaebler's concern and respect for nature and the western landscape.

Excavated pottery shards influenced Rick Dillingham's rich, linear surface embellishment, and in Jens Morrison's *Casas*, they offered references to ceramic tradition. That tradition is evident in Michael Lucero's use of shards as his primary material. Moving to New York in 1979 from his home in California, and without his pottery equipment, Lucero gravitated toward pottery fragments as a temporary measure. What evolved were figures composed of shards. Hundreds of ceramic "leaves" tied together with colored telephone cable and wired to a sectional armature resembling a broom handle provided the structure. Seven or eight feet high, these sculptures, confrontational in scale, presented the human form at its most minimalistic, much like the primitive stick figures of early childhood drawings, an association on which Lucero capitalized. The only volumetric element was a vessel-head (which led to the appellation "pot head").[11] The bent and twisted position of arms and legs gives one figure a Neanderthal stance, another the grace of a dancer. The primitivism of the structure with its archaic references accentuates the power of the human image; the thick layers of shards dramatize the concept of wholeness leading to brokenness and to wholeness again conveying, as Lucero states, "the entire cyclical story of pottery."[12]

Robert Brady's nearly lifesize figures shared the use of vessel-like heads with Lucero. In the early eighties his figures also supported these heads with ambiguous markings. But instead of using shards, Brady built his forms from coils, a method which, when com-

311. ROBERT BRADY
AGROUND
1984. Stoneware and glaze, 70 x 14 x 17". Collection the artist. Courtesy Braunstein/Quay Gallery, San Francisco

312. POLLY FRIZZELL
BUDDY
1982. Low-fired clay; figure on a formica and stainless steel pedestal, height 19". Private collection

The cut-away interior of the torso reveals the essence of the short-order cook's existence. His bland demeanor matches the unpretentious food he offers.

bined with raku firing, allowed him to create the surface appearance of a mummy. The directness of coil building parallels the directness of primitive and naive art which Brady admires. The vessel-head's position on a body lacking a neck recalls early kachina dolls, voodoo figures, and the thin figures in children's drawings, having limbs appearing too frail to support body weight. The truncated limbs of *Seoul Survivor* (1981) speak to pain, sadness, and death as does the dark, charred body of *Ancestor* (1982). The splayed hands of *Alto Mask* (1980) and the mask's bulging eyes once again convey the terror of Edvard Munch's *The Scream*. In a 1985–86 series, a latticework grid, a symbol of the material world, supported or interacted with some of his figures. The intensity of emotion in Brady's earlier figures has softened, but the high level of restless energy remained through his use of rich colors and pitted, scarred surfaces.

SOCIAL MESSAGES

Personal experiences evoking less stressful emotional trauma than those in Brady's figures were realistically portrayed by Jack Earl's

313. JACK EARL
DOG GONE
*1978. Ceramic, china paint,
height 18¼". Collection Katherine Nikoline Keland*

tableaux. After his projects at Kohler Company, Earl returned to his native Ohio. There his depiction of everyday life in rural Ohio in the seventies and eighties was both visual and verbal, his figures' feelings described by lengthy, stream-of-consciousness titles. A young man on the doorstep of a house, bouquet in hand, laments in the caption: "You can take a bath, change you'r underwear and your socks, put on your newest cloths to go see your girl and the first thing her dog comes around sniffing you out."[13] Another poignant scene shows a male figure with the inscription, "Every time she touched him she left a dent." These and other mid- and late-seventies genre sculptures were mocking kitsch or other souvenir figurines that bear neither craftsmanship nor insight.

The juxtaposition of real life and a fantasy life marks many of Earl's early eighties sculptures and later tableaux. Men and women confined in their ordinary houses, living ordinary lives, such as having coffee at a worn kitchen table, dream of mountains, towering trees, meandering streams, a luscious vista detailed on the exterior kitchen wall. Like Gilhooly and Warashina who used surrogate images, Earl's figure of "Bill" represented a composite of his easy-going, passive family members and neighbors. Bill is shown working, resting, thinking . . . just watching life go by. The architecture and interiors of farm homes add character and depth to Earl's unsentimental view of rural life. Earl contrasted the presence of sham in urban sophistication and education with the more straightforward world his figures inhabit.

Though farm women were part of Viola Frey's rural upbringing and figure prominently in her work of the late seventies, their portrayal, in flowered hats and dresses, cloddish sandals, and toothy smiles, is less sympathetic than Earl's. Frey's folksy women hold kitsch figurines, curios familiar to Frey from childhood. While she regarded these objects as the junk art of American culture, they nevertheless inspired an earlier series of frenetic assemblages of simulated curios. During the seventies, the enlargement of the curio figurine became the basis for Frey's lifesize women, grandmother figures holding their kitsch treasures more threateningly than kindly. Frey's women are the opposite of the delicate bric-a-brac they hold. They are women "who had control over their lives, who maintained their power."[14]

The imposing grandmother figures were superseded by seven- to ten-foot-tall urban men and women of the 1980s. Not since Waylande Gregory's 1930s sculptures for fountains had ceramists dealt with fully rounded, larger-than-lifesize figures. But Frey's concerns were quite apart from Gregory's. Power and weakness in today's society became the subject matter. Similar to cartoon characters, the faces of these women with their pompadour hairstyles register wide-eyed, innocent expressions, yet their body gestures suggest a defensive stance. The men, even taller and of greater bulk, represented impassive, authoritarian bureaucrats in suits and ties with malevolent facial expressions and correspondingly threatening postures. These sculptures exposed the overblown middle-class values of ordinary people behind whose empty expressions lies vulnerability and impotency. In *Power Blue Suit* (1982) for example, Frey highlights the ludicrousness of a society primarily impressed with superficial appearances.

In much of her work, abstract, painterly slashes of robust orange, yellow, and blue glazes define a Neo-expressionist, emotional use of color. References to folk art are evident in the figures' stiff positions and frozen facial expressions.

Equally over-lifesize in height, Vern Funk's columnar ballroom dancers of 1985–86 have an Art Deco ambience. In slinky evening gowns, stylized coiffures, and highly polished red nails, the women seem dazed, distractedly engrossed in counting steps; the sleek-haired men appear cool and in control. Funk's own expertise on the dance floor accounts for the realistic details which underscore a concern for appearance and the self-involved, fantasy world of the ballroom. In contrast to this statuesque masquerade, T. J. Dixon's lifesize, unglazed, near-realistic busts and figures of 1985–86 defined a thoughtful mood or a characteristic gesture—a head resting on a cupped hand, a man slouching with hands in his pockets or seated on a crate with elbows on his knees. Most of Dixon's figures are caught at rest, as though waiting for something to happen. On another level, their stance becomes an abstract form, reductive and purged of all details except the sensuousness of evenly textured, terra-cotta clay.

314. T. J. DIXON
FIGURE ON CRATE
*1986. Terra-cotta, 36 x 20 x 25",
lifesize. Private collection*

Dilemma for Ceramic Sculpture

From viewing the development of American ceramics over a twenty-year period beginning in the mid-sixties, there can be little doubt that the ascendance of sculpture transformed the medium. Incorporating the abstract, the architectonic, the archaic, and Minimalism, ceramic sculptors opened the medium to a broad aesthetic vision, or perhaps even revision. Further, figurative sculpture in clay reflected the direction of twentieth-century art in its acceptance of Surrealism, Expressionism, and symbolism. Perhaps one of the most obvious accomplishments of ceramic sculpture generally was the increased volume and scale. Technological advances in construction and firing contributed to overcoming the difficulties inherent in working with clay of great height and weight. Evidence that these problems were successfully and aesthetically surmounted came in exhibitions such as "Large Scale Ceramic Sculpture" at the University of California, Davis campus in 1979. The seventeen guest artists covered the spectrum of abstract, expressive, figurative, and architectural sculpture. Other exhibits such as "The Clay Figure" (1981) at the American Craft Museum in New York, and "Figurative Clay Sculpture Northern California" (1982) at the Quay Gallery in San Francisco, confirmed the strength and importance of figurative expression in clay.

315. TOM RIPPON
STRONG MAN
1981. Porcelain, 20½ x 11 x 10".
Private collection

Like the simplicity of Elie Nadelman's figures of the 1930s, Rippon creates his in basic ways. His choice of forms—squiggles, teardrops, paraboloids and cones—present a figure or bust in its pared-down essentials.

While each show demonstrated the increasing vitality of ceramic sculpture, the exhibit that truly brought national attention to sculpture in clay was "Ceramic Sculpture: Six Artists," which opened at New York's Whitney Museum of American Art in December 1981. Featured were Arneson, Gilhooly, Mason, Price, Shaw, and Voulkos, all of whom had appeared in past Whitney annuals and biennials. In the accompanying catalogue, co-curator Richard Marshall wrote that the artists chosen had "brought the medium into the mainstream of contemporary sculpture."[15] Though not intended as a comprehensive survey, and far less ambitious than the "Century" exhibit a few years earlier, the Whitney show nevertheless attracted critics from major magazines and newspapers. Most of these national reviewers evaluated the exhibit in terms of contemporary painting, though critics from the West Coast, more familiar with the six artists, took their colleagues to task for making the work fit preconceived art-historical categories. Certainly there was much to dispute about the show—the exclusion of certain artists, the choice of examples of work, and the lack of recognition of the vessel—but the heated rhetorical exchanges could not diminish the fact that the Whitney show had, in essence, bestowed museum status on sculpture in clay.

In doing so, the museum was merely catching up on a narrow segment of the clay movement. (Further underscoring this fact was the solo exhibition of Viola Frey's sculpture at the Whitney in 1984.) Among the art-buying world the vision was broader. By the early 1980s, the number of galleries showing work in clay and the number of serious collectors had increased substantially. Some of this activity was due to the precipitantly high prices commanded by contemporary painting and non-clay sculpture, prices which turned collectors toward less costly ceramics. The recognition that collectors formed an essential part of the crafts support network prompted the American Craft Council in the 1980s to institute a collectors' viewing and purchasing event prior to the opening of the yearly ACC Craft Fair. Other accommodations toward collectors were soon instituted by galleries, exhibition curators, and symposia.[16]

The ceramics network, however, continued to suffer from a void in educated, critical attention as well as a broad-based forum to further define the role of the medium in American art. A new publication, *American Ceramics*, appeared in 1982 to provide a platform for stimulating interest in the issues of contemporary work and placing it in an historical perspective. At this juncture, however, the position of sculpture in clay—whether figurative, abstract, archaic, or architectonic—vis-à-vis sculpture in metal, bronze, or wood, remained in a credibility limbo. Further confusing the issue were a group of ceramists incorporating non-clay materials into their sculpture. Precedents for this action date back to the 1960s and 1970s when Daniel Rhodes and Marilyn Levine used fiberglass and nylon fibers to strengthen clay. In the eighties, combinations of clay, wood, organic materials, bronze, and cement, to name just a few, have extended the context of clay beyond historical, traditional connotations. Again, the idea is primary; only here the artist uses clay as the art material to convey transformations in an aesthetic dialogue with materials.

opposite:
316. VIOLA FREY
ORANGE AND YELLOW
HAND MAN (left) and BIG BOY.
*1985–86. Whiteware. (left:) 118
x 60 x 24"; (right:) 120 x 59 x 30".
Collection Stephane Janssen,
Beverly Hills, Calif.*

The artist has used the surface of the figure for broad masses of color which disrupt the form; the expressive, painterly use of clay and glazes contrast with the figure's stiff, authoritarian stance.

above:
317. VIOLA FREY
DOUBLE GRANDMOTHER
WITH BLACK AND WHITE
DRESSES
*1981–82. Whiteware, glaze,
each figure 84 x 20 x 20". Collection Rena G. Bransten*

Chapter 17

PERMISSIVE PLURALISM

Since the 1960s, many American ceramists have been concerned with redefining clay's relationship to art. In the pursuit of recognition for their work in clay, and anxious to be considered serious artists, these ceramists continued the momentum of testing traditional boundary lines. "Pushing the envelope" was not only meaningful terminology for astronauts; the ceramic equivalent of that phrase was the search for what hadn't yet been tried, the results being a diversity of expression for both vessel and sculpture. A cross-fertilization of ideas occurred between the vessel form and sculpture which began to blur the borders previously distinguishing each form. Now the idea had become the primary focus, and whatever form satisfied the concept was legitimate. One of those ideas, the definition of space (a concern ceramics shares with architecture), now included vessel elements, and in this context, both vessel and sculpture grew toward a monumental expression. Highly decorative color was a major component and at times functioned as subject matter. Often criticized for being just an ornamental art, ceramics could now affirm the decorative aspect of its character as a legitimate aesthetic concern.

Architectonic Monumentality

Monumentality in clay comes with the technical ability to sustain height. Clay, to a much greater degree than wood, metal, or stone, is a material subject to the forces of gravity. Early in American ceramic history, large tile murals achieved considerable size because of a supporting wall. Waylande Gregory was probably the first to devise an armature to successfully dry and fire large figures without cutting them into sections. Unaware of Gregory's achievements, Peter Voulkos and John Mason devised other interior and exterior structures to complete their large sculptures and walls. Among the many reasons for the increasingly large work was the influence of Abstract Expressionist painting and its confrontational size.

opposite:
318. TONY HEPBURN
ST. LOUIS GATE
1984. Stoneware, clay, and gold leaf, height 8', width 7', depth 7'. National Museum of Modern Art, Seoul, Korea

above:
319. RON NAGLE
UNTITLED
1980. Multi-fired earthenware, height 3½", diameter 3¾". Private collection

Several companies were invaluable in providing a setting and the equipment for large-scale work. One was the Kohler Company's artist-in-residence program. Another work space opened in the early 1980s in Omaha, Nebraska. In a program initiated by Omaha gallery owner Ree Schonlau, the Omaha Brickworks, a working brickyard, allowed groups of artists to take advantage of their facilities, including a thirty-five-foot diameter beehive kiln. Like the Kohler factory, the brickyard encouraged innovation in the use of mass-produced units, as well as work in an enlarged scale. In 1981, Tony Hepburn, one of the first artists invited to Omaha by Schonlau, held a workshop at the brickyard for twenty participants. Working along with the group, Hepburn, in keeping with his orientation toward ancient monuments, incorporated blocks and bricks for a series of gates whose post-and-lintel construction evoked early Peruvian and Pueblo passage openings.

In 1982, Schonlau invited Jun Kaneko, then head of the ceramics department at the Cranbrook Academy of Art, to participate in the Omaha program. Kaneko agreed, and proposed plans for four oval, dome-shaped *dangos* (dumpling in Japanese), to be constructed at the brickyard. Seven feet long and six feet high, the domes and the equally complex construction of three, thick quadrilateral slabs became the largest objects ever made on that site. The project required six weeks for construction, over three months to dry, and thirty-five

320. JOHN MASON
UNTITLED
1986. Glazed stoneware, 34 x 24½ x 24½". Collection the artist

In this piece, made by Mason in the 1980s as part of a series of architectonic containers, geometric explorations of his 1960s minimalistic cross forms are continued. Here, too, is the mathematical logic of the *Hudson River Series*, along with the monumentality inherent in his earlier work.

321. JUN KANEKO
DANGOS AND SLABS
*1984. Stoneware. Dango, 72 x 84
x 60", weight 5½ tons; Slab 84 x
60 x 12", weight 1 ton. Courtesy
the Alternative Work Site/Be-
mis Foundation, Omaha, Nebr.*

days for firing.[1] Kaneko painted the domes and slabs with bright colored slips in highly decorative geometric patterns and stripes, emphasizing the contours of the domes. Minimalistic in shape, the
domes and the colorful striped platforms were completed in 1983
and subsequently displayed at the Laumeier Sculpture Park in St.
Louis. In one respect, the patterns and color recaptured the spirit of
prehistoric baskets and pottery; at the same time, the blocks of lines
resembled the pattern of color strokes in Jasper Johns's series of
paintings in 1979. The work of Kaneko, Hepburn, and others has
only reinforced Schonlau's commitment to the brickyard as an alternative work space. As Schonlau expressed it, "the artist-industry relationship is one concrete way of realizing the artist's contribution
[to society]."[2]

Japanese-born Jun Kaneko found his mecca for constructing
monumental sculpture in Nebraska. Conversely, American-born
Deborah Horrell found hers in Japan. There she traveled to the Otsuka Ohmi Chemical Company, which had gained a reputation for
its ability to produce industrial porcelain tiles as large as three by
twelve feet, but without the distortion such size usually incurs.
(Horrell was not the first American artist to create work at the company's facilities; in 1982, Robert Rauschenberg spent a couple of
months there producing clay panels.) Horrell's project of 1985, *Passages: Heaven, Hell and the In-Between*, consisted of three nine-foot

entryways leading to a final panel, *Sacred and Profane Transitions*. The low-relief decoration on the panels carved out of thick layers of slip depicted flames, bird wings, a gesturing hand, and fragments of a skull and skeleton. While these images had been part of Horrell's earlier sculpture, in this context they connected the work to medieval and renaissance depictions of hell in Western art.[3] The panels were situated so that the viewer passed from one portal to the next and on to the final panel, the effect being that of a journey through images dealing with the transformation from life to death and the relationship between nature and spirituality.

Affirmation of the strength of architectonic monumentality in ceramics came at the NCECA conference of 1985 in St. Louis where the topic was "Ceramic Art and Architecture." In panel discussions and slide lectures, architects and ceramists discussed how architectural aesthetics were now once again open to ornamentation. Some opportunities for ornamentation, as demonstrated by the work of Frans Wildenhain and Ruth Duckworth, had been available in the past; the present emphasis, however, was as sculpture on an archi-

322. DEBORAH HORRELL
PASSAGES: HEAVEN, HELL
AND THE IN-BETWEEN
*1985. Porcelain, at Otsuka
Ohmi Chemical Co., Japan, 9 x
6 x 18'. Collection the artist*

tectural scale. Part of the reason for the new relationship between architecture and ceramics was the renewed interest in historical preservation.[4] This was spurred to a great extent by the "Art in Architecture" program initiated by the General Services Administration in 1963 (formally implemented in 1972), which required a percentage of the total construction budget for new, federally funded buildings be set aside for art. The program provided funds for both the creation of new work in an architectural setting, and the restoration of artistic ornamentation on existing buildings.

"Architectural Ceramics: Eight Concepts" was the main exhibition at the 1985 NCECA conference, organized in conjunction with the American Craft Museum (formerly the Museum of Contemporary Crafts) and Washington University of St. Louis. For the eight guest artists, the challenge was in defining space and embellishment for either a room, entryway, or a wall. One participant, Tony Hepburn, continued in the direction of his experience at the Omaha Brickworks by producing a handsome, stacked archaic arch, totem, and ritual vessel, *St. Louis Gate*. Mythological and religious themes with amusingly erotic overtones surrounded Akio Takamori's portal flanked by voluptuous male and female nudes. Beth Starbuck and Steven Goldner used handmade tile borders to define the wainscoting, window frames, floor, and table for a small room. But the most unusual decorative panels forming an arch, Cliff Garten's sensitively colored, monumental doorway, produced a barrage of diverse sensations. Incorporating large, winged urns as entrance guardians surrounded by tiled walls and floors, the space examined classical architectural language and its relationship to the vessel.[5] More conventional in form were figurative patterns on walls by Kurt Weiser and Patrick Siler and a garden room by Betty Woodman. In spite of the exhibit's restrictive directive for a wall-oriented format, the show presented the versatile possibilities within architectural ceramics.

Sculpture in a Vessel Context

Cliff Garten's anthropomorphic vessels, done as part of a mural, had developed from a previous series, *Paired Vases*, in which the vessel's relationship to the human figure was underscored by exaggerating two- and three-dimensional curvilinear lines and shapes. Garten's orientation was the historical use of the vessel in landscape as a focal point in gardens, parks, and accents on walls and entrance pillars. Such associations and the vessel's sculptural context also had precedents dating back to the early 1970s in the work of a group of vessel-makers.

LANDSCAPE AND THE ARCHITECTONIC

One of the first to associate the vessel in a landscape context was Wayne Higby. In the early seventies, Higby had translated his affinity for the landscape of the Southwest into slab-formed covered con-

323. Akio Takamori
MAN WITH DOG/WOMAN
*1983. Earthenware, height 16½",
width 23½". Collection Hope
and Jay Yampol*

tainers; grouped like a folding screen to suggest a continuous scene, the assembled rectangular boxes traced the meanderings of a stream flowing below high mountains and steep canyons. Higby's increasing interest in illusionistic depth rather than mere surface relief caused him to shift to another form, the bowl, in 1976. The scenic vista became a dialogue between the bowl's interior space, exterior contour, and a continuous line between both giving the illusion of cliffs deeply eroded by mountain streams. Interaction between form and surface offered Higby the opportunity to fuse the polarities of reality/illusion, near/far, and light/dark as a way of suggesting how opposites work together.[6]

Higby's romantic landscapes contrast with William Daley's unadorned buff surfaces and geometric-constructivist aesthetic. The large scale of Daley's vessels and their interior confluence of squares, octagons, encasements, and stepped levels remove them from both functional and traditional considerations; instead they respond to an architectural context. Similar to William Wyman's temples in their deceptive simplicity and unglazed surfaces, Daley's bowl-shaped structures recall terraced hillsides, ancient amphitheaters, or coliseums. Early in his career Daley had learned of Glen Lukens's use of unglazed clay; in describing his affinity for Lukens's large platters, Daley could have been discussing his own work. Lukens, he wrote, was "dealing with the essential rather than the decorative...[with] a form for describing his response to nature [and] an invitation to the intimate."[7] Daley, too, was responsive to the ambience of the Southwest, especially to the cliff dwellings of the Anasazi. He had visited these ruins when he taught at the University of New Mexico in 1971 and became familiar with the step patterns on native American baskets and pottery. Daley's transformations in clay moved beyond Lukens's use of the plate/platter while still reflecting these influences.

The change in the vessel form had been part of Ken Price and Ron Nagle's concerns for over twenty years. In between making the myriad of objects for "Happy's Curios" in Taos, New Mexico, Price produced a series of *Slate Cups* (1972–77), which were earthenware forms contrasting high color and smooth surfaces with rough, organic, earth-related images. Using the cup form, Price made oblique references to a constructivist mode, but more involved with color than Daley, he projected Color Field painting in three dimensions. Price's next series eliminated organic elements for an architectonic, geometric form that brought his work closer to hard-edge painting. These *Zigs*, as he called them, were small, hollow, porcelain pieces, glazed in striking primary colors confined to their planes by a thin, white line which defined all the edges. An appendage which could be read as a vestigial handle tenuously connected these objects to their origin in the cup. Price thought of these objects as three-dimensional interpretations of the principles of geometry in Mondrian's paintings.[8]

Like Price, Ron Nagle moved into hard-edge geometry and away from the traditional shape of the cup in his work of the early seventies. By 1978, Nagle had simplified the concept of the handle to a small shelf that gave the cup's profile a protruding jaw. Asymmetrical surface treatment and glaze drips poised just above the foot linked the work to Japanese aesthetics. In the 1980s, Nagle's vessels

324. WILLIAM DALEY
CONICAL PROCESSION
1982. Stoneware, unglazed, 21 x 23½ x 22". Collection Jane and Leonard L. Korman

325. WAYNE HIGBY
WHITE TERRACE GAP
(landscape bowl)
1984. Raku, 11½ x 18 x 16½". Collection Wayne and Donna Higby

326. CLIFF GARTEN
HATCH, HATCH
*1984. Earthenware, 67½ x 41½
x 10¼". Everson Museum of Art,
Syracuse, N.Y.*

327. RON NAGLE
UNTITLED
*1982. Ceramic, 6¾ x 3¾ x 4".
Private collection*

moved closer to an architectural expression with a stucco-like surface texture, Art Deco colors, and the splattered patterns and iridescent flecks of the 1950s standard asphalt tile kitchen floor. Since the mid-eighties, the gesture and feel of clay and the emotional appeal of Nagle's multi-layered, sensuous china paints and glazes have all but submerged volume and any sense of vessel. The vessel remained as a memory, a peripheral presence, which Nagle referred to as "a potential form for expression."[9]

Instead of working with the bowl or the cup, Kris Cox, a former student of Paul Soldner's, moved from stoppered raku-fired containers to vessels subordinated by tall, exaggerated handles in the early 1980s. By 1985, the handles had become armatures framing space and supporting a multitude of substructures which resembled ladders, ledges, shafts, and grids. Repetitive grooved lines cut the vessel's surface into ovals, circles, or rhythmic waves. Crusty scabrous textures on rich, saffron-orange and ultramarine-blue glazes added an archeological aura that also connected the vessel to Hugh Robertson and Adelaide Robineau's volcanic glazes. In 1979 a series of lidded vessels with armatures echoed the gabled entryways to a Japanese garden or shrine. Then, in the eighties, unlike Hepburn's post-and-lintel construction, an asymmetrical armature fastened with exaggerated pegs supported beams carrying images of a more personal significance, a ship, a barn, a small figure. As a support for complex post-and-beam attachments, the vessel was increasingly submerged by various guises—as a massive battleship-like image or a futuristic fortress of battlements and gun turrets. More monumental than any of the above vessel-oriented sculpture, Cox's structures incorporated architectural features from the ancient Near and Far East and from the early Roman and Gothic periods for a powerful architectonic statement. Part of that statement involved integrating opposite conditions—controlling the fire, yet allowing for the accidental, planning the structure but making intuitive changes, using shocking and affirming color.

ORGANIC/GEOMETRIC ABSTRACTION

Price, Nagle, and Cox contributed to the ambiguity surrounding definitions of the vessel. Volume appeared to be the only remaining characteristic that would connect their work to the vessel, and for Price volume was becoming questionable. When he moved to Massachusetts in 1982, Price's concerns shifted from the architectural nuances in his *Zigs* to the juxtaposition of the organic and geometric stated earlier in his *Slate Cups*. But in his return to a reevaluation of these forms, volume disappeared; these eighties sculptures resembled diminutive landscapes of rock chunks or crystalline formations. Since the 1960s, edges and right angles at the unexpected junction of massed forms and concentrated areas of color that appear to penetrate down to the core have remained his primary objectives.

Peter Voulkos had retained a biomorphic configuration in his work since the mid-sixties. At that time, he had been exploring stains and firing procedures that would enhance his subtle or harsh, gestural surface marks and indentations. Around 1978, he began fir-

328. PETER VOULKOS
PLATE DRAWING
*1972. Stoneware, diameter 18".
Collection the artist and courtesy Braunstein/Quay Gallery,
San Francisco*

329. PETER VOULKOS
UNTITLED VESSEL
FORM # 28
*1981. Wood-fired ceramic, 40½
x 21 x 19". Collection Modesto
Lanzone, courtesy Braunstein/
Quay Gallery, San Francisco*

ing his stoneware in wood-burning kilns in New York and New Jersey. Deposits of ash and natural minerals, the result of wood firings, produced rich earth tones of ocher shading into orange-browns, smoky grays and blacks which changed from matt to luster in the ridges and rims of his plates. Confining himself to two forms, the oversized plate and bottle, Voulkos treated the surface as terrain for forceful lines, gouged holes, and dynamic eruptions from wads of porcelain, the marks interacting with the wood ash deposits. His stacked vessels, anthropomorphic in scale, projected human body language in a stance that provocatively sagged and bulged.

Abstract biomorphic imagery alluding to landscape or human anatomy assumed monumental proportions in Graham Marks's larger-than-lifesize gourd and melon shapes, which were cut or ripped open to reveal inner, enigmatic structures handbuilt from hundreds of coils (produced by an extruder and then handrolled for variations). The interior geometric maze contrasted with exterior surfaces resembling barnacles, heavy tree bark, the convolutions of the brain, or other biological cellular material enormously enlarged. Marks credits Brancusi and English ceramist Hans Coper for contributing to his sense of abstract form.[10] Some of the interior masses seem imperfect as though decay and decomposition had occurred. While these elements link his work to that of Charles Simonds, Marks allows that the juxtaposition of disparate objects can provide surprising connections and perceptions relating his work to the Surrealists. Some of his mid-eighties sculptures have reduced interior viewing to a small slitlike opening or graceful, linear cracks in the clay surface. Hieroglyphic-like markings, sandblasted on the exterior, made these impenetrable objects all the more mystifying and intriguing.

The gestural stance and the humor implied in Voulkos's vessels take on massive proportions in Arnold Zimmerman's eight- to ten-foot vessels. Inspired by Romanesque architecture, Analytic Cubism, mosaics in churches and monasteries, Zimmerman carves into three- to five-inch-thick stoneware walls for deep reliefs or adds attachments that give movement to the form. Expanding on the terminology of neck, shoulder, and belly in referring to parts of the vessel, Zimmerman exaggerated proportions for distinctly male and female poses. Confrontational monumentality and textured, carved surfaces energized these figure/columns and figure/arches into human parodies.

330. ARNOLD ZIMMERMAN
UNTITLED
1986. Stoneware, 32 x 15 x 15".
Collection the artist

FAVORING THE FIGURATIVE

Zimmerman's subtleties in an organic/abstract context were tackled directly by Rudy Autio, Andrea Gill, and Akio Takamori as figurative vessels. Again, cross-fertilization from figurative sculpture can be credited for these perceptions in the vessel. Autio's drawings of the figure on vessels of the early sixties merged form and surface; the traditional vessel shape yielded to bulges and extensions to accommodate complex compositions of women, horses, dogs, and wolves. In the early 1980s, after completing a project in porcelain at the Ara-

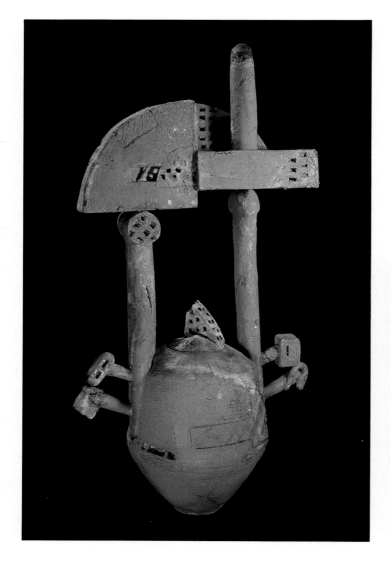

bia factory in Finland, Autio changed to a porcelain body and to a less frontal approach. Seen as clay paintings, the women and animals moved fluidly around the contours of the vessel in brighter, lighter colors. Autio's sensuously painted women have Rubenesque proportions while their association with animals recalls the references to mythology, particularly to Diana the huntress, favored during the Art Deco period. Psychological and sexual overtones play against the lyrical qualities in the leisurely placement and interaction of figures and animals.

In a different approach to the figure, Andrea Gill capitalized on the analogies often made between figure and vessel. By placing the face of a woman at midpoint on the vessel, the top or neck would become a headpiece, and the base a bust. Moving the bust toward the interior of the vessel transformed the space into a decorative niche for a shrine image. Gill flattened the frontal contour of the head, thereby making the severe vertical ridge delineating the nose the only three-dimensional element on the face; this feature and the black lines which described the eyes and mouth linked Gill's wom-

above left:
331. KRIS COX
LIDDED VESSEL WITH
ARMATURE
1982. Low-fired clay, 51 x 26 x 15". Private collection

above right:
332. GRAHAM MARKS
UNTITLED
1982. Earthenware, 32 x 29 x 31". Private collection

333. KEN PRICE
MAGRITTE
1986. Ceramic. (left:) 10 x 3½ x 3½"; (right:) 10 x 6 x 4½". Private collection

en to images in folk and primitive art. An important influence was Gill's year of study in Italy in 1970. There she was introduced to majolica and folk pottery, to Greek drinking cups of fourth century B.C., eighteenth-century face jugs and Toby mugs. The use of pattern painting and decorative surface illusion added to the deliberate blending of painting and sculpture in her work.

Both Gill and Akio Takamori were students of Ken Ferguson's at the Kansas City Art Institute, but there the similarity ends. Takamori inclined toward the calligraphic fluidity of Eastern painting in slips with sgraffitoed lines on textured slabs. Men, women, and animals perform sexual and human/animal transformations between the frontality of the form and the interior and back wall. Secret human desires, the Jungian concept of animals as symbols for basic human needs and sexual energy, and emotions of jealousy and distrust emanated from figures outlined in harsh black lines.[11] Takamori challenged his Japanese cultural heritage, formality, and strict social structure by acting on his conviction that certain cultural myths and moral positions should be defied through aesthetic imagery.

Renewing Earlier Thematic Directions

Among the plethora of directions open and viable to ceramists in the 1980s, a renewed interest in the object, decorative color in a vessel context, and political commentary continued themes explored earlier.

THE OBJECT AS STILL LIFE

Since the focus on the Pop Art object as seen in the casual arrangement of books by Richard Shaw or Marilyn Levine's mail bag hanging from a hook, the object acquired another dimension in a still-life setting. But instead of an emphasis on trompe l'oeil realism, other considerations such as the relationship between objects assumed greater importance. For example, Nancy Selvin's tea bowls of the early eighties rested on long, lacquered, seven-sided forms which could be read either as trays or as lengthy shadows of the bowls. One or several glass rods placed at an angle acted as linear accents reiterating the form of the tray. Airbrushed and spattered with underglaze colors, the four- or five-sided earthenware tea bowls caught the light on drops of glaze on the rims, a composition enriched by the pearlescent color of the trays. By the mid-eighties, Selvin had turned to groups of faceted bottles framed by a small, double-sashed wood window. Equally minimalistic, the window groups verged on an abstract arrangement of volume, line, and plane. By limiting her palette to two or three intense colors and no other decorative elements, Selvin reinforced a ''less is more'' aesthetic.

334. JUDITH SALOMON
TABLE BOWL
1981. Low-fired hand-built white clay, 18 x 11 x 15". Private collection

Joanne Hayakawa's shelves of bottles, jars, and ambiguous-looking objects suggest a more personal context than Selvin's. Whether grouped together in front of a fan-shaped form or a painting, the arrangement focuses attention on the way mirrored or half-hidden images distort perception of familiar things. References to the fan, whose purpose is to half-hide or half-reveal, derive from American-born Hayakawa's Japanese heritage. Hayakawa and Selvin combine wood with clay as does Juta Savage, whose kitchen cups and plates in the 1980s (some in the form of shards) balanced precariously on unstable wooden tables. Even as these ghostlike household objects metamorphose into abstract compositions, they recall familiar domestic rituals.

In many of the settings described, a human presence is implied. This presence is felt most forcefully in Tony Hepburn's 1985–86 series of well-worn boots, dairy and tar cans, shovels, walking canes, and watering troughs. Here the objects reflect the elderly survivors of the shrinking agricultural community around Alfred, New York, where Hepburn lives. Unglazed terra-cotta objects interact with real-life implements; grouped together, they become portraits of the stalwart New England farmer whose worn tools and mud-caked boots testify to endurance and hard physical labor.

SEDUCTIVE COLOR AND PATTERN

Connections between still-life arrangements and the return to vibrant color lie in Karen Koblitz's shelves and wall reliefs. Ordinary objects, realistic in form but painted and glazed in highly unlikely designs—leopard spots, confetti dots, tropical foliage, and geometric patterns—create startling and humorous relationships. Koblitz's groups of objects echo the profusion of images and the overload of media stimulation in contemporary life. Brilliant color achieved through ceramic glazes goes back in time to Hugh Robertson's monochrome glazes and forward to Ken Price's *Zigs*. For Betty Woodman and Judith Salomon, the historical and contemporary merge together. The runny greens, oranges, and blues of Woodman's oversize *Pillow Pitchers* of the early eighties seem like a three-dimensional version of a Jackson Pollock painting, although Woodman actually took this palette from the three-color glazes of the Chinese T'ang dynasty. The form of the *Pitchers* was of major importance. The undulating handles and elongated necks of the pitchers were exaggerated versions of Greek and Etruscan ware Woodman admired when spending summers in Italy. As such, they added a gestural element and expressed the clay's ability to stretch, loop, curl, and swell, reminiscent of George Ohr's flamboyant handles and frilled rims. Along with the pitchers, oversized trays, cups, and baskets humorously mimic traditional tableware, their scale and decorative colors more appropriate for centerpieces celebrating artful food preparation than for functional purposes.

Geometric patterns and grids accented or contradicted Judith Salomon's slightly skewed handbuilt slab vessels. Flat, oval platters, deep-walled bowls on stout, short pillars, or twenty-inch-high rectangular vases were Salomon's standard larger-than-normal forms.

335. RUDY AUTIO
TWO LADIES, TWO DOGS
1979. Slab-built stoneware, height 25". Private collection

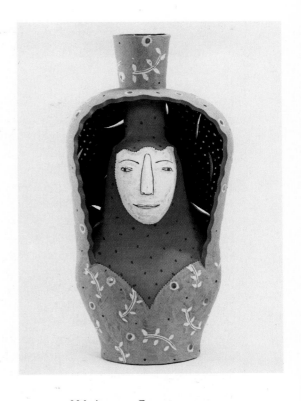

336. ANDREA GILL
WOMAN IN A VEIL
1981. Red earthenware, 22 x 12 x 8". Private collection

Irregular wall heights set up a rhythmic pattern with the rectangles, circles, and squares of primary colors loosely filling in sections of the black-on-white grids. More architectural in form than Woodman's, both Salomon and Woodman's vessels, however, projected a playfulness in their approach to decorative color.

The plate as the ideal ceramic surface for decoration returns this account full circle to the English potters of the eighteenth century whose rhythmic lines of slip crisscrossed Massachusetts redware. A century later, the Pennsylvania Germans and the Moravians each contributed graceful floral designs to establish an American tradition. In the twentieth century, Viktor Schreckengost's Cubist designs and Henry Varnum Poor's paintings on plates added perspective to the two-dimensional surface (see pages 142, 195). Optical confusions were more characteristic of several ceramists choosing the plate as an art form in the late seventies. Although Ralph Bacerra had previously used the plate for a series of Japanese Imari-inspired designs, by 1979 his dominant image was that of birds in flight. Interlocking geometric and organic shapes (reminiscent of a technique used by M. C. Escher) now directed Bacerra's concerns where birds and patterns meld in an overload of visual information. Perceptual ambiguities were also part of Jun Kaneko's series of plates of the late seventies. Slips of lightly colored lines on an oval shape resolved into spiral or concentric circles. Interrupted in some places or converted to dashes and commas, the lines contrasted with a rough-textured background at times so crackled it appeared ready to peel away from the surface. An optical push-pull experience in a minimalistic format allied these plates to similar concepts in contemporary painting.

A different optical sensation based on illusion confused figure and ground in Mineo Mizuno's cast trays of the eighties. Mizuno pitted illusionistic cups against a three-dimensional cup of the same proportions balanced on the rim of the tray. Breaching the relevance of the traditional frame, some trays have the dimensional handles of an illusionistic cup protruding from the rim. Complementary pastel colors are used to further optically alter dimension. Breaking away from the oval or rectangle, James Caswell incorporated geometric Art Deco angles into his irregularly shaped wall plaques. Triangles, concentric circles, and parallel lines in Art Deco pastel colors appeared to float around the frames surrounding a blue basin. The ambience of southern California was suggested through his use of seductive color and pattern, even without the telltale hint of a palm tree.

Designs for the functional plate came during a period of heightened interest in home dining as a social event. In the exhibition "For the Tabletop" (1980), organized by the American Craft Council for the American Craft Museum, a panorama of objects related to the preparation and serving of food and drink was presented. In the handmade category, Beatrice Wood's lustered place settings of 1972 glittered with flashes of iridescent blues, greens, and yellows in contrast to Jim Makin's sensuously thrown, unglazed porcelain place setting of 1980. Decorative elegance and the trend toward colorful patterns stamped Dorothy Hafner's plates and large platters. Inspired by European porcelains and Japanese Oribe wares, Hafner combined de-

337. TONY HEPBURN
MEETING OF MINDS
1986. Clay, wood, 38 x 23 x 20".
Saks Fifth Avenue Corporate
Art Collection

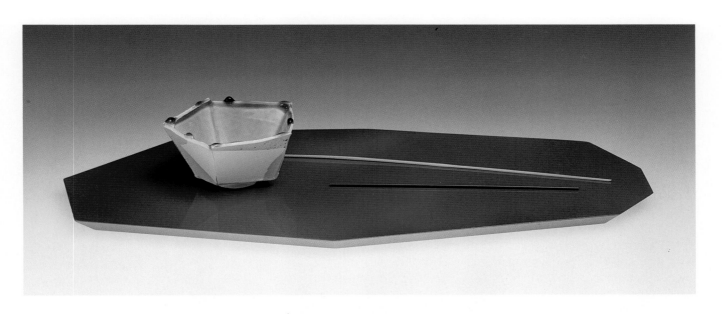

338. NANCY SELVIN
TEABOWL TRAY
1982. Porcelain, lacquered
wood, glass rods, 18 x 10 x 5".
Collection the artist

339. KAREN KOBLITZ
TILED PEDESTAL STILL LIFE
#4 (Wall relief)
1985. Low-fired clay, under-
glazes and glazes. 33¼ x 7 x 14".
Private collection

sign elements from each on modernist shapes. Hand-decorated, slip-cast porcelain dinner services bombarded the senses with high contrast colors of confetti dots, jelly beans, and asterisks. Following in the tradition of Frederick Rhead's Fiestaware, Hafner brought the sophistication, rhythm, and energy of her New York City environment into tableware patterns.

POLITICAL PROTEST

While pattern and color reflected one aspect of the rhythm of contemporary life, certain political issues—human rights, women's issues, environmental concerns, and especially the threat of global nuclear holocaust—demanded that the artist portray this sense of responsibility in his work. The humorous depiction of cultural idiosyncrasies of the 1970s in the work of Gilhooly, Morrison, and Baldwin no longer seemed appropriate. Following in the tradition of Picasso's *Guernica*, Jeff Schlanger's emotional response to those murdered during the political upheaval in Chile in 1973 resulted in a monumental wall of portraits. *Estadio Chile* (1973–78) identified and memorialized over two hundred of the five thousand people imprisoned and tortured by the military junta. In the 1980s, Schlanger produced individual work honoring the innocent victims of the atomic bomb raid on Nagasaki and the war in Vietnam.

Honor for the unknown or ignored women who made important contributions to Western civilization motivated Judy Chicago's *Dinner Party* (1979). The six-year task involved a large group of volunteers who helped complete a forty-nine-foot open equilateral triangular table containing thirty-nine place settings. Each china-

above left:
340. MINEO MIZUNO
SMALL SQUARE WITH CUP
*1982. Glazed earthenware, 11½"
square. Private collection*

above right:
341. JAMES CASWELL
AQUATIC MEMORY
*1983. Low-fired clay, under-
glazes, 20 x 23 x 3". Collection
Edward J. Judd*

342. DOROTHY HAFNER
SATELLITES
*1984. Porcelain prototype for a
line produced by Rosenthal Studio, Linie, Germany. (left to
right:) Sugar, 4¾ x 5 x 2¾"; Teapot, 8 x 11 x 4½"; Creamer, 4½ x
6 x 2¾". Collection the artist*

painted plate represented a different woman as part of a survey
including mythological goddesses, artists, poets, scientists, and
musicians. The plate interpreted the history of women in designs
based on a butterfly or vaginal imagery for its feminist and sexual
connotations. Monumental in format, accompanied by banners,
audio-visual material, and publications, the project toured the country, eliciting intense reactions for its political-feminist statement.
While critical reviews of the work pointed to a lack of aesthetic qualities, on a political and educational level *The Dinner Party* successfully rallied many people in support of the women's movement.[12] In
terms of American ceramics, Chicago focused attention on china
painting's history as a feminist vehicle marking, through her project,
almost a century of social and artistic transformation.

Like Schlanger and Chicago, Richard Notkin also used historical and contemporary events he deemed tremendously significant.
In *Curbing Free Enterprise* (1975) (a visual/verbal play on words worthy of Robert Arneson, his former teacher), Notkin joined Gilhooly
in attacking American commercialism, overabundance, and waste.
In a series of four tableaux titled *Endangered Species* (1978–81), Notkin suggested that not only animals but people were vulnerable to
extinction. In 1981, Notkin commemorated the thirty-sixth anniversary of the atomic bomb over Hiroshima with *Universal Hostage
Crisis*, a group of detailed miniature objects precariously balanced
on an out-of-scale red button. Symbolic of civilization on the brink
of disaster, *Universal Hostage Crisis* points to humankind's captivity by the escalation of nuclear weapons.

David Furman and Robert Arneson take this theme to its ultimate conclusion, the aftermath of world destruction. In the case of
Furman, contemporary ruins are fused with those of past civiliza-

343. Judy Chicago
ISABELLA D'ESTE PLATE
FROM "THE DINNER PARTY"
1979. Porcelain, diameter 14".
Private collection

344. Ralph Bacerra
WALL PIECE
1983. Porcelain, glazes, 24 x 18".
Private collection

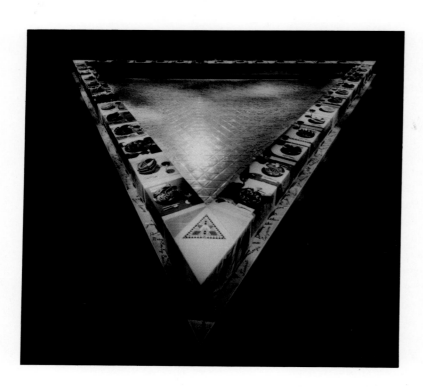

345. JUDY CHICAGO
THE DINNER PARTY
1979. Mixed media sculpture, table 47' each side. Collection the artist

346. DOROTHY HAFNER
ASTERISKS, Coffee and Dessert Service
*1983. Porcelain prototype for a line produced 1983–85. (left to right:) Creamer, 3½ x 5 x 2";
Plate, 6 x 6"; Sugar, 4 x 5 x 2"; Tray, 13 x 14"; Cup and saucer, 5 oz. size; Coffee pot, 8½ x 7½ x 2½". Collection the artist*

tions. In a *Contemporary Archaeology* series (1985), miniature collapsed brick structures connect his work to Charles Simonds's, except for the nature of the debris—the remains of swimming pools, trompe l'oeil crushed beer cans, rumpled candy bar wrappers, and newspapers. Mixed in with these images are pre-Columbian, Peruvian stirrup jars and ancient skeletons, the remains of other, earlier civilizations.

Related to Arneson's *Fragments of Western Civilization* (see page 284), Furman's juxtaposition of past and present took the idea one ironic step further. As for Arneson, ten years after *Fragments*, the nuclear arms build-up in the 1980s had generated images of nuclear destruction. Paradoxically, his bust of George Moscone (*Portrait of George [Moscone]*, 1981), the victim of a political murder, was in part responsible for the anti-nuclear series.[13] Commissioned by the City of San Francisco, the sculpture was rejected for its explicit images of the murder crime. For Arneson, the absurdity of this decision combined with the Star Wars debate and an escalating arms race demanded an equally outrageous response. In a series of drawings, paintings, and ceramics made between 1982–85, he visualized the human consequences of nuclear fallout. Melted by radiation or bearing target marks and wounds, Arneson's series of scarred and ravaged portrait heads transformed the military meaning of "warhead" into images of its charred victims. The primary focus of his outrage was the military-industrial complex, in the form of Colonel or General Nuke and his cohorts. His articulation of the unspeakable made this work all the more potent.

From the post-sixties forward, the customary understanding of the ceramic form, sculpture and vessel, changed and intentionally defied categorization. Architectural concepts applied to ceramics further confused attempts to maintain traditional distinctions. Then, too, the openly decorative stance taken by ceramists in the 1980s returned to clay an aspect of its character denied during the anti-decorative color period of the fifties; ceramists newly intrigued with color and pattern responded by moving into new aesthetic avenues.

In spite of these new alignments in form and ideas, what is clear is that in the making of art, ceramists in the 1980s have demonstrated a willingness to take risks. Sometimes this has meant moving away from the historical context of clay, and risking the connection with clay's roots; or it has meant that the dominance of ceramic sculpture has diminished interest by college students in learning the most primary tool, the wheel. Such conflicting or troubling viewpoints, combined with the pressure from the art establishment that ceramists deny traditional function in order to gain acceptance of their work as a fine art, place the ceramist between the proverbial rock and a hard place. While the majority of ceramists today continue to exhibit within the context of work in clay, an increasingly larger group have joined galleries and participated in exhibitions that include painting and sculpture in conjunction with other materials. There is every indication that in the present aesthetic climate the ceramist will continue to probe the artist's relationship to the values of society and will find new ways to express the human condition.

347. RICHARD T. NOTKIN
UNIVERSAL HOSTAGE CRISIS
1981. Low-fired ceramics, porcelain, silver-plated brass (aerial), 22½ x 20 x 14". Courtesy Garth Clark Gallery, New York

348. ROBERT ARNESON
NUCLEAR HEAD #2
1983. Glazed ceramic, 16½ x 14 x 7". Private collection

349. Elaine Scheer
PEACE THEATER
Slide Ranch, Muir Beach, northern California, 1986. Earth, sod, iron, wire, school desks, 30' x 30'

Conceived as a memorial to the earth, this environmental installation invited participation by social action groups and those in educational programs. Site art is one direction in which contemporary ceramics is moving.

NOTES

For complete citations refer to the Bibliography.

CHAPTER 1 A HANDCRAFT FOUNDATION FOR CLAY

1. Clement 1951, 136.
2. Guillard 1971, 5.
3. Ibid., 35.
4. Vlach, "Slave Potters," 1978, 69.
5. Deetz 1973, 18.
6. Guillard 1971, 30.
7. Barber 1970, 196.
8. Zug 1986, 43.
9. Bivens 1972, 236.
10. Faience or tin-enameled ware was the name given to opaque lead-glazed earthenware in France and central Europe.
11. Rice and Stroudt 1929, 37.
12. Barka 1973, 292.
13. Clement, *Our Pioneer Potters*, 1947, 59.
14. Vlach, *The Afro-American Tradition*, 1978, 76.
15. Ibid., 86.
16. Ibid., 81 for the first quotation. The second quotation was inscribed on a vessel in the collection of the McKissick Museums, University of South Carolina.
17. Sweezy 1984, 54–55.

CHAPTER 2 THE INDUSTRIALIZATION OF CLAY

1. Norton 1972, 5.
2. Kelly 1975, 33.
3. Tracy 1963, 114.
4. The Franklin Institute provided classes in engineering, mechanical drawing, art, and technology useful to craftsmen. It also served as a trade fair for goods made by artisans and industrialists, holding juried exhibitions and offering prizes for quality in design and workmanship. See *Philadelphia: Three Centuries of American Art* 1976, xviii.
5. Spargo 1974, 181–85.
6. Quoted in Clement, *Pottery and Porcelain of New Jersey*, 1947, 12.
7. Watkins 1946, 388.
8. Ibid., 389.
9. Tracy 1963, 110.
10. Curtis 1973, 345.
11. Spargo 1974, 280–81.
12. Goodrich 1966, 29.
13. Schwartz and Wolfe 1967, 29.
14. Guillard 1971, 58.
15. Stradling 1976, 147.

CHAPTER 3 THE ARTS AND CRAFTS MOVEMENT

1. Keen 1978, 5.
2. Pilgrim 1979, 114.
3. Ross 1967, 298.
4. Pentland 1981, 14.
5. Macht 1976, 10.

6. Maria Longworth Nichols and Mary Louise McLaughlin, both members of prominent Cincinnati families, became the leaders of the china painting and art pottery movements.
7. Perry 1881, 835.
8. Quoted in Stradling 1976, 155. See Young, *passim.*
9. McLaughlin 1890, 100.
10. McLaughlin 1938, 219.
11. Perry 1881, 837.

CHAPTER 4 THE EARLY ART POTTERIES

1. Evans 1974, 57.
2. Eidelberg, "Art Pottery," 1972, 129.
3. Swan 1926, 118.
4. Hawes 1968, 24.
5. Bray 1980, 3.
6. Trapp 1973, 194; quotation from Kingsley 1897, 342.
7. Peck 1968, 4.
8. Ibid., 9.
9. Trapp 1980, 17.
10. Ibid., 22.
11. Evans 1974, 105. The establishment of a large number of art potteries is discussed in detail in this book.
12. Ibid., 142.
13. Darling 1979, 172, 181, 189.
14. Fox 1973, 678.
15. Eidelberg 1973, 49.

CHAPTER 5 ART NOUVEAU: FORM AND DECORATION UNIFIED

1. Nelson 1963, 444.
2. Weisberg 1969, 299.
3. Nelson 1963, 442.
4. Darling 1979, 54.
5. Eidelberg 1972, 164.
6. Keen 1978, 31.
7. McLauglin 1901, 178. In 1892, Horace Caulkins produced a small portable kiln capable of achieving porcelain temperatures. McLaughlin may have used the Caulkins Revelation Kiln or a similar model.
8. Ibid.
9. Blasberg 1973, 15; quotation from Ohr's autobiography in *Crockery and Glass Journal*, December 12, 1901.
10. Blasberg 1973, 8.
11. Smith 1965, 9.
12. Trapp 1980, 36.

CHAPTER 6 THE CONSEQUENCES OF THE ART POTTERY MOVEMENT

1. "Editorial" 1901, 161.
2. Observation in the *Mining Gazette*, Houghton, Michigan, n.d. The Pewabic Pottery Papers 1101FOO25, Archives of American Art, Smithsonian Institution, Washington, D.C.
3. Anderson, Moore, and Winder 1974, 23.
4. Binns 1947, 123.

5. For detailed information on Adelaide Robineau's glaze research see Ihrman 1981, 139–58.
6. Blasberg 1979, 26.
7. See Eidelberg 1981, 43–92 for a detailed discussion of the sources for Robineau's designs.
8. "Notes" 1928, 400.
9. Bach 1918, 413.

CHAPTER 7 AMERICAN DECORATIVE ARTS

1. Bennett 1919, 88; Macomber 1918, *passim*.
2. Bach 1920, 117.
3. Arwas 1980, 14.
4. Hunter 1972, 277.
5. Siple 1928, 611.
6. Avery 1928, 238.
7. "Arts and Crafts" 1927, 10; quotation from an article by Elizabeth Cary in *The New York Times*.
8. Viktor Schreckengost, interview with author, Cleveland, Ohio, April 1982.
9. Davidson 1951, 174.

CHAPTER 8 DEPRESSION SCULPTURE

1. Marling 1974, 59.
2. O'Connor 1973, 16.
3. Cowan, "A Potter's View" 1936, 15.
4. Watson 1944, 14.
5. Viktor Schreckengost, interview with author, Cleveland, Ohio, April 1982.
6. Grafly 1933, 338.
7. Edris Eckhardt, interview with author, Cleveland, Ohio, April 1982.
8. Cowan, "The Fine Art of Ceramics" 1936, 3.

CHAPTER 9 THREE DIRECTIONS FOR THE VESSEL

1. Peterson 1978, 91.
2. Goldsmith 1922, 358.
3. Whiting 1933, 441.
4. Auman and Zug 1977, 172.
5. Eaton 1943, 32.
6. Benson 1938, 82.
7. Margaret Fetzer, letter to author, March 1982. Fetzer was on the ceramics faculty with Arthur Baggs at Ohio State University.
8. Ken Ferguson, interview with author, Shawnee Mission, Kansas, June 1982. Ferguson was a student of Harder's at Alfred University.
9. Val Cushing, interview with author, Alfred, New York, September 1979. Cushing was a student of Harder's at Alfred University.
10. Information from articles written by Rhead and quoted in Dale 1986, 121.
11. Ibid.
12. Hennessey 1983, 38.
13. "First California Ceramic Exhibit" 1938, 194.
14. Glen Lukens, transcribed interview with Hazel Bray, Los Angeles, 1966, 36, Archives of the Oakland Museum.

CHAPTER 10 DEFINING A VESSEL AESTHETIC

1. Otto Natzler, interview with author, Los Angeles, 1982.

2. Natzler 1973, 19.
3. Marguerite Wildenhain, transcribed interview with Hazel Bray, Pond Farm, Guerneville, California, March 14, 1982, 22, Archives of American Art, Smithsonian Institution, Washington, D.C.
4. Ibid., 40.
5. Rhoda Lopez, interview with author, San Diego 1979. A former student of Maija Grotell's, Lopez related that Grotell saw her vessels as a reflection of her own physical dimensions. Other information on Grotell from interviews and correspondence with Grotell's former students Martha Lauritzen, John Glick, Jeff Schlanger, and Richard DeVore.
6. Edwin Scheier quoted in "A Path in Two Directions" 1957, 16. Additional information from interview with author, Oaxaca, Mexico, 1976, and the files of the University of New Hampshire.
7. Rudolf Staffel, interview with author, Philadelphia, 1979.
8. Daniel Rhodes, taped interview with Hazel Bray at Ceramics 80 Symposium, June 1980, sponsored by the Student Union, Oregon State University, Corvallis, courtesy Archives of the Oakland Museum.
9. Laura Andreson, notes of interview with Hazel Bray, Los Angeles, 1977, Archives of the Oakland Museum. Other information on Andreson from interviews with author in Los Angeles, 1974 and 1982, and a conversation with Stephanie DeLange, Andreson's former student.
10. Sanders 1955, 319.
11. Carlton Ball, interview with author, Tacoma, Washington, 1979. Overfiring a kiln or a glaze means firing at a temperature higher than that prescribed. But breaking the rules, as Ball discovered, can often lead to new insights.
12. Wildenhain 1953, 43–44.
13. Carlton Ball, taped interview with Hazel Bray at Ceramics 80 Symposium, June 1980, sponsored by the Student Union, Oregon State University, Corvalis, courtesy Archives of the Oakland Museum.

CHAPTER 11 POST-WAR ARTISTIC FERMENT

1. Richard Petterson, interview with author, Claremont, California, 1980.
2. "Jury Statement" 1953, 4.
3. Olmsted 1953, 38.
4. "Craftsman Conference at Asilomar" 1957, 24.
5. Poor 1951, 21.
6. Poor 1954, 29.
7. Grove 1979, 60.
8. Driscoll 1950, 408.
9. Leach 1978, 245.
10. Peter Voulkos, interview with author, Berkeley, California, 1971.
11. Ibid.
12. "The Miami Annual" 1957, 42.
13. Ibid., 43.

CHAPTER 12 TRANSFORMATIONS IN FORM AND SURFACE

1. Peter Voulkos, interview with author, Berkeley, California, 1978.
2. Ibid.
3. See Coplans 1966 and Slivka 1961. Both provide impor-

tant background information for the work of Voulkos and his colleagues.

4. Rudolf Staffel, interview with author, Philadelphia, Pennsylvania, 1979.

5. Cohen 1965, 49.

6. Paul Soldner, interview with author, Claremont, California, 1977.

7. Ibid. Soldner first encountered a raku pot in 1964 when he visited the Freer Gallery Collection in Washington, D.C. By that time he had defined a basic process for himself.

8. Brower 1971, 21.

9. Ken Price, transcribed interview with Michele DeAngeles, Taos, New Mexico, May/June 1980, 24–25, Archives of American Art, Smithsonian Institution, Washington, D.C.

10. Ken Ferguson, interview with author, Shawnee Mission, Kansas. June 1982.

11. Sedestrom 1981, 62. There is some disagreement about the place and date of the first official craft fair sponsored by the ACC. Sedestrom was involved at an early date so I have used her account.

12. Haworth and Beall 1982, 5.

13. Randall 1982, MC3 Box 1, 1–10.

CHAPTER 13   REALISM AND THE COMMON OBJECT

1. Robert Arneson, transcribed interview with Mady Jones, August 1981, 40, California Oral History Project, Archives of American Art, Smithsonian Institution, Washington, D.C.

2. Selz 1967, 3.

3. Foley 1974 (no page numbers).

4. Noah 1977, 5.

5. Howard Kottler, letter to author, 1982.

6. Marilyn Levine, interview with author, Vail, Colorado 1981.

7. Kohler 1974, 75.

CHAPTER 14   THE RESILIENT VESSEL

1. Sweezy 1975, 23.

2. Susan Peterson, lecture on Pueblo pottery, Museum of Natural History, Los Angeles, December 13, 1980.

3. Charles Counts, letter to author, 1983.

4. Ibid.

5. MacKenzie 1981, 7.

6. Ferguson 1976 (no page numbers). The potters in the exhibition were David Shaner, John Glick, Donna Polseno and Richard Hensley, Clary Illian, Carl and Jeanne Judson, and Betty Woodman.

7. Herman 1975, 12.

8. Williams 1980, 99.

9. Riegger 1972, 12.

10. Ken Price, transcribed interview with Michele DeAngeles, Taos, New Mexico, May/June 1980, 37, Archives of American Art, Smithsonian Institution, Washington, D.C.

11. Cardew 1969, 254.

12. Robert Turner, letter to author, 1982.

13. Ken Ferguson, interview with author, Shawnee Mission, Kansas, June 1982.

14. See Lippard 1983 for a discussion of the connections contemporary artists have made with primitive cultures.

15. Elena Karina, interview with author, Los Angeles, 1980.

16. Kuspit 1981, 79.

17. MacKenzie 1980, 12.

18. Higby 1982, 11.

19. "Function, Nonfunction" 1980, 45.

20. Bettelheim 1982, 38.

CHAPTER 15   ABSTRACT AND ARCHITECTONIC IMAGERY

1. In the early 1930s, Viktor Schreckengost's decorative plates (such as *Leda*, fig. 119) became wall plaques. A decade later, Waylande Gregory produced plates meant for walls rather than tables. Both artists were ahead of their time in moving toward an architectural expression.

2. Ruth Duckworth, interview with author, Chicago, Illinois, November 1981.

3. Tony Costanzo, interview with author, Oakland, California, October 1986.

4. George Geyer and Tom McMillin, joint interviews with author, La Jolla, California, 1981.

5. John Roloff, interview with author, Oakland, California, October 1986.

6. Abadie 1977, 12. "Body art" was a term that emerged in the late 1960s, so called because artists turned to their own bodies as subject matter. In *Landscape-Body-Dwelling* (1971), Simonds built tiny structures on his prone form.

7. Montgomery 1985–6, 30.

8. Jens Morrison, interview with author, Los Angeles, 1984; the artist mentioned a discussion with ceramist Jack Thompson in which Thompson coined the phrase "academic folk art" in reference to Morrison's structures.

9. Mel Rubin, interview with author, Los Angeles, October 1983.

CHAPTER 16
FIGURATIVE IMAGERY AND THE HUMAN CONDITION

1. Jens Morrison, interview with author, Ann Arbor, Michigan, 1980.

2. Fleming, quoted in Weeks 1982 (no page numbers).

3. Bova 1987, 38.

4. Robert Arneson, interview in Wechsler 1984, 20.

5. Robert Arneson, transcribed interview with Mady Jones, August 1981, 99, Archives of American Art, Smithsonian Institution, Washington, D.C.

6. Robert Arneson quoted in Wechsler 1984, 20.

7. Johnson 1983, 83.

8. Patti Warashina quoted in Wechsler 1981, 127.

9. Nancy Carman, letter to author, 1983.

10. Stephen DeStaebler, interview with author, Berkeley, California, February 1980.

11. Zimmer 1982, 26.

12. Michael Lucero, quoted in Haulk 1982, 16.

13. Tableau title quoted in Bourdon 1978, 155.

14. Viola Frey quoted in Wechsler 1981, 73.

15. Marshall and Foley 1981, 8.

16. For example, gallery director and art historian Garth Clark founded the Institute for Ceramic History which, beginning in 1979, sponsored biennial symposia designed in part to interest collectors by offering a myriad of ceramic exhibitions, prominent speakers, critics, and panel discussions.

CHAPTER 17 PERMISSIVE PLURALISM

1. Schonlau 1984, 50.
2. Schonlau's remarks paraphrased in Falk 1984, 46. The Archie Bray Foundation, a brickyard where Peter Voulkos and Rudy Autio began their careers in the 1950s, is still in operation, an early example of an alternative workspace.
3. Horrell 1987, 34. See also Wells 1986, *passim*.
4. Jensen 1985, 11.
5. Rubin 1985, 12.
6. Wayne Higby, interview with author, Alfred, New York, 1979. See also Klemperer 1985, 32–37.
7. William Daley, letter to author, August 1982; Daley stated that he views himself as Glen Lukens's heir since his former teacher, Charles Abbott (at the Massachusetts College of Art) and his former colleague Aurelius Renzetti (at the Philadelphia College of Art) both championed Lukens and his use of "the inherent aspects of the material, its tooth, its ability to be compressed."
8. Ken Price, transcribed interview with Michele DeAngeles, Taos, New Mexico, May/June 1980, 34, Archives of American Art, Smithsonian Institution, Washington, D.C.
9. Ron Nagle quoted in "A Short Survey" 1984, 29.
10. Graham Marks, interview with author, Rochester, New York, November 1983.
11. Nasisse 1986, 32.
12. Richardson 1981, 20.
13. Fineberg 1983 (no page numbers).

BIBLIOGRAPHY OF WORKS CITED

BOOKS AND CATALOGUES

Abadie, Daniel. *Charles Simonds*. Buffalo, N.Y.: Albright Knox Art Gallery, 1977.

Anderson, Timothy J., Eudora Moore, and Robert W. Winder, eds. *California Design 1910*. Pasadena, Calif.: California Design Publications, 1974.

Arwas, Victor. *Art Deco*. New York: Harry N. Abrams, Inc., 1980.

Barber, Edwin Atlee. *Tulip Ware of the Pennsylvania-German Potters*. New York: Dover Publications, Inc., 1970.

Binns, Charles F. *The Potter's Craft*. 1910. Reprint. New York: D. Van Nostrand Co., Inc., 1947.

Bivens, John Jr. *The Moravian Potters in North Carolina*. Chapel Hill, N.C.: University of North Carolina Press, 1972.

Blasberg, Robert W. *Fulper Art Pottery: An Aesthetic Appreciation 1909–1929*. New York: Jordan-Volpe Gallery, 1979.

———. *George E. Ohr and his Biloxi Art Pottery*. Port Jervis, N.Y.: J. W. Carpenter, 1973.

Bray, Hazel. *The Potter's Art in California 1885–1955*. Oakland, Calif.: The Oakland Museum, 1980.

Cardew, Michael. *Pioneer Pottery*. New York: St. Martin's Press, Inc., 1969.

Clement, Arthur W. *Our Pioneer Potters*. York, Pa.: The Maple Press Co., 1947.

———. *Pottery and Porcelain of New Jersey 1688–1900*. Newark, N.J.: Newark Museum, 1947.

Coplans, John. *Abstract Expressionist Ceramics*. Irvine, Calif.: University of California, 1966.

Dale, Sharon. *Frederick Hurten Rhead: An English Potter in America*. Erie, Pa.: Erie Art Museum, 1986.

Darling, Sharon S. *Chicago Ceramics and Glass 1871–1933*. Chicago: Chicago Historical Society, 1979.

Davidson, Jo. *Between Sittings*. New York: Dial Press, 1951.

Eaton, Allen. *Handcrafts of the Southern Highlands*. 1937. Reprint. New York: Dover Publications, Inc., 1973.

Evans, Paul. *Art Pottery of the United States*. New York: Charles Scribner's Sons, 1974.

Ferguson, Kenneth. *Eight Independent Production Potters*. Kansas City, Mo.: Kansas City Art Institute, 1976.

Fineberg, Jonathon. *War Heads and Others: Robert Arneson*. New York: Allan Frumkin Gallery, 1983.

Goodrich, Lloyd. *Art of the United States: 1670–1966*. New York: Whitney Museum of American Art, 1966.

Guillard, Harold F. *Early American Folk Pottery*. New York: Chilton Book Co., 1971.

Haulk, Tom. *American Clay II*. Baltimore, Md.: Meredith Contemporary Art, 1982.

Hawes, Lloyd E. *The Dedham Pottery*. Dedham, Mass.: Dedham Historical Society, 1968.

Hennessey, William J. *Russel Wright American Designer*. Cambridge, Mass.: M.I.T. Press, 1983.

Herman, Lloyd E., ed. *Craft Multiples*. Washington, D.C.: Smithsonian Institution Press, 1975.

Keen, Kirsten H. *American Art Pottery 1875–1930*. Wilmington, Del.: Delaware Art Museum, 1978.

Kelly, Alison. *The Story of Wedgwood*. London: Faber & Faber Ltd., 1975.

Leach, Bernard. *Beyond East and West*. New York: Watson-Guptill Publications, 1978.

———. *A Potter's Book*. London: Faber & Faber Ltd., 1940.

Lippard, Lucy, ed. *Overlay: Contemporary Art and the Art of Prehistory*. New York: Pantheon Books, 1983.

Macht, Carol. *The Ladies, God Bless 'Em*. Cincinnati, Ohio: Cincinnati Art Museum, 1976.

MacKenzie, Warren. *Minnesota Pottery: A Potter's View*, edited by Valerie Tvrdik, 6–9. Minneapolis, Minn.: University Gallery, 1981.

Marling, Karal Ann. *Federal Art in Cleveland 1933–1943.* Cleveland, Ohio: Cleveland Public Library, 1974.

Marshall, Richard, and Suzanne Foley. *Ceramic Sculpture: Six Artists.* New York: Whitney Museum of American Art, 1981.

McLaughlin, M. Louise. *China Painting: A Practical Manual for the Use of Amateurs in the Decoration of Hard Porcelain.* 1877. Reprint. Cincinnati, Ohio: Robert Clarke & Co., 1890.

Nelson, Glenn. C. *Ceramics.* New York: Holt, Rinehart & Winston, Inc., 1960.

Norton, R. W., Art Gallery. *American Porcelain Tradition: 18th, 19th and 20th Centuries.* Shreveport, La.: R. W. Norton Art Foundation, 1972.

O'Connor, Francis V., ed. *Art for Millions.* Greenwich, Conn.: New York Graphic Society Ltd., 1973.

Peck, Herbert. *The Book of Rookwood Pottery.* New York: Bonanza Books, 1968.

Peterson, Susan. *The Living Tradition of Maria Martinez.* New York: Kodansha International, 1978.

Philadelphia: Three Centuries of American Art. Philadelphia: Philadelphia Museum of Art, 1976.

Ramsay, John. *American Potters and Pottery.* New York: Tudor Publishing Co., 1947.

Rice, A. H., and John B. Stroudt. *The Shenandoah Pottery.* Strasburg, Va.: Shenandoah Publishing House, Inc., 1929.

Riegger, Hal. *Primitive Pottery.* New York: Van Nostrand Reinhold Co., 1972.

Ross, Ishbel. *Taste in America.* New York: Thomas Crowell Co., 1967.

Rubin, Michael. *Architectural Ceramics: Eight Concepts.* St. Louis, Mo.: Washington University Gallery of Art, 1985.

Sanders, Herbert H. *The World of Japanese Ceramics.* New York: Watson-Guptill Publications, 1967.

Schwartz, Marvin, and Richard Wolfe. *A History of American Art Porcelain.* New York: Renaissance Editions, Inc., 1967.

Seltz, Peter. *Funk.* Berkeley, Calif.: University Art Museum, 1967.

Spargo, John. *Early American Pottery and China.* New York: Century Co., 1926. Reprint. Rutland, Vt.: Charles E. Tuttle Co., 1974.

Sweezy, Nancy. *Raised in Clay.* Washington, D.C.: Smithsonian Institution Press, 1984.

Trapp, Kenneth. *Ode to Nature: Flowers and Landscapes of the Rookwood Pottery 1880–1940.* New York: Jordan-Volpe Gallery, 1980.

Tyler, Christopher, and Richard Hirsch. *Raku.* New York: Watson-Guptill Publications, 1975.

Vlach, John. *The Afro-American Tradition in Decorative Arts.* Cleveland, Ohio: Cleveland Museum of Art, 1978.

Watkins, Lura W. *Early New England Potters and Their Wares.* Cambridge, Mass.: Harvard University Press, 1950.

Wechsler, Susan. *Low Fire Ceramics.* New York: Watson-Guptill Publications, 1981.

Weeks, Edward F. *Personal Mythologies.* Birmingham, Ala.: Birmingham Museum of Art, 1982.

Wells, Gary. *Deborah Horrell.* Columbus, Ohio: Ohio State University, 1986.

Young, Jennie. *The Ceramic Art: A Compendium of the History and Manufacture of Pottery and Porcelain.* New York: Harper & Brothers, Publishers, 1879.

Zug, Charles III. *Turners and Burners.* Chapel Hill, N.C.: University of North Carolina Press, 1986.

ARTICLES

"Arts and Crafts." *The Art Digest* 1, no. 10 (March 15, 1927): 10.

Auman, Dorothy Cole, and Charles G. Zug III. "Nine Generations of Potters." *Southern Exposure* 5, nos. 2–3 (Summer/Fall 1977): 166–74.

Avery, Louise C. "International Exhibition of Contemporary Ceramic Art." *Bulletin of the Metropolitan Museum of Art* 23, no. 10 (October 1928): 232–38.

Bach, Richard F. "Mobilizing the Art Industries." *American Magazine of Art* 9, no. 10 (August 1918): 412–18.

———. "Museums and the Art Trades." *Arts and Decoration* 14, no. 2 (December 1920): 116–17.

Barka, Norman F. "The Kiln and Ceramics of the 'poor potter' of Yorktown." In *Ceramics in America*, edited by Ian M. G. Quimby, 291–318. Charlottesville, Va.: University of Virginia Press, 1973.

Bennett, Charles A. "Wanted: A National School of Industrial Art." *American Magazine of Art* 10, no. 3 (January 1919): 85–88.

Benson, E. M. "Chicago Bauhaus." *Magazine of Art* 31, no. 2 (February 1938): 82–83.

Bettelheim, Judith. "Ceramic Art in California: The 1970s." In *NCECA San Jose '82*, edited by Marcia Chamberlain, Judith Bettelheim, and Jay Kvapil, 37–41. San Jose, Calif.: NCECA, 1982.

Bourdon, David, "Jack Earl at Portnoy." *Art in America* 66, no. 6 (November/December 1978): 155.

Bova, Joe. "Night Fishing in Texas." *Ceramics Monthly* 35, no. 3 (March 1987): 33–40.

Brower, Catherine. "Don Reitz." *Ceramics Monthly* 19, no. 10 (December 1971): 19–26.

Clement, Arthur W. "Ceramics in the South." *Antiques* 59, no. 2 (February 1951): 136–38.

Cohen, Harriet Goodwin. "Exhibitions: The Teapot." *Craft Horizons* 25, no. 3 (May/June 1965): 49–50.

Cowan, R. Guy. "The Fine Art of Ceramics as Exemplified in the 1936 Exhibition of Ceramic Art at the Syracuse Museum." *Design* 38 (November 1936): 3–7.

———. "A Potter's View of American Potters." *Art News* 35, no. 4 (October 24, 1936): 15.

"Craftsman Conference at Asilomar." *Craft Horizons* 17, no. 4 (July/August 1957): 18–24.

Curtis, Philip. "The Production of Tucker Porcelain 1825–1836." In *Ceramics in America*, edited by Ian M. G. Quimby, 339–74. Charlottesville, Va.: University of Virginia Press, 1973.

Deetz, James J. F. "Ceramics From Plymouth 1620–1835: The Archaeological Evidence." In *Ceramics in America*, edited by Ian M. G. Quimby, 15–40. Charlottesville, Va.: University of Virginia Press, 1973.

Driscoll, Harold. "Bernard Leach—Mills College Workshop." *Ceramic Age* 55, no. 6 (June 1950): 408, 410, 414.

Eaton, Allen. "Worcester Museum Handcraft Exhibition."

Craft Horizons 2, no. 2 (November 1943): 23–25, 32.

"Editorial." *Keramic Studio* 3, no. 8 (December 1901): 161.

Eidelberg, Martin. "Art Pottery." In *The Arts and Crafts Movement in America 1876–1916*, edited by Robert Judson Clark, 119–86. Princeton, N.J.: Princeton University Press, 1972.

———. "The Ceramic Art of William Grueby." *The Connoisseur* 184, no. 739 (September 1973): 47–54.

———. "Robineau's Early Designs." In *Adelaide Alsop Robineau: Glory in Porcelain*, edited by Peg Weiss, 43–92. Syracuse, N.Y.: Syracuse University Press, 1981.

Falk, Lorne. "The Omaha Brickworks." *American Ceramics* 2, no. 4 (1984): 44–47.

"First California Ceramic Exhibit." *Bulletin of the American Ceramic Society* 17, no. 4 (April 1938): 194.

Foley, Suzanne. "Robert Arneson II." In *Robert Arneson*, curated by Stephen Prokopoff (no page numbers). Chicago: Museum of Contemporary Art, 1974.

Fox, Claire G. "Henry Chapman Mercer: Tilemaker, Collector, and Builder Extraordinary." *Antiques* 104, no. 4 (October 1973): 678–85.

"Function, NonFunction." *Ceramics Monthly* 28, no. 10 (October 1980): 44–47.

Goldsmith, Margaret O. "Jugtown Pottery." *House Beautiful* 52, no. 4 (October 1922): 311, 358–60.

Grafly, Dorothy. "America's Youngest Art." *American Magazine of Art* 26, no. 7 (July 1933): 338.

Grove, Nancy. "The Visible and Invisible Noguchi." *Artforum* 17, no. 7 (March 1979): 56–60.

Higby, Wayne. "The Vessel: Overcoming the Tyranny of Modern Art." *NCECA Journal* 3, no. 11 (1982): 11–12.

Horrell, Deborah. "Working at Otsuka." *Ceramics Monthly* 35, no. 2 (February 1987): 31–38.

Hunter, Penelope. "Art Deco and the Metropolitan Museum of Art." *The Connoisseur* 179, no. 722 (April 1972): 273–81.

Ihrman, Phyllis. "Robineau's Crystalline Glazes." In *Adelaide Alsop Robineau: Glory in Porcelain*, edited by Peg Weiss, 139–56. Syracuse, N.Y.: Syracuse University Press, 1981.

Jensen, Robert. "Architectural Art: The New Possibilities." *NCECA Journal* 6 (1985): 11–12.

Johnson, Lin. "News and Retrospect: Annual Southwest Conference." *Ceramics Monthly* 31, no. 7 (September 1983): 81, 83.

"Jury Statement." In *Designer Craftsmen USA 1953*, Charles Nagel, Director, 4. Brooklyn, N.Y.: Brooklyn Museum, 1953.

Kingsley, Rose G. "Rookwood Pottery." *The Art Journal* 60 (December 1897): 342.

Klemperer, Louise. "Wayne Higby." *American Ceramics* 3, no. 4 (1985): 32–37.

Kohler, John Michael, Arts Center. "Fantasy at Kohler." *Craft Horizons* 34, no. 12 (December 1974): 75.

Kuspit, Donald B. "Elemental Realities." *Art in America* 69, no. 1 (January 1981): 78–87.

MacKenzie, Warren. "Criticism in Ceramic Art." *NCECA Journal* 1, no. 1 (1980): 12

Macomber, Percy. "The Future of Handicraft." *American Magazine of Art* 9, no. 5 (March 1918): 192–95.

McLaughlin, M. Louise. "Losanti Ware." *Keramic Studio* 3, no. 8 (December 1901): 178–79.

———. "Miss McLaughlin Tells Her Own Story." *Bulletin of the American Ceramic Society* 17, no. 5 (May 1938): 217–25.

"The Miami Annual." *Craft Horizons* 17, no. 3 (May/June 1957): 42–43.

Montgomery, Susan. "Witness the Spirit of William Wyman." *American Ceramics* 4, no. 3 (1985–86): 30–35.

Nasisse, Andy. "The Battleground of Eros." *American Ceramics* 5, no. 1 (1986): 30–35.

Natzler, Otto. "Immortal Clay: The Exploration of a Medium." In *Form and Fire: Natzler Ceramics 1939–1972*, edited by Lloyd E. Herman, 17–23. Washington, D.C.: Smithsonian Institution Press, 1973.

Nelson, John Marion. "Art Nouveau in American Ceramics." *Art Quarterly of the Detroit Institute of Arts* 26, no. 4 (1963): 441–59.

Noah, Barbara. "Lichtenstein's Ceramics." *Artweek* 8, no. 11 (March 1977): 5–6.

"Notes: John Cotton Dana and the Newark Museum." *American Magazine of Art* 19, no. 7 (July 1928): 400.

Olmstead, Anna. "Ceramics." In *Designer Craftsmen USA 1953*, Charles Nagel, Director, 37–39. Brooklyn, N.Y.: Brooklyn Museum, 1953.

"A Path in Two Directions." *Los Angeles Times* (August 25, 1957): 15–17.

Pentland, Heather. "Sara Worthington King Peter and the Cincinnati Ladies' Academy of Fine Arts." *Cincinnati Historical Society Bulletin* no. 1 (Spring 1981): 6–16.

Perry, Mrs. Aaron. "Decorative Pottery of Cincinnati." *Harper's New Monthly Magazine* 62, no. 372 (May 1881): 834–45.

Pilgrim, Dianne H. "Decorative Art: The Domestic Environment." In *The American Renaissance 1876–1917*, Michael Botwinick, Director, 111–51. Brooklyn, N.Y.: Brooklyn Museum, 1979.

Poor, Henry Varnum. "Design: A Common Language." *Craft Horizons* 11, no. 3 (November 1951): 19–21.

———. "Tile Mural." *Craft Horizons* 14, no. 6 (November/December 1954): 28–30.

Richardson, John. "Strictly From Hunger." *The New York Review* (April 30, 1981): 18–20.

Schonlau, Ree. "Jun Kaneko: Omaha Project." *Ceramics Monthly* 32, no. 6 (June/July/August 1984): 49–50.

Sedestrom, Carol. "American Craft Enterprises." *Studio Potter* 9, no. 2 (June 1981): 62–63.

Sewell, Darrel. "Introduction." In *Philadelphia: Three Centuries of American Art*, edited and curated by Darrel Sewell, xv–xxii. Philadelphia: Philadelphia Museum of Art, 1976.

"A Short Survey of San Francisco Bay Area Potters and Artists." *Studio Potter* 13, no. 1 (December 1984): 21–46.

Siple, Ella S. "The International Exhibition of Ceramic Art." *American Magazine of Art* 19, no. 11 (November 1928): 602–619.

Slivka, Rose. "The New Ceramic Presence." *Craft Horizons* 21, no. 4 (July/August 1961): 31–37.

Smith, Dolores. "Echoes from the Past: George Ohr's Pottery." *Popular Ceramics* 18 (September 1965): 8–11.

Stradling, J. G. "American Ceramics and the Philadelphia Centennial." *Antiques* 110, no. 1 (July 1976): 146–58.

Swan, Mable M. "The Dedham Pottery." *Antiques* 10, no. 2 (August 1926): 116–21.

Sweezy, Nancy. "Tradition in Clay: Piedmont Pottery." *Historic Preservation* (October–December 1975): 20–23.

Tracy, Berry B. "The Decorative Arts." In *Classical America 1815–1845*, Katherine Coffey, Director, 108–115. Newark, N.J.: Newark Museum, 1963.

Trapp, Kenneth. "Japanese Influence in Early Rookwood Pottery." *Antiques* 103, no. 1 (January 1973): 193–97.

Vlach, John. "Slave Potters." *Ceramics Monthly* 26, no. 7 (September 1978): 66–69.

Watkins, Lura W. "Henderson of Jersey City and his Pitchers." *Antiques* 49, no. 50 (December 1946): 388–96.

Watson, E. W. "Waylande Gregory's Ceramic Art." *American Artist* 8, no. 7 (September 1944): 12–14, 34, 39.

Wechsler, Susan. "Views on the Figure." *American Ceramics* 3, no. 1 (1984): 16–25.

Weisberg, Gabriel. "Bing's Salon of Art Nouveau." Part 2, *The Connoisseur* 172, no. 694 (December 1969): 294–99.

Whiting, Frederick A. "Native Craftsmanship Will Come Into Its Own In The Southern Appalachians." *American Magazine of Art* 26, no. 10 (October 1933): 441–42.

Wildenhain, Marguerite. "Potters Dissent: An Open Letter to Bernard Leach." *Craft Horizons* 13, no. 3 (May/June 1953): 43–44.

Williams, Gerry. "The Role of the Traditional Potter in Contemporary Society." In *Transactions of the Ceramic Symposium 1979* edited by Garth Clark, 97–103. Los Angeles: Institute of Ceramic History, 1980.

Zimmer, William. "A New Figure on the Horizon." *American Ceramics* 1, no. 1 (1982): 26–29.

UNPUBLISHED MATERIAL

Haworth, Dale, and Karen Beall. "Notes Toward a History of NCECA [1982]." NCECA Archives, Scholes Library, Alfred University, Alfred, N.Y.

Randall, Ted. "Outline History of the National Council on Education in the Ceramic Arts [1982]." NCECA Archives, Scholes Library, Alfred University, Alfred, N.Y.

Sanders, Herbert H. "Selected Decorating Processes in Pottery: With Original Examples Illustrating the Process." Ph.D. diss., Ohio State University, 1955.

INDEX

PHOTOGRAPH CREDITS

The author and publisher wish to thank the owners and custodians for permitting the reproduction of works of art in their collections. All photographs were provided as credited in the captions unless cited below. All numbers refer to figure references.

Courtesy Alternative Worksite/Bemis Project, 318, 321; courtesy *American Ceramics* magazine, 226; courtesy American Crafts Council, 154; courtesy Archives of Howard Tilton Memorial Library, Tulane University, New Orleans, 81, 94; courtesy Robert Arneson, 225; courtesy Robert Arneson and Frumkin/Adams Gallery, N.Y.C., 219; courtesy Arthur E. Baggs Memorial Library, Ohio State University, Columbus, from the Carlton Atherton Collection, 108; courtesy Asher/Faure Gallery, Los Angeles, photo Douglas M. Parker, 302; © Morley Baer, 170, 222; © Morley Baer, courtesy California Design, 92, 93; Baker photo, 180; Dirk Bakker, 321; courtesy Berkley/Lainson Studio, 291; Ben Blackwell, 294; Jon Bolton, 313; courtesy Braunstein/Quay Gallery, San Francisco, 218, 311, 317, 328, 329; courtesy C.D.S. Gallery, N.Y.C., photo Scott McCue Photography, 309; John Carlano, 324; courtesy *Ceramics Monthly* magazine, 171, 189, 194; © 1979 Judy Chicago, photo Michael Alexander, 345; courtesy Cincinnati Historical Society, 38, 39, 54; Geoffrey Clements, 134, 138; courtesy Cleveland Museum of Art, 119, 137; courtesy College Archives, New York State College of Ceramics at Alfred University, 146; Cooper-Hewitt Museum, Smithsonian Institution, 70, 80, 83; courtesy Cross Creek Gallery, Malibu, photo © 1985 Johsel Namkung, 270; Anthony Cunha, 253, 260, 269, 320; Cuyahoga Metropolitan Housing Authority of the Works Progress Administration (WPA), 125–26; courtesy David Stuart Gallery, 191; courtesy Dorothy Weiss Gallery, San Francisco, photo Brian Oglesbee, 337; courtesy Ruth Duckworth, 274; © 1986 Lisa Ebright, 273; courtesy

Elements Gallery, New York, photo John Beckman, 293; © George Erml, pp. 2–3, 42, 46, 48, 52, 63, 67, 73, 79, 86, 91, 150, 230; M. Lee Fatherree, 141, 178, 315, 317, 328, 348; © Courtney Frisse, 58, 62, 100–103, 107, 111, 114–15, 123, 129, 144, 149, 153, 159, 163, 166, 174–75, 177, 183, 187, 197–98, 205, 232, 247, 252, 256, 272, 290, 330; Charles Frizzell, 312, 338; courtesy Frumkin/Adams Gallery, N.Y.C., photo eeva-inkeri, 221, 295, 296, 348; courtesy David Furman, 281; courtesy Galerie St. Etienne, N.Y.C., 136; courtesy Garth Clark Gallery, Los Angeles/New York, 76, 87, 133, 135, 195, 207, 226–27, 251, 253, 257, 260, 267, 269, 298, 323, 344, 347; Roger Gass, 327; courtesy George Geyer and Tom McMillin, 278; courtesy Andrea Gill, 336; Fred J. Griffith, 242; Robert Grove, 186; © Dorothy Hafner, photo S. Baker Vail, 346; courtesy Hansen Fuller Gallery, San Francisco, 220; courtesy Hansen Fuller Goldeen Gallery, San Francisco, Calif., 213, 224; courtesy Helen Drutt Gallery, Philadelphia, 201, 332; courtesy Holly Solomon Gallery, N.Y.C., photo Paul Sanders, 255; © Scott Hyde, 82; David N. Israel, 268; John Jackson, 349; courtesy James Corcoran Gallery, Santa Monica, 206, 333; courtesy Jan Turner Gallery, 340; courtesy Jessica Darraby Gallery, Los Angeles, 314; courtesy John Berggruen Gallery, San Francisco, photo M. Lee Fatherree, 287; courtesy John Michael Kohler Arts Center, Sheboygan, Wis., 303; courtesy Jordan-Volpe Gallery, N.Y.C., 44, 56–57, 59; courtesy Karen Karnes, 215; © Nancy Kaye, 124, 193, 299, 316, 341; courtesy The Kessel Collection, photo Bill Scott, 263; © 1982 Allen Laughmiller, 267; photo courtesy Mel Rubin, 286; © Schecter Lee/Esto, 4, 14, 18, 20, 22, 24, 27, 33–35; courtesy Lee Nordness Galleries, N.Y., 223; Elaine Levin, 108, 162, 192, 243; Elaine and Clare Levin, 30, 112; Doug Long, 297; courtesy Louis Newman Galleries, Beverly Hills, 331; courtesy L. A. Louvrer, Venice, Calif., photo Colin McRae, 275; © 1982 David Lubarsky, 310;

courtesy Michael Lucero, 310; courtesy Tom McMillin, 277; Michael McTwigan 259; Frederick Marsh, 322; Fred Marvin, 147–48; Edward Matalon, 332; Robert Mates, 122; Beverly Mayeri, 298; courtesy Meredith Gallery, Baltimore, 261; courtesy Michigan State University, 87, 89; Eric Mitchell, 271; Steve Myers, 250; National Archives, 69–AN–242–P1036 and P1038, WPA Federal Art Project, 127–28; National Museum of American History, Smithsonian Institution, Washington, D.C., 2–3, 5, 7, 15–16, 19, 25, 168; © Gail Reynolds Natzler, 6, 155–58, 169, 237, 265; Nobody Prints by Joe Nobody, 295; courtesy Mrs. Boyd O'Dell, 151; courtesy O. K. Harris Gallery, N.Y.C., 239; Old Salem Restoration, Winston-Salem, 1, 6; courtesy estate of Waylande Gregory, photo © R. A. Pike, 139; Dean Powell, 244; Sally Bowen Prange, 264; courtesy Pucker Safrai Gallery, Boston, 268; courtesy Regina Roditi, 169; courtesy Rena Bransten Gallery, San Francisco, 276, 315, 319–20, 327; T.K. Rose, N.Y., 323; Mike Rothwell, 339; Joe Samberg, 93; San Francisco Museum of Art, 207; courtesy Scholes Library, Alfred University, 106; Mark Schwartz, 334; courtesy Sharpe Gallery, N.Y., photo © 1986 David Lubarsky, 300; Bob Shimer/Hedrich-Blessing, 274; Stan Shockey, 228, 235; Paul Soldner, 190; Phil Starrett, 258; courtesy Susan Cummins Gallery, Calif., photo Beth Changstrom, 248; © Grant Taylor Photography, 257; Frank J. Thomas, 195–96; Jerry L. Thompson, 212, 308; © Charles Tompkins, 145, 238; courtesy University City Public Library, 104; courtesy University of Southern California Archives, 184; Tom Van Eynde, 282; R. Vigiletti, 216; Tod M. Volpe, 69, 82, 85, 99, 118; courtesy Peter Voulkos, photo Oppi Untracht, 188; Frank Wheat, 292; © 1984 White Line Photography, 311; courtesy Whitney Museum of American Art, 289; William Wyman, courtesy estate of the artist, 204; Patrick Young, 161; courtesy Zabriskie Gallery, N.Y.C., 307–308, and the artist, 306.